DARK CUPBOARDS, DUSTY SKELETONS

∞

Elizabeth Wehrfritz
is married with a daughter,
two sons, a granddaughter and two grandsons.
A member of the Society of Genealogists living
near London record repositories, she researched family history
before records went online, putting together a genealogical tale of the direct
female line. *Dark Cupboards, Dusty Skeletons: A Post War Upbringing*
is a sequel to *Letters From Lwów*, her mother's letters
and diaries from a year in pre-war Poland.
But enough of secrets: time to spill
the beans !

∞

$\mathcal{D}ARK\ CUPBOARDS,\ \mathcal{D}USTY$
$SKELETONS$

A POST-WAR UPBRINGING

1940s & '50s

ELIZABETH WEHRFRITZ

Wolverwood Books 2022

For Jo, Steve, Carl, Lucy, Rolf, Ben, Becky and Arthur.

A recipe for survival:
   To see a World in a Grain of Sand,
   And a Heaven in a Wild Flower.
   Hold Infinity in the palm of your hand.
   And eternity in an hour.   *William Blake*

© Elizabeth Wehrfritz 2022
First published 2022
by
Wolverwood Books
Email: eliz@wehrfritz.co.uk

The moral right of the author has been asserted.
All rights reserved.
No part of this publication may be
reproduced in any form (electronic, mechanical,
photocopying, recording, or otherwise) without prior
written permission of the copyright owner and
publisher of this book.

ISBN:

978-1-3999-3102-1

Cover and text design by the author.

Printed by:

Parchment Print Oxford,
Kingston Business Park, H4+H5,
Kingston Bagpuize, Abingdon OX13 5FB.

Contents

Prologue: Post-War World	1
Before Memory: Wartime Marriage	8
Moves & Changes: Snapshot Memories	35
Total Disruption: Catholic Boarding School	76
Precarious Normality: Roehampton 1	143
Settled but Only Temporarily: Roehampton 2	208
Disaster & Collapse: Putney High School	297
Epilogue: A Better World Emerging	309
List of illustrations	311
Index	313

Overleaf: R.S.P.C.A. certificate awarded to "Elizabeth Wallace", "June 1956"; blue fountain pen ink has faded over six-and-a-half decades. The essay was written in class at Roehampton Church School.

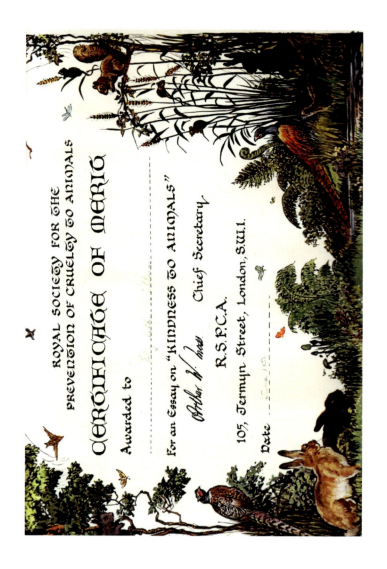

Prologue: Post-War World

Seventy-seven years ago I was born into an unbelievably different world. In 1944 Britain was still at war, V2 rockets exploded on London bringing death and destruction, including on Gower Street where we lived. On the Normandy coast 'D' day landings had begun, atomic bombs yet to be dropped on Hiroshima and Nagasaki. This world has since changed out of all recognition, is hardly the same planet as wartime, and post-war, Britain. Attitudes have changed enormously; people are nicer to each other, less prejudiced, a happier world created.
Attitudes to health were very different. Many potentially deadly illnesses and disabilities carried considerable social stigma: tuberculosis, cancer, mental illness, all unmentionable, would be kept secret, never spoken of. There was no National Health Service. If you became seriously ill and couldn't afford to pay – you died. Antibiotics weren't generally available until the mid'50s. The disabled were often hidden away by their families. Unwelcome in restaurants, thought to put off other customers, they might be asked to leave.
The Welfare State as we know it wasn't up and running. Workhouses, still felt to be hugely shameful and dreaded, existed into the '50s as a last resort for those falling on hard times splitting families: children from parents, husbands from wives. In 1948 a network of volunteer welfare services were merged into a new system, the beginning of Britain's current Welfare State.
When I was born which class you belonged to was immensely important: being middle class opened doors, gave rights and privileges. If you considered yourself middle class maintaining this was felt to be vital. And you had to speak with the right accent: the minute anyone opened their mouth a working class accent would be instantly condemnatory to middle class ears.

Dark Cupboards, Dusty Skeletons

In the late '40s and early '50s one rarely, if ever, saw a person of colour, immigration only really getting going in the mid'50s with the *Windrush*. White working class Irish weren't acceptable. Even in the late '60s notices for rented rooms could still be seen stating:
"No black or Irish need apply." That was the way things were.
Many went to church on Sundays as a mark of respectability; parish vicars and curates would personally visit their parishioners at home.
Employment for women often wasn't an option in the late '40s and '50s. In the interests of getting returning troops settled back into civilian life the rule was one job per family. This made sense: the last thing the government wanted was an army of men, traumatised and brutalised by war, used to military discipline, hanging around getting drunk, or whatever!
For middle class women nursing, teaching and secretarial work were often the only respectable career options; they would never have contemplated shop work or, heaven forbid, scrubbing floors. If a woman did go out to work she would earn considerably less than a man for similar work. The middle class norm became the ideal 1950s housewife spending many hours each day keeping house immaculately, with a few new mod cons such as fridge and hoover, competently cooking delicious meals for her husband when he came home from work, diligently warming his slippers in front of an open coal fire.
A woman had to be very careful before committing herself to a marriage she might find it hard to get out of. Divorce was a major scandal difficult to obtain and expensive. Marital separation also stimulated gossip; having the piece of paper – the wedding certificate as Mother had – conferred some degree of respectability. The disgrace of a broken marriage might lead to social ostracism except for bohemians and the exceptionally confident. But an imbalance of women over men due to war and colonisation meant many women were condemned to a life of spinsterhood, never finding the husbands and families they longed for.
Sex before marriage and illegitimacy might also lead to social ostracism. Mothers could be forced to give up illegitimate children for adoption. Veils of secrecy surrounded any 'dodgy' family situation. Children weren't told of family 'scandals': they might talk, spread things around. So, of course, fertile gossip abounded.
Within marriage contraception wasn't easily available, abortion against the law. Many babies weren't wanted; they came anyway. Wives, frequently

Prologue: Post-War World

brought up in ignorance, often couldn't enjoy sex; rape within marriage wasn't illegal. With troops returning came a 'baby boom' in families separated for so long. I was slightly ahead of this, born before the war ended.

Childbirth in hospital was becoming more common. In 1944 my mother was the first generation in our direct female line to give birth in hospital rather than at home. Visitors usually weren't allowed and, heaven forbid, absolutely *NO* fathers admitted to that inner sanctum of the delivery room.

If a woman couldn't conceive and adopted, the adoptee wouldn't be told. Left to find out as adults through accidentally discovering documentation many felt deceived, receiving no help from authorities with finding natural parents, or counselling if they did. Without fertility treatment adoptive parents were more available, although less carefully screened.

Infant deaths had sunk from Victorian levels but were still not as uncommon as now. So a fat baby was thought to be healthy, an object of pride to be shown off. Being small, premature and not a good eater, much to Mother's chagrin I never fitted this ideal.

Physical care of babies meant a good deal of hand washing. There were no disposable nappies, no plastic panties, although the rubber ones available did cover the thick terry-towelling nappies. Babies might be held on a pot from an early age in the hope of 'catching' it, avoiding a messy nappy. Rigid routine feeding at set times made 'catching' more likely. Serious potty training began at a much younger age than now.

Babies were usually breastfed; if they needed a bottle this would be glass and curved slightly with a hole to let air in at the opposite end to the rubber teat. I remember in pre-school years having my baby bottle to play at feeding my doll family. Babies might be put outside in their prams in the fresh air to sleep during the day. My husband, awake, bored and active, managed to demolish his; it had to be rebuilt for his sister. Not everyone fed new babies at night; they might be left in a separate room to cry it out.

Economically life has become what in that post-war era could only have been dreamed of when food was rationed and in short supply; you had a buff-coloured ration book with coupons limiting what could be bought and, therefore, eaten. Obesity wasn't an issue.

Clothes weren't easily come by, many women, as in earlier times, still made their own. Holes in socks were darned to make them last longer, trousers patched, outgrown worn children's clothes handed down to

Dark Cupboards, Dusty Skeletons

younger children, jerseys hand-knitted. Everything would be painstakingly hand-washed and hung up to dry outside on a washing line, including babies' numerous terry-towelling nappies. An immovable stain would be a ruinous disaster it being too costly to throw things out, buy new.

Most schools practised formal class teaching in front of a silent class, the teacher writing with white chalk on a blackboard. Rote learning was the norm relying on corporal punishment, sometimes rather a lot, to enforce learning and discipline. Many parents agreed with this, felt children couldn't be properly brought up without corporal punishment.

Most secondary schools were single sex. Sex education, not part of the curriculum, would be rudimentary in the extreme. Parents didn't want their children to know where babies came from – brought in the doctor's bag, hidden under a gooseberry bush, discovered in a stork's nest – often found this topic impossible to mention. Mother's class at St Paul's Girls' School in the 1920s had had a talk about the nuptials of the earthworm by an obviously highly embarrassed young lady teacher. Post-war, sex education hadn't changed much.

Boarding school for middle class boys from age eight or even younger was the norm – where they had to cope with beating, bullying and, in their teens, homosexuality – believed to be the correct way for boys to be brought up. Girls might also be sent away to board. Great Britain was still a colonial power: colonialism had always split families children being separated from parents and sent back to England to boarding school. During the war large numbers of children had been evacuated from cities likely to be bombed to live with strangers, their lives changed forever. This was the environment I was born into, to some extent explaining my childhood experiences.

On the continent the British had a – probably justified – reputation for not treating children very well. However, during the war some savvy families did manage to move out of London, find work in rural areas and stay together. Others, like my mother-in-law, bravely refused evacuation, staying in London throughout the blitz to keep the family together.

With no TV to entertain and few organised activities even middle class children when not in school would be allowed to roam outside for much of the day, with sandwiches, until teatime, becoming semi-feral, playing on bombsites or open countryside. "Health and Safety", "Conservation", "Environment", or "Climate Change" were all unheard of phrases.

Prologue: Post-War World

In the world I was born into dealing with feelings meant learning to ignore them. They got in the way, didn't exist, one just wasn't supposed to *have* feelings. Even as a little girl I felt crying was shameful. You never saw a man cry. Now men cry on television in front of millions. And why not? Wiping feelings under the carpet was how many dealt with wartime trauma whether away fighting on the battlefield or living through bombing raids at home. When my mother and father linked up again after a long separation she once (tactlessly I thought) teased him, laughing, reminding him of hiding under a table during a bombing raid. He'd shown fear.

Men were expected to be "manly", which also meant not being seen to have anything to do with babies. Mother said my father told her he'd do anything to help her in the house but wouldn't be seen out with me. Babies just didn't go with the desired masculine image. It was the '60s which changed all that; one was allowed to have feelings, be emotional. We really needed the '60s.

Although they didn't yet have the vote, eighteen-year-old boys were conscripted into the army where, under military law and military discipline, they had no control over their personal lives, whether they lived or died. Sent abroad to places they may never have heard of, some never came back or injury changed their lives forever. Why were so many mothers, like mine, so desperate to have a son, felt disappointed with the birth of a daughter? When our daughter was born a lovely elderly couple at Wanstead Quaker Meeting told us,

"We like little girls. People say boys are cannon fodder."

For their generation, remembering the slaughter of the Great War, boys *were* cannon fodder. During the Second World War there was more tolerance of Conscientious Objectors – my father-in-law was one – but they were still a stigmatised, socially isolated group, having to go through an unsympathetic military tribunal to register as a CO.

Murderers could still be hanged until 1965: several crimes including treason remained punishable by death until 1998. The last woman hanged was in 1955. I would have been ten, twenty when the last hanging of a male murderer took place. Not much interested in the news I don't remember hearing about either or perhaps, as it was just part of life as we knew it; I didn't find a hanging particularly remarkable. Male homosexuality was still a prosecutable offence until the 1967 Sexual Offences Act after which homophobic laws tended not to be enforced in

Dark Cupboards, Dusty Skeletons

many cases. Female homosexuality was never against the law. Queen Victoria had apparently said, "Ladies don't do things like that," and refused to sign the bill.

This, then, was the world I was born into, explaining a lot of childhood experiences. In the seventy-seven years since 1944 – the year I was born – attitudes have changed out of all recognition; stigma and secrecy are no longer skeletons hidden in cupboards, no longer big issues for much of what is mentioned in this book.

*

A brief word on how this probably rather too-lengthy epistle was put together, an autobiography of early life from a multitude of jottings made over twenty-five years while memories were still fresh, some returning only briefly to be quickly noted down before possibly lost forever. These needed endless sorting, ordering and then rewriting in coherent English. Memories of incidents were clear, sequences not always clear, memories of *which* stories had been written up often forgotten so written up again, resulting in two slightly different versions to be amalgamated.

Pieces written about earlier childhood may seem unrealistically sophisticated. They're based on my own sharp flashback memories still vividly clear, added to information gleaned from Mother's brief date diaries linked with incidents she briefly mentioned – interpretations put together with adult insight from these sources.

Stories come in different writing styles some written for autobiographical creative writing exercises at Birkbeck College, University of London, where we were encouraged to 'fictionalise' to add interest. Others written in old age seem more prosaic. All stories, 'fictionalised' or prosaic, are basically true as remembered. Some are written in different 'voices': a child's 'voice' as I remember feeling at the time. Others, written in my seventies when writing coherent sentences has become trickier, relying on earlier jottings as *aides des memoire*, are probably more boring . . .

As some recollections are undeniably candid many names have been changed, especially less common, easily identifiable names.

Why write about childhood? Firstly as a way of paying tribute to those who helped giving support emotionally and materially through crises, including the unknown Great British Tax-Payer helping someone they never knew existed. Re-living childhood has helped me realise just how kind some

Prologue: Post-War World

people were, how lucky I was, the kindness of those I knew and of strangers. A second reason is to try to gain closure about trauma I was expected to 'forget'. In Mother's day and age many did 'forget', or at any rate never felt able to confide. Her generation dealt with emotional pain in this way especially wartime trauma. One just wasn't supposed to *have* feelings, they got in the way, were best ignored. Talking about terrible experiences was silenced, counselling for closure not yet dreamed up.

Perhaps Mother couldn't cope with my distress leading to her not allowing talk about certain episodes of my early life. And she didn't want people to know of mistakes which would reflect badly on her ability to cope. Her two big sisters tended to imply that Ruth, the baby of the family, couldn't cope. She tried to prove them wrong. Being less 'difficult' than she believed I went along with her need for traumas to be hidden. She would put words into my mouth about my supposed thoughts and feelings; I was expected to agree or at any rate fall silent letting her imagine agreement. Consequently at seventy-seven traumatic episodes still fester in my mind.

And I've always had a problem verbalising, words tending to jumble in my head muddling what I really need to say. Writing being slower, putting pen to paper gives time to sort jumbles, put down what I really want to say.

A further reason for writing about childhood is to productively while away coronavirus lockdown, the Wallace side of the family having always been talented, hard working, and very driven.

And last but not least, writing might hopefully help future generations avoid similar problems, repeat mistakes.

Enough of secrets, time to spill the beans, reveal what could never be spoken of, drag dusty skeletons out of pitch-black cupboards to dance uproariously, to lay childhood ghosts . . .

Before Memory: Wartime Marriage

Pigeons in Russell Square clustering round my park bench squabbling over crumbs in the sunshine perhaps descendants of the first seen brought in my pram to watch them fluttering back after the blitz? Wheeled from my parents' flat in Gower Street aged five months in the spring of 1945, the only spring the three of us were together as a family before she left him after just nineteen months of married life? What happened in that time I don't remember? Which had so much impact on all our lives. Why did she leave?

Behind me, through tall limes the square grey blocks of Senate House tower. That was where they met, where it all began, when they both worked in the Ministry of Information set up in the newly built University library. She felt very safe there she said: when working late she was allowed to sleep in the basemen. Bombs wouldn't penetrate the massive slabs.

They worked in the Balkan section, he as a news sub-editor preparing bulletins for broadcast to enemy occupied territory, she as Assistant Specialist, Foreign Division. A faded photo shows the team: six women to just two men. Men were in short supply, most being in the forces. There was a good spirit in the section, a feeling they were needed to pull together for Britain and freedom.

They had both lived in London during the blitz. He'd been an Air Raid Protection warden digging people out.

"Oh Yes, I've picked up the pieces." he would say, reminiscing.

He'd also worked in a factory south of London repairing aircraft engines. The factory was bombed, a splinter in his skull led to concussion and a spell in hospital.

She'd done a brief spell of nursing she wasn't cut out for. The white head-square with embroidered Red Cross she kept, used by me to play doctors and nurses with dolls.

Before Memory: Wartime Marriage

Ruth Isabelle King married George Carlton Wallace, who called himself "Bill", quietly at Holborn Registry Office on 30th October 1943. At forty Bill was more than ten years older than her. He'd wanted to just get married without telling anyone but she felt her parents would be upset. They were there; her father witnessed the wedding certificate. She never met Bill's relatives: he'd cut himself off from his father after a row, his mother who'd had health problems died when he was in his teens.

She knew the unmentionable though, that he'd been divorced. He'd had to tell her that, his marital status had legally to go on the marriage certificate: "The divorced husband of Margaret Helen Wallace formerly Grant." Did she ever know he'd been twice divorced and the father of at least three children?

It was a practical wartime wedding. She told me she wore maroon gloves with matching maroon bag. When later reminded she laughed mischievously,

"Oh *did* I?"

She had by then joined the army and moved to Bletchley Park to work on decoding German ciphers. She chose to stay there; he remained in London at the Ministry of Information.

A letter from Bill to Ruth written soon after their marriage in October 1943, on his return from a visit to Bletchley Park, found decades later among papers in her flat:

London: 21st November, 1943.
Ruth darling,
Extraordinary things happened about the train yesterday morning. I got to the station at about half-past eleven, and was told that an express to London would be within a few minutes. The train duly arrived, and I got into an empty compartment which I had to myself all the way to London. I was in the flat by 1. p.m. Goodness knows which train it was meant to be; it came from Carlisle. The journey was almost up to peacetime standard.

It was a pity the train didn't get in a bit earlier, though, because then I could have dashed down to Cambridge Circus by taxi and got you a scarf. As it is, you will have to wait until Monday. The barometer suggests that the present weather will go on for sometime; the pointer is hovering over

Dark Cupboards, Dusty Skeletons

'Very Dry', a sign that whatever weather conditions prevail at the moment will go on prevailing.

Enclosed is my duty sheet for the next three weeks. You will see from it that I do not get three days off after all, because I have to do a day duty on Tuesday. I must go into this duty question and see if I am doing more than my whack. Anyway, the week's leave is duly recorded, and I see that I have two days off on December 10 and 11. If your own duty is not something awkward at that time, I will speed down to Bletchley again. I know you will not be having a day off so soon after your leave, but we could have an evening together or something.

My two days with you did me much good, darling. My back seems to be clearing up rather more quickly than usual. When I first arrived at Bletchley I was very tired, due I think to the fact that I had completed five duties in a row and that the cold weather had caught up with me half way through them. The few hours with you were very happy ones, and I came back feeling full of life. There has been no rush of news over the week-end; in fact, things are so quiet that I am writing this in the office on one of the F.O. machines. This afternoon and evening are to be devoted to work; if only Mary Airey comes on Monday, I hope to have a nice large chunk of script ready for you to read when you come to London.

Goodbye for now, darling. Take care of yourself. And I will get the scarf to you just as soon as I can. All my love.

Bill.   [Typed, except signature.]

And her diary records that Bill told her:
"I feel so safe with you, Ruth, as though I will never be hurt again."
What did they expect of marriage? In a play he'd seen as a boy, he told her, the young hero had wanted to take the girl he loved away from other people and live on a hill alone with her.
With pipe and trilby he looked like Ruth's father, the father she felt she'd never been close to, acutely disappointed his third daughter wasn't the son he'd hoped for.
She was ten years younger than Bill, daughter of a second headmaster at Latymer Upper School, educated at a convent, top girls' public school

Before Memory: Wartime Marriage

and Oxford. Innocent, trusting, convinced Oxbridge graduates were the best; a pioneer role not acceptable to men.

Her philosophy of life was in tune with Bertrand Russell's *In Praise of Idleness* – if you couldn't be happy working it's better to be idle.

"If you were not in such a hurry to avoid the raindrops you would see how beautiful they are." was a Chinese proverb she copied into her tiny leather diary.

A joint bank account meant loss of financial independence for this emancipated woman. And still the bombs were falling. "Bomb at Goodge St. at 1.00 p.m." she recorded in her diary on Monday 19th June.

Ruth and Bill
Venue unknown, likewise ownership of the cat. Had Ruth adopted a bombed out stray? Possibly a garden behind the Gower Street flat or an inn garden near Bletchley c.1943.

And on Saturday 4th July, "My childhood was very short" he told her. Son of a self-made theatrical manager always "on tour" he'd run away from home to escape his sometimes violent father, alone in the world, qualifications grindingly achieved at night school financed by full-time job.

"Trouble is an old friend of mine," he'd said, "like the wolf at the door who comes in and sits at the table."

"He used the withdrawal method," she told me in a rare moment of intimacy, "which wasn't very satisfactory."

In March 1944 she became pregnant. They began flat hunting in London looking at cheap rented accommodation vacated by those able to move away from the

Dark Cupboards, Dusty Skeletons

bombing, setting up home at 45 Gower Street, the address on my birth certificate.
Bill had never been a stranger to hard work. He worked frenetically at his full-time job in the Ministry of Information, sometimes on night shifts. Nevertheless the war created jobs and financial security after the 'thirties recession when he'd struggled to survive as a crime fiction writer.
"I didn't understand his work."
What did she mean by that? He would get up in the early hours to write, having built his own tea-making machine triggered by their alarm clock. Then he'd leave for Senate House and a full day's work.
On Monday 10th July her diary notes they "Delivered *Elizabeth*", the play he'd been writing, to the publishers. It wasn't accepted. She was then four months pregnant. His 'baby' didn't make it. Unused to failure she felt humiliated, unable to give support.
Words were part of their married life, the pithy phrase, the clever plot, hard intellectualism. Words full of deep meaning, yet meaningless. Heavy tiring words leaving the listener spent. To prove something. Lacking the spontaneity and vibrancy of the London streets outside, energising, life-giving.
"The charming, scholar's mind . . . will be the end of you, darling," wrote a close friend.
Non-practical, she tried to learn to cook with rationed food, entertaining his friends, hating the embarrassment of inedible desserts emerging from the oven. He could do better.
Air raids exhausted and hardened her.
"Cooked stew in flat with bombs about."
She laughed at him, once scared enough to crawl under the table. She'd been brought up never to mention sex. He didn't want children, wanted a physical relationship though, "all the time." she noted.
Yet despite bombing and rationing they seem to have had a good time together in wartime London during the five-and-a-half months between June 1944 until my birth in November. They saw plays: he wanted to go to the theatre often to keep ideas running through his mind, he said. They went to Kew Gardens, Regents Park and Hampstead Heath, shopped in the West End, ate out in pubs, Chinese restaurants and hotels, went to an art exhibition and a concert. Her diary records they cycled in Surrey

Before Memory: Wartime Marriage

when visiting her parents in Hindhead, took two weeks holiday at the end of July at Ross-on-Wye. Bill developed his own photos; she had music lessons and went to the hairdresser every two or three weeks; they entertained friends, played bridge, had long evening discussions; read novels; listened to the radio; bought furniture and kitchenware for the flat.

"I've seen so much of the bad side of life. Now I'm seeing some of the good," he told her.

I pour over her tiny black leather diary trying to decode scribbled fading ink. Brief phases holding fragments of another world.

"Bomb at Goodge Street at 1 p.m." is recorded in June 1944, amongst many such entries.

She, tiring quickly, non-energetic, felt he worked too hard.

"She was never a very energetic person, was she?" he said, trying to remember, when I caught up with him decades later.

*

Mother couldn't conceive of the idea that I might not be a boy, she was used to things going right for her, to success. Everything bought was blue; I was to be "David" or "Martin". Girls' names weren't considered.

The baby was turned in the womb to avoid a suspected breech delivery. This led to a premature birth on the 20th November at 10.30p.m. in boiler rooms beneath St Thomas's Hospital, converted into an air raid shelter. The tiny infant girl almost died the first week. Matron wouldn't allow her to be moved or picked up. Twelve days later Ruth went back to the flat, leaving the baby in hospital overnight. Less than a week later came another disruption to the marriage relationship when Ruth and the baby were sent to St Thomas's Baby Hostel in Surrey. For the next month Bill visited at weekends until she and the baby came back to Gower Street in the New Year.

She registered the birth. Perhaps because my father was a writer my mother hopefully put "Bloomsbury" on my birth certificate and his favourite girl's name, "Elizabeth". Her mother had said she didn't want a grandchild; her father was delighted. With Ruth's two older sisters well into their thirties and unmarried, he probably felt his chances of becoming a grandfather were slim.

Life continued at Gower Street with the baby: New Year to mid-May 1945. The three of us spent just four-and-a-half months together.

Dark Cupboards, Dusty Skeletons

I turn the diary pages, secrets exploding. Tiny, black leather embossed with gold, brief entries, fragments of another world, brief phrases, so little telling so much. About a time I can't remember. Happenings with so much impact on me, my life. Four-and-a-half months of family life before she left.

He did all the washing, even terry toweling nappies. A good cook – chemists seem good at mixing things – he complained,

"I've lost three pounds on your cooking," alarming with wartime food rationing. He'd help with anything in the flat he told her, but wouldn't be seen out with a baby.

Winter with a small weak baby – she always hated bad weather – few outings are noted in the scribbled faded ink, visits from friends, her relatives: parents, sisters, aunts to see the baby, regular entries about taking "E." to be weighed. At the end of February 1945 came,

"News of Pa's illness."

Bill went alone to Hindhead. Then on Friday 2nd March,

"To Hindhead to say Goodbye to Daddy."

And three days later,

"Daddy's funeral at Woking."

And a further separation while she stayed with her bereaved mother. Sunday 25th March, Palm Sunday, "10.30 p.m. Rocket falls near Gower Street."

Nights were disrupted by air-raid warnings and dashes to the shelter. Too tired to cope with a crying baby she left me in the flat:

"You were asleep, so we just had to leave you and hope for the best."

Why did she tell me?

Never a very energetic person she was exhausted by childbirth and the demands of a tiny premature baby. These weren't the only demands,

"I want it all the time," he told her.

She became afraid of becoming pregnant again.

Friday 6th April 1945: "Like a [illegible word] in a dream."

And what had she discovered when she wrote:

"The loss of everything."

Tuesday 1st May 1945: "B.B.C. announces Hitler's death at 10.30 p.m. E. crying."

Perhaps with reason. With the ending of war, not fighting a common cause, people no longer gelled together in the same way.

Before Memory: Wartime Marriage

"I suppose people will start being nasty to each other again," commented Ruth's Auntie Bella.
Tuesday 8th May: "V. E. Day."
Then just two weeks later relief wafts from the tiny page saying briefly on Wed 23rd May:
"Came to Hindhead."

*

"Why did you marry him?" I would say, when old enough to ask, trying to probe the mysteries of a time I couldn't remember which seemed so important.
"You don't understand," would be the inevitable adult reply, "in the war you met people you wouldn't normally meet."
She often came out with things I didn't understand which shut me up while I mulled over them. Sometimes for years, bringing her relief from questions she didn't want to answer. I eventually figured out she meant 'class'.
Many marriages were rushed into during the war. People were separated, not knowing when they would meet again; death might intervene; they had to grab opportunities, live life while they could.
He'd wanted her to go she said, when pressed, to get married again.
"Why did you leave?" I persisted.
She said simply, "I was tired of crying."
Stunned into silence my questions ceased. Her words hung, blocks of floating ice deep in a frozen subterranean sea. I dared not touch them.
Father, when aged seventeen I caught up with him, took a more jovial approach.
"And one day," he bantered, "she decided I was too awful to live with, so she tucked you under her arm and left."
He had by then, of course, found someone else. When he died though, he was still legally married to Ruth and visiting frequently.
A colleague at the Ministry of Information had said,
"Bill, you will always love Ruth and she will never leave you."
"And then " she said, during her last illness in hospital aged eighty-five, "I left him."
She still felt guilty, as though it was her fault. She should have managed the situation better. Knowing what I did, what I'd found out from the Public Record Office, I tried to reassure her. Whether it was genes, or

Dark Cupboards, Dusty Skeletons

upbringing in a theatrical company constantly on the move, he was forever a nomad, forever moving on from job to job, place to place, person to person; thriving on change. There wasn't much she could have done about that.

But I am tired of struggling with raw emotion, of, *"Who's Afraid of Virginia Woolf"* and the Bloomsbury Group, the knife turning, a matrix of pain and sorrow. It was all a long time ago. The pigeons are going up to roost, the café is closed, the Square darkening. Time to leave this bench and walk past Senate House to my creative writing class at Birkbeck, to find relief in writing it all down.

*

May 1945 to March 1946 – reconstructed from letters, diaries, and what Mother told me.

When Ruth left Bill she travelled by train and bus to her mother, Bertha's, cottage "Brambletye", in a state of nervous breakdown. Her mother, in her mid-sixties, never energetic herself, trying to adjust to widowhood after thirty-eight years of marriage, put Ruth and the baby into Heathersbank Nursing Home. During the three weeks Ruth spent there her six-month-old baby was looked after separately. She saw her only for a few minutes towards the end of her stay. Her diary records: "Saw E. today." Not, apparently, an everyday occurrence. Also that the baby gained no weight.

*

Ruth's first breakdown had struck after her finals at Oxford, the second while working for *The Times* newspaper when she was told she "wasn't suited to the hurly burly of office life." Eldest sister, Janet, far away teaching in Scotland, also suffered breakdowns.

Back at Brambletye her sister Kay visited, took photos on a sunny summer's day in the riotously flowering back garden. At this stage, it seems from letters below, Ruth hadn't realised her marriage had ended, that she wouldn't be going back to Gower Street. We weren't wanted there.

Their mother, Bertha, had said she didn't want a grandchild although Mother told me she later became fond of me. Seeing little of her I wasn't aware of this. In Bertha's letter to Bill (below) she mentions getting on with her own life. We weren't wanted at Hindhead either.

Before Memory: Wartime Marriage

"And you do it all?" asked Mother in amazement decades later about my own marriage. She'd found it hard to cope with domesticity.

Looking more herself again after three weeks in Heathersbank Nursing Home. Ruth with Elizabeth in the garden at Brambletye Hindhead. There's no photo of grandmother with her only grandchild, none of a family group.

Herbaceous border planted and tended by grandfather before he passed away the previous February.

A proper pram with sunshade! (Possibly paid for by Grannie.) A pram could have been put in the guard's van on the journey to Hindhead.

And a terry toweling nappy – no plastic panties – no plastic in the mid-1940s – why Mother has something covering her dress.

Dark Cupboards, Dusty Skeletons

The following is a fictitious account written as an exercise in dialogue for a creative writing course. It's fact that that her father had died after suffering a stroke while building a bonfire; that when in hospital having lost his speech he tried to say something about Ruth. She thought this may have been to do with money. Ruth did say her mother, Bertha, had alienated her in some way when she left Gower Street and went back to Hindhead although she didn't say exactly how, that she'd moved with me to Potter's Bar. The conversation below is speculative.

As youngest daughter Ruth had felt closest to her mother as mother's "Little Ouffie". Her mother had always coped, picked up the pieces, done the housework however soul-destroying. She would know what to do. Ruth arrived exhausted from night bombing, from trying to keep the baby quiet while her husband struggled as a writer, from rows and tears over her inability to cope with domesticity, from surviving on very little money. But sitting in the lounge with its faded antique chairs, her mother started:
"Ruth, what are you going to do? You've a young baby. Where are you going to live? What are you going to do for money? You can't afford to give that child a decent start in life."
Ruth said hesitantly, "Well . . . I'm not sure . . . I don't know."
Had her mother forgotten that when she'd married, Grandfather had already bought her marital home for her to move into after the wedding?
"Why did you leave Bill? He was helping you in the house, doing all the laundry. Your Father never gave me that kind of help. If Bill wasn't violent and supporting you, you had better go back. If you think he may not always be faithful, well, you've made your bed, you'll just have to lie on it. Many men are like that, their wives cope. You'll just have to sort things out between you. Why did you marry him if you're not temperamentally compatible, as you put it?"
Had her mother also forgotten, Ruth wondered, that she herself had married a poor schoolmaster when Grandfather had wanted a wealthy match? Almost the same situation.
"It's different now Mother, the war's changed everything. One meets people one wouldn't normally meet. In London no one knows if they'll even be alive next day."
"We had to cope with war too, black-edged telegrams arriving, a whole generation of young men lost. We coped, so can you. I was tired like

Before Memory: Wartime Marriage

you. I had to do everything: meals, cleaning, keeping the kitchen range alight for heating and cooking, having soldiers on leave billeted on us. *And* bringing up three under fives."

"But there wasn't bombing every night."

"Ruth, all this is a great worry to me. My headaches are worse. What are you going to *do*?"

"Well . . . I don't know . . ."

She looked hesitantly sideways at her mother.

"You seem so vague, to have no definite plans."

"You've got room here. There are three bedrooms and only you now Daddy's gone."

"We bought this house to retire to. I've been happy here getting on with plans for my own life. I'm sixty-four. I want some time for myself before it's too late."

She stared vacantly at the gold-framed crystal clock ticking on the mantlepiece.

"What would the neighbours think? There'd be gossip."

The Thomson family, thought Ruth, had always been anxious to present an unassailable front to the world, ever since Grandfather had made money and they'd tried to be accepted by a different class of people.

Her mother's blue eyes stared unseeingly at a piece of fluff on her Davenport. Flicking it away, she crumpled her embroidered handkerchief tightly before pushing it deep into the pocket of her tight-bodice dress.

Ruth said, "I was worried about you, being on your own, now Daddy's not here any more."

Covering her face with her hands she watched her mother through gaps in fingers, wondering whether it would have been different if the baby had been a boy, the boy her parents had hoped for when she was born, their third attempt.

"I'll have to put her in a residential nursery," Ruth said, twisting a strand of hair round her little finger. Surely Mother would relent, suggest she stayed?

Upstairs the baby began to cry. According to the Truby King routine her next feed wasn't due for another half hour. Her grandmother, barely hearing, continued:

"We did everything for you. All that money spent on your education at that top girls' public school, then at one of the better Oxford colleges. The one *you* wanted to go to, not the one that offered you a scholarship. We made so many sacrifices. I went without fashionable

Dark Cupboards, Dusty Skeletons

clothes, without electric light being put in. The neighbours had that. I had to scrape and save even on food and coal. Your father was terribly upset when we visited you and saw the conditions you were living in. He'd done so much to give you a better start in life than he'd had. Then saw his only grandchild born into worse. He had the stroke soon after, building a bonfire in the garden to try and forget for a while. The worry killed him, he died trying to say something about "Ruth", struggling to communicate. Spent his last days wondering where he'd gone wrong, what he should do now, feeling responsible in some way. He'd be here now if it wasn't for all this."
Ruth stared paralysed at the rust-coloured carpet.
"I'll write to Bill and tell him I do not intend to shoulder his responsibilities indefinitely. And ask him what he thinks he is going to do about you and the baby."
Soon after Ruth moved into rented accommodation in Potter's Bar. Her little girl had only sporadic visits to her grandmother's, growing up with hazy memories of a vacant relationship.

*

Brambletye, Linkside, Hindhead, Surrey. 7/17/45.
Dear Bill,
As Ruth is so vague about her plans perhaps you will let me know what your plans are with regard to Ruth and the baby as I do not intend to shoulder your responsibilities indefinitely. The whole thing has been a very great worry to me but I was glad to be able to help her and she was quite ill when she came to me, but now she is well I want something definite from you. So please write and let me know what you intend to do – so that I can get on with my own plans for the future.
Awaiting your reply.
Sincerely yours
Bertha King.

Bill didn't answer, instead sending Bertha's letter to Ruth with a rather curt note saying he wouldn't dream of discussing this matter with a third party. So that was that!
However he appears to have found the rented accommodation at Potters Bar Ruth shared with another tenant, Olga, who sometimes looked after me. Mother told me the reason she left after four months was that the owners, who'd moved somewhere safer during the bombing, wanted their house back. Olga moved to Bristol.

Before Memory: Wartime Marriage

Then, diary entries show, Ruth had another try at living with her mother in the winter of '45 to '46. Again this didn't work; she looked for somewhere to live locally in the Hindhead area. She found a place nearby and asked her mother to invite the prospective landlady round to assure her Ruth came from that all-important, good, social background. Ruth said living near might have worked well, but her mother had said, "I never mix business with pleasure."
The arrangement fell through.
Gossip may have been why Grannie didn't want us at Brambletye, gossip generated by a single mother with no father around; perhaps she still hoped to persuade Ruth to go back to Bill; she may also have felt Ruth's dislike of domesticity would lead to doing a lot herself – Bill also found this difficult – combined with Grannie's own proneness to become quickly tired. She'd had enough.
But the Thomson family network still operated in the spring of 1946 when Mother was again looking for somewhere to live. That was how we met Auntie Gladys who made such a difference to my life. Mother's Auntie Elsie, living in North London, wanted to see me – her sister Bertha's only grandchild. Mother, taking me to visit, talked to her aunt about her problem finding somewhere to live. Elsie chatted to her other sister, Daisy – Bertha didn't get on with Daisy or communicate much – Daisy played tennis with a friend, a Mrs Gladys Mary Hamilton (née Coles), recently widowed, living alone in a four-bedroom, detached house in Roehampton and looking for a tenant to live with her.
At this stage the Thomson family network was still close enough to look after its own whatever tensions or personality clashes marred relationships. Ruth would become increasingly detached as the years went by. I have no memory of Auntie Elsie, she died when I was still young, but she seems to have had a profound effect on my life changing it for the better. And I barely remember Auntie Daisy although a ten-shilling note would unfailingly arrive in the post on my birthdays.
Auntie Gladys had married late in life – in 1928 turning forty – and to her disappointment no children had come along. She later talked about her husband, Jack, who'd died at the end of the war from natural causes. Everyone was celebrating but it wasn't a happy time for her. And so, according to Mother's diaries, towards the end of March 1946 when I was about sixteen months, we moved in with our new landlady who

Dark Cupboards, Dusty Skeletons

wanted me to call her "Auntie Gladys", and who would eventually become a family friend, taking the place of grandmother. We became her family, the family she'd never had. According to census returns she would have been fifty-eight. She took us in when we were what might now be termed "homeless". At first Mother paid rent. To jump ahead to 1952 when we went back to live permanently with Auntie Gladys, she didn't charge anything. Mother had had tuberculosis and couldn't work for a while; she'd tell people we 'shared' a house.

Auntie Gladys's four-bedroom detached house graced an upmarket part of Roehampton. In the social circles the Thomson family aspired to contacts had to be made through the *right* people. Auntie Gladys seems to have been happy to have us, for us to come and go: Mother was always chopping and changing. Although I didn't realise it at the time, geared up as I became to moves, changes and loss of contacts, Auntie Gladys became very fond of me, an adopted grandmother.

Clearly Ruth's uncertainty and depression led to her being in a very unsettled state. World post-war shortages created cuts in food rations. Shortages led to queues. That life became a financial struggle before state benefits became available for mothers on their own, is evident in her letters.

In November '46 government statistics showed a "tidal wave of divorce sweeping Britain" as a result of hasty wartime marriages. Divorce was still scandalous invoking gossip behind closed doors. The only grounds in the late '40s were adultery, physical cruelty, desertion or incurable insanity. One of these had to be proved in court. It would be many decades before rape within marriage became illegal. After separating their relationship continued by post. I was totally unaware of the existence of this. My father was simply a non-existent non-entity. My world revolved round my mother. I don't think I was even aware that most children *had* fathers and I hadn't; at a young age it never occurred to me that I *should* have had one. In retrospect I should perhaps be grateful that he supported us financially at a time before state benefits were available, making it possible for me to stay with her. This, of course, in my infant world I took for granted. Bill's previous wife, Helen, had left their son Billy in a 'baby's hotel' from the age of twelve months, then with a foster mother he wasn't happy with, until he was eight.

Before Memory: Wartime Marriage

The following letters show a balanced approach to the situation on both sides, both probably aware of the possibility that letters might at some stage be read by solicitors or produced in court.

45, Gower Street, W.C.1..
[Telephone] MUSeum 9905
24th June, 1945.
Ruth dear,
Thinking over what we said on the telephone this morning, I am wondering if you really ought to come up to Town on Wednesday, because I feel that since you wrote your letter of June 10 you have changed your mind and are going to suggest that we resume our life together.
If that is the case, I am sorry Ruth, but it is impossible. There are some hard times ahead of me now that the war in Europe has finished, and I know that if we attempted to resume the old life, I simply would not be able to cope. The consequences, financial and otherwise, would be disastrous. The reasons why it cannot be were given in my previous letter to you. I have thought that letter over as carefully as I can, and there is nothing in it which I can now go back on.
In these circumstances, and if your Mother is making it difficult for you, would it not be better for you to fix yourself up somewhere else down in Hindhead for the time being? So long as it is not too ruinous, I will dig up the money somehow. If you could find somewhere not too impossible, you would have time to think and make plans – something you have not yet been able to do.
In any event, it would not be a good thing to try to talk about our affairs now. I am feeling pretty wretched about the whole business, and I expect you are too, and to attempt any sort of discussion at this stage would only lead to recriminations and bad feeling. If all this sounds a little ridiculous, I am sorry – I am only trying to do what is best. Of course, if you want to come along for a few things and a cup of tea, you are more than welcome – but it would be as well to keep off problems. My Instinct warns me that this is a bad time to try to deal with them.
Yours, Bill.

Dark Cupboards, Dusty Skeletons

45, Gower Street, W.C.1. Museum 9905   12th July, 1945.
Dear Ruth,
Thank you for your two letters. Enclosed is another wad of boodle [cash].
I am terribly sorry that you have that feeling of resentment in the back of your mind. I was afraid something of the sort would happen, and hoped in some way to avoid it; it is a thing that does no good to anyone. I can see only too clearly your difficulties, and it was my first impulse on reading your letters to fall in with your suggestion about letting you have this flat for a time. But I am afraid I have had to decide against it finally. You see, much of the work I am struggling with now is work that I should have tackled 12 or 18 months ago. I did not do so, and circumstances have to some extent overtaken me. The position is that I have had to agree to stay on at the Ministry [of Information] while trying to make up the leeway. I am aware, however, that the job will not go on for ever, and in the meantime competition is growing week by week in what is at the best of times a highly competitive profession. [Journalism] I want to be able to say that the money I am able to send you now will go on indefinitely, and in the course of time will be increased; but I cannot say this if I get moving about from place to place. People who do not know me very well get tired of that sort of thing; they think it is a sign of instability, and are not slow to make a change to someone a little less mobile. Apart from all this (and if it does not persuade you, I am sorry, but I do know my profession so well), I simply cannot move tons of reference books and papers to hotels and so on, even temporarily. In the old days when I was writing cheap fiction it was another matter; the work I am doing now needs much study and research, and simply cannot be dashed off in any odd corner and without my familiar sources of information.
And so, beastly though it seems (and I do not feel at all kindly towards myself about it), I am going to stay on at this flat, and it is therefore not available to you. That must be regarded as definite. In this connection, I suggest it would be a good thing if, with your permission, I arrange for the furniture that is yours to go into store until you are ready to use it. You must let me know about this. There is one other point about this flat − I notice that you are still retaining the keys; and so that, in a moment of difficulty with your family you will not be tempted just to move back here (a circumstance that would be very bad for both of us), I am having the locks altered. It sounds a horrible thing to do, and if it is any consolation to you, I am feeling pretty ashamed about it, but my

Before Memory: Wartime Marriage

feeling is that I must isolate myself in every possible way from any awkwardness of the kind I feel could easily occur, if I am to be able to carry on making the money which is just as much necessary to you as to me.

Another point arises about the money question. What you are getting now is the limit of what I can manage. I am told that it is very much more than could be obtained by recourse to a Court, where (as circumstances are now) the amount which can be ordered is only £2.5.0. [two pounds, five shillings]. I may be wrong about this; doubtless a lawyer (if you are disposed to consult one) can advise you more impartially. Of course, if ever the position arises that you have grounds to petition for a divorce, the matter is different. I am dealing with this matter of money because I want you to appreciate that the sum you are getting now is a substantial one, and I do not propose to increase it; to do so would merely run the risk of having to cut down later, when perhaps you may have involved yourself in running liabilities which would not stand any cut. It is better to know exactly where you stand financially than to have the worry of ups and downs; and to make your arrangements according to your known means.

In connection with your future plans, I will do some hunting next week and see if I can fix a furnished flat or some sort of accommodation for you temporarily. You did not say how much you were prepared to pay, however. Perhaps you will let me know. Accommodation in London, even in hotels, is almost impossible to get, and I can promise nothing; but I will do the very best I can. If I have any luck, I will let you know.

In your letters you had some personal criticisms of me, and raised the thorny question of responsibility. My dear, it is not wise for us to start throwing things at each other; both of us have so many things to throw. In general, however, on the question of responsibility, I will always help in a real emergency, so long as it _is_ a real emergency. I hope this deals with the specific point on the question of responsibility that you raised. The tendency is bound to be in time that you cope with your own emergencies; but for the time being, until you get settled in some way, I will try to do what I can, so long as it does not interfere with what can be called the long-term security arrangements I now have in hand. That is for your benefit as it is for mine.

It is a pity all this has come up at this time. It has not, I feel, done any good. I think we are both doing our best to avoid the trouble that most people get into at such times as these – we are trying to keep the whole thing on a friendly basis, and not make a silly fight out of it. At all costs

Dark Cupboards, Dusty Skeletons

that must be avoided. For that reason I for one shall not write any more of these letters. If on your side you are feeling very angry about the whole business, I can only make the suggestion that you write to me again, cramming all the anger that is in you into the letter. Writing is a very good way of getting things off your chest. I shall not reply to such a letter; in fact it will be forgotten just as soon as possible, and never spoken about. Maybe this suggestion will help you to resolve your resentments and face the future in better heart; it seems worth trying, anyway.

That is all, I think. Let me know about the furniture and your clothes, and about the price you want me to arrange for the temporary accommodation. As I say, the way things are, I cannot promise anything, but I will do what I can.

Yours, Bill.

45, Gower Street, W.C.1.
31st July 1945.
[Telephone] MUSeum 9905
Dear Ruth,
I shall be meeting your train at Waterloo on Thursday. I had rather hoped to be able to see you right through to Potters Bar, but I cannot do that on the Thursday, because in addition to it being my first night on the new service, my duty hours are from 5 p.m. to 3 a.m., and I am going to get quite tired enough before I am done. It is just bad luck that the move and the new duty should happen to coincide.

Your finance and your morals both seem to be in a state of confusion. So far as the money I am sending is concerned, you have always had £4 – £3 to you in cash and £1 into your bank. In future you are getting £4 in cash direct, but paid monthly at the rate of £17. 10. 0 [seventeen pounds, ten shillings] per month. All right? But any time you feel that £4 is too much, be sure to let me know!

When writing to you, I ought to head part of my letter (if not the whole of it) 'Joke Section'. My reference to being immoral was meant to be funny. But perhaps you really knew that, only were feeling cross when you wrote. Anyway, being quite specific, I did not want you and the infant to stay the night at this time because I am working like a horse to get my book into the hands of the agents by the date promised, and 24 hours of you and the infant in this place would throw me completely out of gear for two or three days. When I have got some of the awful pile of work cleared up, maybe things will be different (assuming we are

Before Memory: Wartime Marriage

even on speaking terms by then), but just at the moment I am resisting anything which is likely to cause an upheaval in the smooth progress of my days.

I don't suppose you feel particularly happy about our relationship – whatever it is supposed to be now. Nor do I. In fact, when I think about it, the whole thing tends to worry me sick – so I try not to think about it too much. My suggestion is that, when you do get down to some thinking at Potters Bar, you get the whole thing ironed out in your mind. That is easier said than done, of course, but you ought to make the effort. Some time or other we have both got to look rather hard into the future, find out what we are going to do, and then get the tangle straightened out. Anyway, when you are ready, it is something we can deal with by discussion.

Yours, <u>Bill.</u>

P.S. The cot mattress should be at your new address by the time you arrive. The cot itself will be in the cloakroom at Potters Bar Station. If you want me to fix it up, and can do without it on the Thursday night, I will come along Friday – early in the morning – and do my stuff.   B.

45, Gower Street, W.C.1.
Museum 9905
13th August, 1945.
Dear Ruth,
I know you will never do anything about your clothes if left to yourself, so I am packing them and they will be in the cloakroom at Potters Bar station some time tomorrow, and the cloakroom ticket will be in the post. Enclosed are the keys.
Yours, Bill.

The letter below is a draft or copy. It's not clear whether the second part is definitely a continuation of the first.

110 Quakers Lane,
Potters Bar,
Mlddx.
Sept. 20th. 1945
Dear Bill,
Thank you for your letter & also for sending my shoes. I feel that now the worst has happened. At least I can't at present imagine anything worse. The resentment & recriminations which as you said, generally arise at such times & which we both hoped to avoid, have come. I can

Dark Cupboards, Dusty Skeletons

only hope that, as you suggested earlier to me, the expression of your feelings in a letter may have made you feel slightly better.

I have felt your irritation gradually increasing during these last months. Maybe I could have lessened it, had I realised how strongly you felt about a quick acknowledgement of money sent to me by you. I see that I have been at fault here, but also that you have much exaggerated the matter, & that there is here a case to be made for me, but at present there would be no point in making it. I see now that you have been sending me money voluntarily but never willingly. I did not realise this before, though it is natural enough if you feel that I have merely used you for my own ends, & that you cannot have from me in return the things you should have from a wife.

The middle section of this letter seems to be missing, the following written on the same note paper as the first with the same pen.

. . . bank to pay the balance (£25) into your account as partial repayment of the money you have given me.

I am sorry all this has happened. I had hoped while here at least to do small things for you. I had laid up some stores of rationed food for you for the winter. I had planned the necessary coupon expenditure for Elizabeth & myself, & had put by some for you. I had hoped you would come here sometimes, or that, being within reach of London, we would meet. I had given myself during this short period, an intensive training in cooking and housekeeping, hoping that later you would sometimes benefit from it. I had hoped, as preserving bottles are not obtainable, to collect from the flat some empty jam jars & bottle some fruit for you for the winter. I had hoped also that you would be glad to feel that Elizabeth was having good living conditions. But at present I realise that whatever I do or say, you will assume I want to persuade you that we should live together again. I do not want that any more than you do. I suppose, if you do believe me when I say that, you will think it is because I have got what I wanted. If it is any satisfaction to you to know it, I am just as unhappy as you are. And I am sure that none of us can have much happiness in the future, neither you, nor I, nor Elizabeth, until your feeling of resentment is dispelled.

I would have been about sixteen months when we first moved to Roehampton with Auntie Gladys in March 1946 until the autumn of 1947. For the next few years we came and went as Mother chopped and

Before Memory: Wartime Marriage

changed. At least she then mostly kept me with her; one has to be grateful for small mercies!
Mother was able to have a bedroom to herself, a large room upstairs at the back of the house. I was put in the smaller front bedroom next to hers above the porch. Kitchen and bathroom were shared with Auntie Gladys, also the large back garden with sweeping lawn and herbaceous borders beautifully kept by a hired gardener.

Claremont, Highdown Road, S.W.15.
April 3rd 1946.
Dear Bill,
Many thanks for the cheque and the hot water bottle.
As you know, I don't want to have a divorce, but also I will certainly go ahead with it, if you are quite sure that you want it. It won't make much difference to me, because whether we are married, separated or divorced, our marriage goes on being my life and work, even if it has to consist of only the one aspect of it, bringing up Elizabeth. But if you want to make a complete break & start afresh, I wouldn't want to hinder you.
Basic difference of temperament you say – I see that – and other things too. I just don't believe that it is impossible for us to get together. Not to go back to the kind of life we had in Gower Street, of course not. But I shall never feel that it is right to give up completely because that was a failure. We know now that we can't ever give each other all we want. But my [illegible] is that we can have a better life together than apart . .
.

Dark Cupboards, Dusty Skeletons

Summer 1946, aged about 18 months: John Chaloner, Mrs Chaloner's elder son next door at Roehampton, asked Mother if he could take some photos as I played in the driveway. An artist, he wrote and charmingly illustrated children's picture stories under the name of Jon Chalon: *The Flying Steamroller*, *Sir Lance-a-Little and the Knights of the Kitchen Table*, and *The Story of the Green Bus* with protagonists Jane and Stephen – his own children's names.

Before Memory: Wartime Marriage

Draft; undated; typewritten with many errors; probably May or June 1946.

Dear Bill,

I am sorry that I didn't either ring you or let you know last Sunday. I intended to ring but was not free till rather late in the evening (E. did not get to sleep) and felt it better not to disturb you in case you had gone to bed early.

What I want to say is quite simple. Perhaps you realise that I shall never get adjusted to our being apart. If not you had better know now and that, as you said earlier on about your own decisions, nothing can be done about it. It is over a year and I miss you just as much. But this doesn't mean that I shall attempt to alter your decision or hinder you in any way such as in the matter of a divorce. Like you I feel that nothing is worth having if it has to be taken and is not given freely.

Recognising the basic difference of temperament I just don't believe it is impossible for us to get together. Not to go back to the kind of life we had in Gower Street, of course not. But I shall never feel that because that was a failure we need give up completely. We are neither of us good at personal relations, but we both feel drawn to the vocational way of life, or as you said the life of service is the only one that is really worthwhile. That is a basic similarity. But we differ in method and the need for adjustment comes in, for creating suitable circumstances. It is in that for both of us in marriage, that the emphasis should be. The personal side would then fall into place. Or again, as you said in the beginning, the main point is that we have a family business. Lack of experience and immaturity accounted for many of my past mistakes, and now largely through having Elizabeth I am older and wiser and a better person, and I feel sure I could give you what you need, as much, and more than any other woman, and that we could achieve something worthwhile together. But as you are convinced that in any circumstances you would be too irritable and frustrated, then nothing can be done about it

So the future is bleak for us both. Believing as I do that our marriage was not a mistake, it goes on for me consisting of only the one aspect, the bringing up of Elizabeth. And if I do this job you will probably think I shall change later on. Certainly it will be very difficult. Since you are not willing to make adjustments my aim will be to do the best for her. If I make a life of my own I shall in some way have to give up Elizabeth and should feel that were her loss as well as mine. If I do the job of being a mother as well as possible I must give up the things I need as a person,

Dark Cupboards, Dusty Skeletons

and then get nothing for it later on, (wanting another child, since she will have yr temp. [your temperament?]) However, I think that will be the best way. And for you there is the financial burden. I will do my best to ease that as soon as possible.

Post-war economy pushchair with rear wheels only !
Playing in Auntie Gladys's back garden with two little boys,
Colin and Michael, who lived on the corner of Highdown Road and
Dover House Road. Summer 1946

To move on from this sunny summer's day: January 1947 saw the "big freeze", exceptionally cold weather causing serious problems in living

Before Memory: Wartime Marriage

conditions with power cuts to rationed supplies when the country was still recovering from war. I would have been two in November '46, so don't remember the cold but do remember being told about it. Years later Mother said,
"Auntie Gladys and I eeked out the heating," alternating during the day with three types: I think the coke boiler in the kitchen in the morning which also heated water (the house had no radiators) and a coal fire in an open fireplace in one room. In the afternoons Mother had a small open, one-bar electric fire. In the evening one tall, black, cylindrical paraffin-burning heater "the oil stove", moved between bedrooms. Houses never normally had night heating making do with hot water bottles: solid, beige stoneware, now sometimes seen in antique shops, known as 'stone pigs'.
Coke and coal were in short supply, power cuts may have limited the time an electric fire could be used, paraffin probably only available in limited quantities. The gas stove would have provided for heating food and drink. Auntie Gladys's relatively large house must have been difficult to heat. At least there was a proper bathroom and coke boiler to heat water. As late as 1950 a government survey found only 46% of households had a bathroom.
Public transport was cheap. In Roehampton Mother wasn't far from friends and relatives in southwest London. Barnes, where she'd grown up, was just a bus ride away. Her first cousin, Audrey, still lived there. Also a single mother, family-minded Audrey had the idea that her daughter Vanessa and myself should be brought up as sisters, both being close in age and similar fatherless situations. Over the years we visited often.
Mother met her lifelong friend Daphne shopping in Roehampton Village in the mid '40s, a friendship lasting until Ruth died in 1999, although the family, Daphne, her husband Ivan and daughter Ann a year older than myself, moved away from Roehampton in 1953. Mother's university friend, Sheila also a single mother with two young children, Jonathan and Sarah, lived in Wimbledon again easily accessible from Roehampton by public transport.
Mother's sister, Kay (Kathleen) lived in rented rooms in North London. We saw her regularly, if infrequently.

Dark Cupboards, Dusty Skeletons

Reliable cheap public transport to Hindhead meant Mother could get to her mother's for weekends, I don't remember my grandmother ever visiting Roehampton.

We moved six times before I was five: from Gower Street to Hindhead, to Potters Bar, back to Hindhead, to Roehampton, to Headington, Oxford with Auntie Janet, returning briefly to Roehampton in school holidays. Then still before I was five I was away at boarding school where you move six times a year between home and school. Moves weren't too much of a problem as long as Mother was there; boarding, although coped with at the time, a different can of worms entirely leaving a huge empty vacuum. More of which later.

Looking lively despite ups and downs.

First portrait, aged two, 1947.

Moves and Changes: Snapshot Memories

In my childhood 'family' no one got on with anyone else: a generation constantly putting each other's backs up. Mother's elder sisters, Janet and Kathleen, my maiden aunts, never got on with each other. As a child Ruth had been close to Kathleen (Kay), but felt her sister found it hard to cope when she'd married and had a child. Mother, struggling financially, was upset by supposed criticisms of her care of me:
"Is that coat warm enough, Ruth [for Elizabeth]?"
Janet, the eldest tended to snap, scold, and glower venomously, Victorian public schoolmistress style – in a way that would have done credit to a rattlesnake with toothache – Mother seemed intimidated by her. Controlling elder sisters assumed the youngest couldn't cope. Mother struggled on determined to prove them wrong.
Kathleen had fallen out with her mother over risqué relationships with men, her liberated life-style provoking embarrassing gossip for a respectable teaching family; Ruth fell out with her mother over leaving Bill. Grandfather died soon after my birth. Grannie, a fulltime housewife described as "nervy" and "never very strong" had put everything into bringing up her daughters, was perhaps suffering from burnout while adjusting to bereavement.
So Mother moved in with a non-relative. Auntie Gladys's detached, characterful, four-bedroom, indisputably middle-class house, "Claremont", graced quiet, gentle Highdown Road leading off Dover House Road, which climbed the hill from Putney to Roehampton. All the houses in surrounding roads were detached with names – nothing so vulgar as numbers! – neatly planted front gardens and built to accommodate at least one live-in servant. Claremont possessed three entrances to choose from, each with separate gates onto the pavement: a low wooden gate in the centre opening onto a

Dark Cupboards, Dusty Skeletons

paved path to porch and front door for exclusive use of residents – us – and visiting guests. To the right a separate tradesmen's entrance led to the back kitchen door, its 'vulgarity' hidden from the front garden by a trellis. This was used by the milkman, coalman, and other delivery men, trade not being socially upmarket enough for the front entrance. The paperboy did use the letterbox in the front door to push Auntie Gladys's daily newspaper through early each day to read with her breakfast, the kitchen door having no letterbox. To the left of the front garden was a low double gate opening onto a short concrete driveway to the garage. Auntie Gladys didn't own a car so rented her garage out to a uniformed chauffeur with care of a large, expensive shiny, black model. Attitudes to class have become less rigid; that was the way things were then.

I grew to love the large back garden surrounded by its high wooden fence. A terrace with steps led down to a neatly cut lawn with four apple trees, herbaceous borders down each side, at the end vegetable beds and a small wooden tool shed. The large greenhouse had a rain water tank inside to fill galvanized metal watering cans (water being eternally fascinating to a small child) an attached cold frame and rusting unused boiler outside.

Highdown Road houses, all of similar size, had been built in the 1920s in, I believe, William Willett style, less expensive than some of his local designs but with enough differences to be characterful. In an age when class was important, it was suitably middle-class for an Oxford graduate from a respectable, socially aspiring family.

Claremont was a lovely house to grow up in and, during frequent moves and changes, became more of a home than anywhere else, somewhere we always came back to. Mother longed for somewhere of her own, often talked about uprooting, but Auntie Gladys and I both loved that house, thought of it as "home". When you're a child who actually owns a house isn't meaningful, and Auntie Gladys was the kindest, most easy-going landlady.

One winter's evening in Letchworth Mother went through her black and white photo collection. She held up a large view of the front of Claremont given to her by Auntie Gladys.
"You don't want this, do you?" she stated.
Absorbed in some other pursuit, I absently agreed,
"No."

Moves and Changes: Snapshot Memories

Always safer to agree with such categorical assertions. Now I wish she'd kept it.

This inexpert depiction is as I remember Claremont.
To the right is the tradesmen's entrance; in the centre the grey stone birdbath; to the left next to the Chaloner's house, the driveway with drain for hosing down a car. The roof (well above my child's level of vision) isn't accurately remembered. The half-hexagon gable roof drawn here was actually a simpler V-shape although the bay windows beneath definitely had three parts as shown. Three small trees grew to the right of the drive which couldn't all be drawn in without obscuring the house. The little round window intrigued me from early childhood – other homes didn't have one – the downstairs lavatory. Above is the stained glass, art-deco window where the staircase turned halfway up.

Dark Cupboards, Dusty Skeletons

Auntie Gladys on the terrace looking at me taking the photo.

Our immensely kind, easy going, landlady opened her home to us.

Summer 1955.

A few very early snapshot memories of Roehampton flash vividly back, probably from age 2¾ as I remember being left at day nursery in Putney, more of which later, which happened according to Mother's diaries in October 1947 before my third birthday. Pictures of situations and feelings are still clear, interpretations below pieced together later.

I must have been very small, memory and consciousness just dawning. Round, pleasant, motherly Florrie came to look after me for short periods to give Mother a break. Perhaps when Mother went to the lavatory she normally left me outside, maybe Florrie thought I might cry. I remember her taking me in with her to the ground floor lavatory at the front of Auntie Gladys's house with its small, intriguingly circular window, totally unlike the usual rectangular shape. I stood by the hand-basin wide-eyed, solemnly watching the unfamiliar sight of Florrie lifting her voluminous brown skirt covering flounced white petticoats beneath, sitting herself on the 'throne' all the while chatting companionably:

"I must go to the lavatory, mustn't I? My Mummy would be cross if I wet my knickers, wouldn't she?"

Moves and Changes: Snapshot Memories

My only clear memory of Florrie, still vivid at seventy-seven!
Another early memory is of growing up with polished surfaces, being taught from a young age to be very careful with Auntie Gladys's beautifully shiny wooden dining table, *never* to do *anything* which might leave – horror of horrors – a *scratch*.
This table is also linked with a memory of Auntie Gladys's mother, "Old Auntie". She used to walk round, slowly slowly, one hand on the surface to steady herself – for exercise, it was explained. I must have decided to help as I remember getting behind, putting my hands on the small of her back, leaning forward to push, saying, "Exercise! Exercise!"
Mother, quite rightly, quickly told me to stop. Auntie Gladys dived out of the room exploding with laughter. She had a wonderful sense of humour.
I remember Mother's efforts to keep my face clean, being washed with a clean white cloth handkerchief wetted with spit. Post war there were no paper tissues, no wet wipes, no polythene bags to pop a wet flannel in.
Early on I was taught to clean my teeth. Toothpaste came in circular, shallow tins. You took off the lid and rubbed your toothbrush bristles across the pink flat surface to get paste on it. Non-fluoride, of course.
A brown paper parcel sat in Mother's bedroom brought by the postman. In no hurry to open it she said it was just her bicycle basket she'd lent to a friend. I must have been old enough to know parcels were exciting. To humour me she gave way and opened it. I wasn't disappointed. Tucked inside were a creamy-white, hand-knitted, woollen lamb and small black gollywog neatly dressed in jacket and trousers. "Lamby" became one of my favourite toys. His neck, its stuffing soon shifting into head and body, became thin and elongated, just right for a small hand to grip for carrying him around, amusing a young lady visitor who laughed.
I remember playing in the driveway of Auntie Gladys's house, an aeroplane roaring overhead, becoming frightened, starting to cry. Unconscious memories of a wartime baby perhaps? Mother, determined not to encourage fear, said it was nothing, walked away indoors; an early lesson in staying stiff upper-lipped – as expected to continue.
A dim memory flashes back of coming into Auntie Gladys's kitchen on a cold day after playing in her garden, feeling warm and glowing. Mother, deciding I must be chilled, produced a white enamel bowl filled with hot water, insisted I take off my shoes and socks and sit with my feet it – a standard technique to warm someone up. This happened only once, perhaps

Dark Cupboards, Dusty Skeletons

I wouldn't sit still for long. I have no memory of actually feeing cold or the warm water making much difference.
Always independent some earliest memories are of running off; when out with Mother and another relative delightedly streaking away. Shortly after, to my horror, a brand new harness with reins appeared suddenly, made of thick light-brown, polished leather, the front chest piece decorated with bells and beads; probably quite costly in that post-war era so perhaps paid for by Grannie as I think we were at Hindhead. Horrified I made a fuss about wearing it. Mother relented saying don't run away again. I never did when out with her, never wore the awful thing. It hung around for years long after I was far too big to wear it.
Another time I remember Vanessa's mother, Audrey, taking cousin Vanessa and myself for a walk near Barnes Station – running off – Audrey leaning over a parapet high above telling me crossly to come back. I did. She sounded so annoyed.
But the time I must have caused Mother most worry was at Roehampton. Aged two? Quite small anyway. Playing by myself in Auntie Gladys's front driveway, I suddenly took it into my head to nip out of the front gate and run to the corner of Highdown Road then, deciding to explore a little further, turned right down Dover House Road to Crestway and having got started, kept going. (I do remember where I went; street names were learnt later in junior school). The other side of Crestway a council estate drifted down the hill with rows of small, identical, terraced houses grouped round public greens. Carrying on, running happily down the hill, I eventually found a green where older girls were playing. They spoke to me. I stayed with them until they had to go in for lunch, disappearing suddenly. Still not unduly perturbed I stood by myself in the middle of the green having forgotten the way home, a wait not long enough to feel frightened. Mother soon arrived having borrowed a black sit-up-and-beg bicycle from the Chaloner's next door, then asked people if they'd seen me. Of course I'd taken it for granted she'd be there when I needed her – and she was. She wasn't angry just obviously rather shaken, said I mustn't do that again. We walked back up the hill to Auntie Gladys's house, she wheeling the bicycle.

*

Mother's bible for child rearing was *Feeding and Care of Baby*, by guru of the time, Sir F. Truby King, C.M.G, MB, B.Sc. who tended to dictate *what* "the child" should eat (the ideal diet), *how much* "the child" should eat,

Moves and Changes: Snapshot Memories

and at *what times of day*. I still have Mother's tattered beige copy of this manual for new, and unsure, mothers. Post-war food, still rationed and in short supply, was extraordinarily unappetising, often plain boiled vegetables with gristly red meat. Not surprisingly there were very few fat children in post-war Britain. Parents and schoolteachers were more concerned about getting children to eat whatever was available. Below is Truby King's recommended diet for a two year-old: a vast amount. I'm not surprised Mother was worried. She'd been brought up in a schoolteacher family to be bookish and respect 'authority'. Truby King was gospel. My own children, who thrived and grew, ate nothing like so much at two. During the war, in 1942, Truby King's baby manual was revised and re-published: some foods recommended weren't easily obtainable such as oranges and fresh eggs.

Feeding and Care of Baby, p.139
"Suggested meals for a 2 year-old child:
On waking:
The juice of half an orange, or grape-fruit, or tomato juice
Breakfast:
1-1 ½ slices crisp wholemeal toast, buttered.
4 – 5 tablespoons of porridge or cereal with milk, or stewed fruit, with dry cereal and milk in hot weather.
1 rasher of grilled bacon occasionally
Cup of milk (6oz.)
Piece of raw ripe apple to complete meal
Dinner:
1 egg or steamed or baked fish, brains, chicken or rabbit – 1 flat tablespoon
Green vegetable (well mashed) – 1 ½ flat tablespoons
Other vegetable (well mashed) – 1 flat tablespoon.
Potato (baked or steamed in jacket – 1 flat tablespoon
With gravy made from vegetable water to which marmite may be added
Junket, custard or milk jelly 2 – 3 tablespoons, with 1 – 2 tablespoons of stewed fruit or baked apple
Small cup of milk
Piece of raw ripe apple to complete meal
Tea:
Thin crisp toast (and or) wholemeal bread sandwiches of honey, marmite, lettuce or tomato

Dark Cupboards, Dusty Skeletons

2 – 3 dates or raisins
cup of milk (8 oz.)
piece of lettuce or apple to complete meal
Give nothing but fruit juices and water between meals."

To be fair he does add:
"Individual appetites vary considerably and although most children would be amply satisfied with the amounts specified, *others may demand more."*
[my italics]

Later when child psychology got underway psychologists would say eating might become a power struggle between mother and child. I don't remember any feeling of power or awareness that Mother was acutely anxious, something only realised later. I just didn't want to eat, or not as much as she thought she thought was "right" for "the child". I have no memories of feeling hungry or being pressurised into eating. But after reading Truby King no wonder Mother was worried!

Mrs Chaloner next door at Roehampton, comfortably round and motherly, with three grown up children of her own, managed to reassure Mother a little. She'd written books with a relaxed attitude to bringing up children under the pseudonym Len Chaloner rather than Leonora (as men were more likely to get published). Googling shows titles included *The Mother's Encyclopaedia,* and *Feeling and Perception in Young Children.* She helped us a lot, mother and child on our own. Now is a good opportunity to pay tribute.

In 1947 I started nursery school. Mother's diary notes this momentous event in October, so it would have been a few weeks before my third birthday. Wartime day nurseries had been set up in response to need, mothers being involved in war work on the home front while fathers were abroad serving in the forces. The only school run Mother ever had would be our daily trip on the number 30 bus down the hill to the Upper Richmond Road. After that I took myself to another nursery next door when we lived in Oxford, then to boarding school. They say memory doesn't really begin until three but I have clear snapshot pictures of this wartime day nursery, easier to remember in my seventies than what I ate for lunch today or a name.

I remember being walked to the bus stop at Crestway to catch a big red double-decker bus down Dover House Road, down the hill to Putney,

Moves and Changes: Snapshot Memories

where the bus turned right into the Upper Richmond Road to the bus stop. We got off there then walked back the way the bus had come past the junction with Dover House Road to cross the Upper Richmond Road. The nursery school was on the ground floor of a big house on the south side of the Upper Richmond Road (I've just checked compass directions) with a large back garden we played in.

Another picture is of sitting next to Mother on the bus, the conductor standing in front of us. He has two shiny metal 'boxes' on thick brown leather straps round the shoulders of his navy uniform, one with interestingly coloured tickets. Mother would give him large brown pennies, he'd take two tickets, slot them into the other shiny 'box', press something to punch holes then give them to her. She'd pass them to me to hold.

we get the big red double decker bus – down the hill – watch conductor in navy clothes and peak cap – take mummy's large brown pennies – take pink and yellow tickets from his rack (wanted red ones) thick brown leather straps round his shoulders – watch him punch holes in tickets – give them to mummy – hand jingling in a pouch – change for mummy – where are we going – she doesn't smile . . .

Mothers weren't allowed to stay while children settled. Another clear picture is of being left for the first time, sitting on a bare wooden floor, crying. A young lady in nurse's uniform sat on a hard, straight-backed chair a yard or so away. Other children in the room run around. One little boy ran up to the nurse and spoke to her. She smiled, replied. I'm crying but she takes no notice. I want to stop but tears keep coming so I shut my eyes hoping that will stop them. Having learnt the futility of crying – I was going to be left anyway – in future I never did.

sitting on floor – where's mummy – bare boards in big room – tears keep coming – want them – to stop – nurse sits near – white blue uniform – on hard chair – little boy runs up – she smiles, chats – doesn't see me – want to stop crying – shut my eyes – perhaps tears will stop – they push their way – under lids . . .
mummy comes – we – get on the bus – more tickets – given to me – I want to be home

Dark Cupboards, Dusty Skeletons

There are other snapshot pictures of nursery. One is of a dazzlingly bright sunny day. The doors of the large nursery room at the back of the house are open to the garden. Unusually tables have been put outside for lunch. I'm sitting at one on a small, wooden, child-sized nursery chair in front of a white china plate of boiled white fish and boiled potatoes. Hot sun blazes down, blinding. I screw my eyes up, know I should eat dinner, but can't. The sun is so bright. At last someone mercifully removes the plate and we go indoors again away from the sun.

My eyes have always been sensitive to light. In those post-war days no one thought of sunglasses, sunhats or sun-protection cream; Wychhazel lotion a standard remedy to soothe burnt skin. I don't remember any trouble with sunburn.

lunch time- a table – outside in the big garden – bright sun – can't see – a white plate – boiled white fish – can't eat – screw eyes against – light – mercifully – someone – takes plate away – small canvas beds – with blankets – put – on floor – sleep – know nothing – time passes

I remember Mother arriving one afternoon to fetch me. There was a white iced birthday cake, mine, the first I'd seen; I hadn't known it was my birthday. The nurse wanted me to stay while everyone had a piece.

I remember Mother, tired, irritable, not seeming pleased about the cake; perhaps she hadn't had a good day. She said we couldn't stay, had to leave *now*. The nurse insisted I at least cut the cake, so someone helped me hold the knife handle and push down through the brown inside. Then we left without eating any to catch the bus back up the hill.

tea time – birthday cake – mummy comes – seems cross – won't wait – we must go – NOW – a nurse says "she must cut the cake" – my hand held – round the big knife handle – helping me push down . . . we leave – other children have – the cake

*

At nursery I picked up the usual infectious diseases most children caught in that post-war era, going down, aged three, with measles in the spring term of '48 (no measles immunisation available) which possibly left a slight, lifelong hearing problem. On top of measles came whooping cough but without the 'whoop' as I'd just had the inoculation which apparently worked to some extent. I remember waking in my cot alone in my room above the porch at Roehampton, feeling better, climbing out to play with a

Moves and Changes: Snapshot Memories

hobby horse, Mother rushing in saying I wasn't better yet, putting me back in the cot. After that at some point I also developed tonsillitis.
Medics were resisting removing tonsils as without antibiotics post-operative infections had led to deaths but Mother, worried I wasn't eating enough, thinking a tonsillectomy would solve the problem, persuaded a specialist near Hindhead. Perhaps the operation was paid for under the new National Health Service set up in July '48, or grandmother may have paid for private treatment.
No one considered it damaging for a three-and-a-half year old to be left in a strange place. But this hospital did at least allow occasional visitors as I remember Grannie sitting by my bed, giving me a blue handkerchief, trying to persuade me to eat a hard-boiled egg (unsuccessfully). Auntie Kay told me years later she'd heard I'd said,
"Where's Mummy?" over and over. Many hospitals believed children became too distressed, crying inconsolably, when a visiting parent had to leave so visitors just weren't allowed. Perhaps it was felt Grannie would be more neutral, less likely to be upsetting.
Food Feud (below) was a piece of creative writing written for a course at Birkbeck College, University of London. Everything in it is a definite, clear memory. I remember being put into pyjamas and into bed in a ward with young children in beds down each side; then left as Mother slipped out of the door, afraid to call out, trying to beckon her back; some other children in the ward and the nurses; being taken into theatre for surgery – not knowing at the time only realising with hindsight piecing together snapshot memories. I remember leaving the hospital, being taken to Brambletye in a taxi (probably paid for by Grannie) building up to a massive tantrum, Mother reacting angrily, bottling my anger down. The next snapshot memory is of Mother looking at me across Grannie's dining table where just the two of us sat opposite each other, her annoyance when I still wasn't eating much, saying exasperatedly,
"Oh! You're supposed to be eating now! You've had your tonsils out!"

FOOD FEUD

Aged three.
In a hospital bed.
Mother slips
through the door.
Afraid to call
I beckon
frantically
to come back. She doesn't.

Wheeled out of the ward.
Strange man in white coat
holds black thing to my face.
says "Talk into the telephone".
I hold my breath.
He sighs.
...darkness......lying down....
...my mouth is open........
.....try to close it.........
..a 'spoon' down my throat......
....is hastily withdrawn......
........................know no more.

"I can get out of bed"
says a boy next to me.
He does.
"You can't" he says.
Indignant, I try.
At once
the nurse is there
to put me back.
Why?

Another boy
cries and cries.
He has a toy windmill.
I have never seen one before.
I don't have a toy.
Because
I don't cry?

It's dark. (Night)
A nurse sits at a small table
with a dim light.
When I sit up
she comes.
But not for long.

Grandmother comes.
Sits by my bed.
Gives me
a blue handkerchief.
Wants me to eat boiled egg.
I won't.
Say "Where's Mummy?"
again and again.
Grannie's not the same.
Doesn't fill the emptiness.

The taxi home.
A huge rage
wells up.
Mother is cross.
Stamps. Crushes.
I push the rage
down, down.

Lunchtime
I move the food
Round my plate
Mother is angry.
"You're supposed to eat now."
"You've had your tonsils out."
I don't.

Moves and Changes: Snapshot Memories

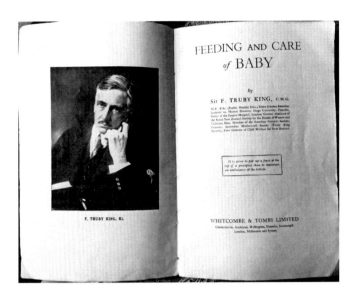

Mother's 'bible' *Feeding and Care of Baby*
by a rather grim-looking Sir F. Truby King.
Feeding baby clearly wasn't something
to approach in a relaxed way.

In those post-war years in Roehampton Village rationed food came from small, family-run, shops, the same familiar shopkeepers serving each day. Roehampton High Street had a combined Post Office and bakery, a greengrocer, wet fishmonger, Addison's hardware store, a chemist and small café doing post-war teas and hot meals, plain and unappetising by modern standards. Also a riding stables where horses came and went leaving the smell of manure drifting round open, exposed food shops, generally accepted as unremarkable.

Next to Addison's was a flight of steps leading down to more small shops, a sweet shop run by an elderly lady outside which the number 72 bus terminated, a newsagent, bank, and butcher's. The largest Village shop was a grocer's with different counters for different products. You had to queue at each of these for different items – no self-service. The number 30 buses from Putney and beyond parked outside before turning round the horses' drinking trough and public fresh water fountain to begin their return

Dark Cupboards, Dusty Skeletons

journey. A very small shop in Medfield Street sold knitting wools and a few clothes, probably handmade. I was hardly aware of the Village pubs throughout the many years spent in Roehampton hidden as they were behind tall plain wooden fences; probably serving only alcoholic drinks non-male customers weren't encouraged. It goes without saying *we never visited*. Decades later Mother was horrified I rehydrated my family's vegetarian Christmas nut roast with *wine!* Definitely the first step down the slippery slope into alcoholism . . .

Few homes had fridges, Auntie Gladys didn't have one; frozen food wasn't available so fresh meat and fish had to be shopped for every two or three days, Mother walking the half-mile to the Village with shopping bag and myself in pram. Roehampton had no supermarket just small shops with loose produce set out on trays in front windows with handwritten price tags. Plastic bags didn't exist. Meat, fish and greasy items might be wrapped in greaseproof paper. Butter being an expensive luxury Mother usually bought margarine. Both would be passed over the counter hand-wrapped in greaseproof paper. I'd watch as bacon was sliced by turning the handle of an interesting, shiny, circular machine on the counter, then wrapped to be handed over for Mother to put in her shopping bag. Tea came loose in packets until the mid '50s: no tea bags! We had a standard brown ceramic teapot, put in a couple of teaspoons of tea then poured in boiling water from the kettle heated on the hob. The teapot lid got dropped and broken:

"Oh, what a catastrophe!" A replacement would cost.

And there was no pre-packaged fruit or veg. Shoppers took their own bags, with a separate one for earthy potatoes which came unwashed. You had to ask the shopkeeper for what you wanted and tell him roughly how much. I would watch him choose from his stock of apples or potatoes, then weigh them on his scales – the old type with curved metal tray one side and solid metal weights on the other to balance – in pounds and ounces. He'd lift the tray from the scales and tip them straight into the bag Mother held out. Apples might merit a brown paper bag. You couldn't pick the rosiest apples or check quality – you had to be *served!* Years later, when I caught up with him, my father Bill, told me a greengrocer had once weighed out apples one of which was rotten. He'd pointed this out. The shopkeeper had said, "You'll have what you're given, mate!"

Moves and Changes: Snapshot Memories

Bill flew into a rage and got the rotten apple changed – probably given to someone who didn't protest.

The elderly lady in the sweetshop would weigh out the boiled sweets Mother had chosen from one of the tall glass jars filled with brightly coloured sweets on shelves behind the counter, and put them into a small white paper bag, twisting the top so they wouldn't fall out. I watched her take the few large brown pennies placed on the counter and give the bag to Mother. Then she picked up a large pair of scissors and carefully cut out a greenish square printed on the dull beige utility paper of our ration book before handing it back.

Shopping provided social life. We met Daphne and her daughter Ann, while queuing in the greengrocers. There were no toddler clubs where mothers with young children could meet and chat. Mother developed a life-long friendship with Daphne. Auntie Gladys would come home from shopping in the Village with the latest gossip (of the milder kind!)

Raw meat and fish would be selected, cut and weighed by the shopkeeper. Both were displayed exposed to air. You might be given a very fatty joint; Auntie Gladys would complain at lunchtime, the main meal of the day, about what she'd been sold. The one fishmonger in Roehampton, in the High Street, set out the unfrozen raw fish on an open exposed stand sloping towards the pavement, to entice customers. With little traffic air was less polluted; even so modern Health and Safety would have had a fit. When purchased, fish would often be wrapped just in newspaper; print had to be washed off after unwrapping. Meat would be wrapped first in plain white greaseproof paper, then newspaper. Occasionally thick red juices leaked into the shopping bag.

Payment would be made with loose coins or paper one-pound notes – no plastic credit cards – or, for the wealthier and more trusted, put on account to be paid for later.

Milk was delivered each day by the milkman in glass bottles with foil tops, left by the tradesmen's back door early in the morning before breakfast. So Auntie Gladys had fresh milk for her breakfast as well as a newspaper to read. Empty bottles had to be rinsed in cold water and put out to be collected next day.

With no fridge or freezer food preservation and use needed careful planning. A joint of meat might be roasted the day after being brought

Dark Cupboards, Dusty Skeletons

home, then eaten cold next day; any tough, stringy remains would be put through the mincer, or stewed, or both. Nothing was wasted.

Auntie Gladys's scullery had a large, airy walk-in larder with a tiny window for light and ventilation, the lowest shelf tiled white for coolness and hygiene. A large, fine mesh, wire cover would be placed over a plate of meat to keep flies off in summer. Milk might be kept in a bucket of cold water in warm weather. Tins, jars of jam and packets of non-perishable food like tea were kept separately in a cupboard in the kitchen.

Cooking was done on the gas stove in the scullery, a relatively modern contraption sporting blue and white enamel with flat metal gas taps for the four burners, a grill with tray under burners, an oven below lit with matches. It stood on the floor on four long metal legs. Saucepans were bare grey metal with metal handles which could burn when hot if one wasn't careful.

The kitchen and scullery both had large rectangular porcelain sinks with wooden draining boards. Auntie Gladys would stand at the kitchen sink washing up looking out over the back garden. After being washed, knives, forks, spoons, plates, cups, saucers, and saucepans, had to be dried with stripy cotton tea towels, and put tidily away. Crockery was all made of china (no plastic); a breakage was a major catastrophe for Mother with so little money for replacement. We had non-matching odds and ends, some showing white chips from accidental knocks and bangs.

With hindsight I realise Mother worried terribly that I might not be eating enough. Perhaps she had some justification having had a small, premature baby, but maybe young children's bodies use food more efficiently: provided what's eaten is nutritious and a child's well and lively, quantity needn't be such an issue. And at that time it was still a bit of a status symbol to have a plump small child – no worries about survival from memories of a higher Victorian infant death rate – unlike today's worries about obesity beginning early in life. To have had a premature baby as small as myself had been a bit demeaning for Mother. But after a visit to the clinic she recorded in her diary,

"E. is exactly average height and weight".

With a mother who found coping difficult, hated domesticity, had low energy levels, never a 'do-er', traumatised by war and a broken marriage, being an only child probably gave me a better start in life. In her early thirties she still had the energy to nurse me through illnesses and other

Moves and Changes: Snapshot Memories

early childhood setbacks. With all the difficulties I never had to cope with a younger sibling or an older one bossing me around always that little bit ahead and better at everything. Except that perhaps she had too much time to worry about perceived problems such as eating.

Another early problem was talking. She told me later I didn't talk until three then came out with a whole sentence. This doesn't tally with diary entries mentioning earlier attempts. She said she'd thought I wasn't going to talk. I've always found verbal communication difficult – when stressed, angry or upset and needed most – a considerable disadvantage. Did she realise children need to hear speech, to be talked to? Or think speech just *happened?* I remember her talking to me when a little older. Children were taught baby names so biscuits became "biccys", horses "gee-gees", dogs "bow-wows", cats "poozas" or "pussies" (without present day connotations), birds "dicky birds". Bodily products were your "big job" or just "bigs", what came out of one's nose "bogeys" – eternally interesting to small children. I remember having trouble pronouncing some words, being aware of this, wanting to get them right: for "apple" only managing "appley", and yellow being "lellow" for a long time.

*

Below is Ruth's undated draft of a letter to Bill; she rarely put dates. Probably written in summer as she mentions plans to get a teaching post in the autumn, and probably in '47 when I would have been rising three. As always both were careful to avoid strong feeling should letters be read by a solicitor.

Claremont, Highdown Road, Roehampton. S.W.15
Dear Bill,
I have not yet made any definite arrangements for the autumn, but expect to get something fixed up.
Sometime ago you wrote suggesting that it was time I stopped ignoring the broader realities of life in case I should get overtaken by circumstances & In a panic come to you for help. I don't think you need worry that I should do that. At least I believe that I have now learnt thanks to you to be sufficiently self-reliant.
It is true I have been sitting quietly in Putney [Roehampton] because any other course would have been too expensive while Elizabeth was still a baby.

Dark Cupboards, Dusty Skeletons

Since last summer, apart from paying £1 a week for rent from my reserves, I have lived entirely on what you have sent. It hasn't been easy with the cost of winter fuel, but it has been possible. Now you suggest is the time to take up a career. Well, I haven't already got a career which I can take up again and am not in a position to start a fresh one (too old to train) so I must have a job which will give some financial security, & this I've decided must be teaching, or some work connected with education, as only in this way can I have the necessary free time during the school holidays. [A graduate in the 1940s and '50s was qualified to teach without further training.]

You suggest also that I should think of marrying again. Here also practical considerations make it extremely unlikely. But fundamentally I suppose it is because I don't believe I'll ever get adjusted to our being separated. Maybe you'll say this is because I've not made enough effort. It seems to be how I'm made & how I feel & nothing can be done about it, as you said earlier about your own decisions as to no compromises. But I am sure also that this doesn't mean I shall attempt to influence you at all. Like you I feel that nothing is worth having if it has to be taken, & is not given freely. Certainly I agree that our life together in Gower Street was a failure or more accurately perhaps my failure – but because of that I shall never feel it was right or necessary for either of us to give up completely, or that to get married was a mistake.

That being so I realise that I must now be mainly a mother, with very little chance of personal life, since the two will not be compatible, & that I shall get very little for it later on.

About the broader issues. First, yes I have been sitting quietly in Putney, because any other way of living wd [sic] have been more expensive. Since last summer apart from drawing £1 a week for rent (from reserve), inclusive of elect. gas & fuel, I have lived entirely on what you have sent.

Now I intend to take a resid. teaching post from next autumn for about 2 years, if poss. in a school wh. takes children from 3 years, & that Eliz. will also be there. This will not be easy to find, as my qualifications are not to teach in a nursery or prep. school. [Or] I shall take an ordinary teaching post & shall send Eliz. to a resid. [residential] nursery school. Apart from pers. feelings, I think that any child is better with its mother until at least about 5 years old, but these are the only 2 alternatives & the arrangements must be made within the next few weeks. After she is about 5, I should like if poss. to do part-time teaching, or coaching & make a home, Eliz. to go to a day school or *[illegible?]* as a weekly boarder.

Moves and Changes: Snapshot Memories

You suggest I shd. take up a career. This I shall not do. For one thing I'm not the sort of women to have one, except marriage. Even in diff. circs, that is without the child, I know I cd never really put my heart into it. As things are, I must have work wh. will provide the bread & butter for adult & child, & wh. will give me free time in the school holidays. Therefore teaching. I can see no alternative, & shall hope to do the job adequately. If you can [illegible] to send me some money, it will be welcome.

You suggest also the poss. of marrying again. I wdn't like to be so definite about this, as about the career, but I am pretty sure that it is also out of the question. For one thing I shall be far too busy for the next 2 or 3 years, & by then be that much older. I can't imagine being without a man for the rest of my life, & can foresee the poss. of getting involved in a few years time with someone who wd prob. be married & have a family. Also having made the rearing of Eliz. my main business, I suppose I'll feel v. much the need of another baby. But the main reason is that I don't believe our mar. was a mistake & nothing can be done about it.

I know, & have known for a long time, that the best life for me is to marry & be able to co-operate in my husband's work.

But at least it is poss. for me to be positive & not fatalistic about it, since I have the power of choice. I could choose to take up my own life by putting Elizabeth in a residential nursery.

All this is in answer to your suggestions. What of yourself. I don't think my decisions really affect you. I imagine that for both of us our present life is in many ways intolerable. Your greatest problem just now is, I suppose, a financial one, & in this I could perhaps help a bit by becoming more independent financially. This I will try to do.

Then there is Elizabeth. Do you still feel the best course is for you not to see her. I don't agree with this at all. I think it would be much better for her to know you naturally, as she grows rather than suddenly later on, & she is bound to eventually. It would also be better for me.

Recognising basic diffs of temp [differences of temperament] I still believe that we cd on the basis of having a family business with adjustment make the good life possible for ourselves as you said.
RW.

*

One day Mother announced, "Janet's coming back from Carlisle". She often tended to speak thoughts aloud as though unaware I was there. I could see she looked pleased. Her eldest sister, teaching Greek and Latin in upmarket girls' schools, had spent a year at Carlisle County High School

Dark Cupboards, Dusty Skeletons

for Girls after leaving St Leonard's School (girls' boarding) in St Andrews Scotland. She now moved back south to Headington School for Girls in Oxford. Mother felt she would help us and she did. It was Auntie Janet who rented the ground floor flat we moved into with her, next to a lovely nursery school.

That year is the only time I remember three of the family living together, otherwise it was just the two of us or I was sent away on my own. But even so I don't remember Auntie Janet ever sitting with us to eat meals as Auntie Gladys did; she tended to live a separate life. Auntie Gladys, in many ways, became 'family', but with Mother so unsettled anyone might disappear forever from my life at any time. Bill didn't want us; Ruth's mother didn't want us; now Janet tried to help. We spent the summer of '48 at Roehampton before moving to Headington in the autumn.

I remember arriving at 17 Stephen Road (address learnt when older) one sunny day, an elderly lady called Miss Woods welcoming us in her garden. This backed onto that of Hunsden House Nursery School; as she owned both properties the fence between had a door linking the gardens. Slim and neat, she had greying hair and wore a beige outfit with fashionable calf-length skirt. She tried to introduce me to Deborah, the little daughter of Mary and Archie Utin (pronounced "Yootin") who ran the nursery. But Deborah was screaming and screaming, and Miss Woods's friendly calls of "Hello" across the fence went unheard. Apparently Deborah, sitting in a child seat on the back of her mother's bicycle, had caught her foot in the spokes of the wheel. However we did meet next day. Deborah had dark curly hair, was slightly younger than me, and had two older brothers, Timothy and Jonathan whom she called "Yonna". We became good friends and over a year spent a lot of time playing together, both in and out of school hours before I was sent to boarding school, after which our friendship fell apart.

Then aged three and three-quarters I remember Miss Woods only as the elderly lady who owned the house. I've since discovered online that after her father, a Fellow of St John's College Oxford, had died, her mother had bought the plot of land and built the house – 17 Stephen Road – we moved into. Miss Woods had founded the nursery school in a room in this house. When her mother died she'd had the present nursery built separately in its large garden. Online history shows it was always run on progressive, open air lines with windows and doors opening south and east, a model for other

Moves and Changes: Snapshot Memories

nurseries: "The atmosphere of a school should be an extension of the home atmosphere, not an 'ordering about' atmosphere."

Mary and Archie Utin had then been running Hunsden House School for five years. Aged three, accepting this as normal, the way of the world, not knowing much else, I never realised how lucky I was, that it would be the happiest year of early childhood. Seventy-five years on a memento of Miss Woods is the needle-case she hand-embroidered with my initials, "EW". Treasured and still used.

Auntie Janet rented a ground floor flat in Miss Woods' house. We entered from the garden into a sunroom with two doors, one leading to Auntie Janet's large bed-sitting room overlooking the front garden, another to a small room overlooking the nursery garden where Mother and I slept on low canvas beds. Our bedroom led to the kitchen with small table and hardback chairs where we ate, a gas stove, and large white porcelain sink. The kitchen doubled as bathroom with bath at one end hidden by a curtain for privacy and a highly temperamental, Ascot gas water-heater, which only ever produced tepid water. The other end of the kitchen led into the hall with the only downstairs lavatory, another door to Auntie Janet's room, a door to the back of the house let to a Polish family with several young children, and stairs to Miss Woods's rooms. I remember once being invited upstairs with Mother and once into the Polish family's kitchen otherwise never venturing into these forbidden precincts. Heating was provided by an open coal fire in Janet's room and small electric bar fire in our bedroom.

The flat was more cramped than our rooms at Roehampton. Mother used Janet's bed-sitting room for entertaining visitors while her sister was teaching (our small bedroom had no chairs), had to share a bedroom with me – and then there was the bath situation, more of which later.

Each morning after breakfast I would lift the latch on the door in the high wooden fence – the door between home world and nursery world. The sky seemed infinitely blue. Birds wheeled and soared above. Leafy buds leaned trustingly towards the sun's rays. Once through the door I'd race across the lawn to the nursery to spend the day with Deborah amongst twenty or so other three to five-year-olds. In fine weather we spent a lot of time in the large garden achieving new feats on the climbing frame, dressing dolls on the patio, pushing doll's prams behind the house where, under the shadow of tall leafy trees, we could watch the chickens scratching in their wire run – Deborah and I, mothers together with our babies. Deborah's mother,

Dark Cupboards, Dusty Skeletons

Mary (we nursery children knew the couple who ran the nursery as "Mary" and "Archie") picked up the eggs and showed them to us: some cracked, some with small chunks of shell already missing, tiny windows revealing glimpses of fluff and beak inside. Mouth open I stared in wonderment. Mary picked a tiny piece of shell off one, then said, "This one's not quite ready yet!" I sensed she didn't want to disturb the chick by taking too much off. Better to let nature take its course. Best were the fluffy yellow chicks already hatched, running amongst the big brown grown up hens.
Then indoors for morning milk drunk with paper straws poked through the silver foil tops of transparent glass bottles. We held them in both hands sucking, then chortled at the rude bubbly noises from the last few drops. Archie Utin sat nearby at a real artist's easel, painting – though he often helped Mary in the nursery – surrounded by other canvases with finished pictures. We watched him dip his brush in the colours on the palate then magically turn them into trees, houses, people. The wartime day nursery in Putney I'd been taken to on the bus was became a fast-fading haze.
After elevensies Deborah and I might go off to explore the garden pond reputed to have a live frog hiding inside an old pipe. We waited impatiently for him to appear, then spotted frogspawn amongst the rushes and water lilies, tiny black circles inside transparent jelly with a few wriggling tadpoles nearby. I'd been given some spawn of my own to keep in a jar on our bedroom windowsill and watch them hatch, but they didn't. Mary said it was because I'd handled them too much. Probably true.
Bored with the non-appearing frog we might go on the swing for a bit. The older boys chased round earth paths behind a couple of small sheds and bushes, shouting to one another.
One day, indoors again for lunch, Deborah and I gleefully chanted, "Yum, yum, yum!" until Mary told us to stop. No child was ever smacked, ever shouted at. We sat at small tables to eat, gobbled lunch – there was never any pressure to eat – then went outside again to play in the sunshine.
I remember once a brown horse being brought in, standing next to it near the house, Mary showing us the harness, saddle and blinkers. At any time I could have taken myself home through the door in the high wooden fence but never wanted to, sometimes coming through out of nursery hours to play with Deborah and the toys. On wet days we all played together in the big nursery room with windows right along the length of one wall

Moves and Changes: Snapshot Memories

overlooking the garden. There were drums, tambourines, triangles to experiment with; indoor apparatus to climb on, a long low table to sit round and draw. We weren't taught letters or numbers. I think I learnt colours mostly at home. I don't remember sitting down much except occasionally in a circle or being read to. I had books at home bought by Mother to encourage me – with hindsight – to feel positive about starting nursery school. Well meant but not making much difference to the earlier trauma of being left at nursery in Putney: *We go to Nursery School* (A Barbara Bateman Book, published by University of London Press, price 3/6) and *Jimmy Jumbo's Journey* about a little elephant who doesn't want to go to school and runs away, has various unpleasant experiences, goes home, then has a lovely time going to school letting his new friends ride on his back.

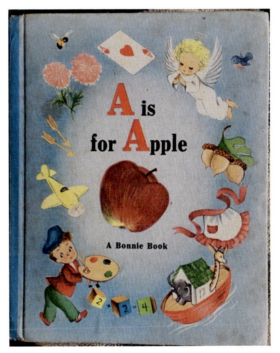

It's unlikely a modern alphabet book would include pictures of an angel or that archetypal symbol of the unliberated housewife – a frilly apron. Other dated images are a candle, darning a sock, a bottle of ink, games of jacks and marbles, a quart jug and a thimble.

Dark Cupboards, Dusty Skeletons

"At Nursery School in Oxford"

Hunsden House Nursery School,
Headington, winter/ spring 1948-9. I'm in the front
row second from right, wearing pale blue leggings under
my skirt as Mother was anxious about my health; my tendency to
catch colds (with no tonsils !) For all her anxieties about eating I don't
look smaller than the other girls. The seven girls are all wearing skirts: *never*
trousers in the 1940s. Some of the thirteen boys have ties; they wore short
trousers above the knee in all weathers. My first little best friend,
Deborah, is holding the doll. Her parents Mary and Archie Utin
ran the nursery and lived in the flat above with their three
children. The photo shows all, or almost all,
the children at the school – about twenty.
Names have faded from memory.

I remember a lot of running round and playing, being happy with Deborah; adults occasionally being cross: when on one non-nursery day Deborah and I took off all our clothes and bathed in the semi-stagnant water of the small concrete paddling pool, having to be thoroughly washed in clean water. Never feeling fear, never feeling terrified of adults. That was yet to come.

Moves and Changes: Snapshot Memories

Unlike at the nursery in Putney we didn't have to lie down for an afternoon rest. Mother thought I should so after lunch Mary would take me upstairs to their flat on the first floor to rest in Deborah's elder brother Jonathan's bed. This stopped when it was realised I no longer went to sleep.

At the end of the day – when other children's parents arrived to collect them – I would walk back across the lawn to the door in the fence for tea with Mother. Later, Auntie Janet would come home, but cooked and ate separately; I've no memory of the three of us ever sitting down to eat together. In the flat's kitchen Mother and I would sit at the small table to eat our meals sometimes with one of my dolls with her own plate in front of her. Dolls were still very real to me, secretly alive but not letting us know. Once, my doll had a piece of boiled egg on her plate. Would she eat it when we weren't looking? I must have turned away briefly as Mother unexpectedly said,

"Oooh! Look! She's eaten the yolk!" Sure enough it had gone. Mother knew I preferred the yolk. So did the doll!

I would be put to bed in the room Mother and I shared with two low camp beds. After she'd put the light out she'd kneel on the floor beside my bed as I lay drowsily drifting into sleep and sing in her musical voice. She usually sang only the first verse:

> "Do you want the moon to play with?
> And the sun to run away with?
> They'll come if you don't cry . . .
> Oola loola loola loola loola loola . . . "

or:

> "Golden slumbers kiss your eyes,
> Smiles awake you when you rise,
> Sleep pretty baby do not cry
> And I will sing a lullaby."

or perhaps:

> "Dark brown is the river
> Golden is the sand
> It flows along for ever
> With trees on either hand."

Dark Cupboards, Dusty Skeletons

I remember *Bobby Shaftoe*, *Greensleeves*, *Do You Ken John Peel*, and a Christmas carol *Away in a Manger*. She knew several verses of *Good King Wenceslas*, so I would try and persuade her to stay and sing more than the first holding, onto her arm, but she only once sang it all through. More often she might relent enough to sing the second verse then pull free and slip away into the lighted kitchen. The words were a series of sounds I only half understood. It was the tunes that stayed in my dreams from her voice softly singing in the darkened room. Bedtime enchantment.

*

Deborah and I spent a lot of time together out of nursery school. Mother sometimes took us to Bury Knowle Park along a little sunken alleyway at the end of Stephen Road, riding our tricycles or scooters to the playground with swings, slide and a roundabout. We each had an identical red scooter. Deborah, younger than me, was better at balancing and could cruise all the way down the long asphalt path in the park without putting down a foot. She also had a better tricycle with proper chain and pedals unlike my cheaper one with pedals attached only to the front wheel limiting speed. Deborah, although younger, always outstripped me. I wanted to go faster, wished for a trike like Deborah's. The smaller one was probably all Mother could afford: the shape of things to come growing up in a one-parent family.

Once we decided to put on an 'exhibition' of our 'paintings' in the sunroom, holding them up one by one. I'd gathered together our 'audience' of Mother and Auntie Janet who, when asked indignantly, assured us she *was* looking while obviously reading her newspaper.

Needless to say we weren't always good. Once we crept
through the hedge behind the chicken run into next-door's garden!

Deborah had a knitted, blue square, wool 'comforter' to have in nursery school. I asked Mother for one. She produced a ball of blue wool to knit but until she had time I took the ball instead.

The Utin's had a sun lamp (ultra-violet) under which Deborah had sessions. Mother felt this would improve my health so asked if I could join her. Deborah and I sat next to each other on a bed under the lamp with no clothes on giggling and chatting. I don't remember whether we wore protective goggles as we should have done.

Moves and Changes: Snapshot Memories

Above: Miss Woods' house, 17 Stephen Road. Left: sunroom & door in fence to nursery garden. The large window is Auntie Janet's bedsitter.

Below: Auntie Kay visited with friend Alfred; the swing is in the nursery garden. Rarely, all three sisters were together. Looking towards Miss Woods' house. Aged 4, 1949

Playing on my own in Miss Woods' garden I explored the garage and adventurously climbed onto the seat of Mother's black sit-up-and-beg

Dark Cupboards, Dusty Skeletons

bicycle which leant precariously against the wall, once there realising with alarm it might fall over and I couldn't get down. But there wasn't long to wait before Mother missed me, rushed in looking worried, held the bike and helped me off.

Another time, playing alone in the garden, I suddenly realised I knew the way to Bury Knowle Park and could take myself to the swings, roundabout and slide. Which I did. Again, I'd barely got happily settled on the roundabout – cone-shaped, balanced on a tall pole, thrillingly going up and down as well as round and round – before Mother arrived looking less than happy but not alarmingly cross and took me straight home. Yet another running away escapade.

We often went to the library in Bury Knowle Park to borrow adult books for Mother and to the clinic next door to collect post-war government rations of children's orange juice and powdered egg. The orange juice had a distinctive taste, quite sharp, different from any tasted since and the powdered egg had to be mixed with water to make a nourishing thick yellowish 'soup'. It came in blue rectangular tins. I remember Mother once producing something alien-looking, telling me enthusiastically – at her most persuasive – that this was,

"A real egg!"

I viewed it with intense suspicion, cautious about eating this strange unfamiliar food preferring the powdered egg that my post-war generation was brought up on.

I remember being taken on some interesting outings that year in Oxford, all enriching first experiences. Archie Utin once walked with us to the football ground in Headington, later Oxford United Football Ground. We stood in the empty stalls watching a casual game whilst he and Mother chatted.

Another time I was taken to my first concert in a large hall, stared at the gleaming golden organ pipes, listening to loud music booming forth.

Then there was the outing with Mother and Auntie Janet in a punt on the river from under Magdalen Bridge. I was taken down the steps beside the bridge to where several punts were moored and told to get into what looked like a very unsafe, wobbly small craft. And told to get in *first! Before them!* Nervously I protested I'd thought it was going to be a big boat (like one I remembered cruising on, on the river at Richmond). They didn't want any trouble: I was told sharply to get in, which I did, soon acclimatizing and feeling safer.

Moves and Changes: Snapshot Memories

Another outing leaving a clear picture was being taken to look through huge ornate metal gates into Magdalen College Park, seeing for the first time brown deer, antlers lowered to graze, and scurrying red squirrels racing up and down tall trees.

I was once left at a Sunday School in Headington, probably at St Andrew's Anglican church. After Mother had gone a nice lady welcomed me, explaining the impressive model of a church with imitation stained glass windows older children were busy putting together, a magnificent construction involving paints, brushes, scissors, cardboard, and transparent coloured paper for the windows. Wanting to join in but a bit too young and not sure what to do, I just stood and watched waiting for Mother to come back. She was late; the other children had all gone home.

We shopped for food in Headington once calling at the toyshop to buy a small green clockwork frog. I remember being taken into Oxford to a Music Department where mother worked, probably doing secretarial work.

*

Mary Utin asked Mother if she would take in a stray kitten. Few cats were neutered then: homeless kittens proliferated. He was mostly all-black, half-grown. I never knew where he came from, he just appeared in the nursery garden.

"What do you want to call him?" Mother asked.

"Tommy!" I replied at once.

Aged four, I had a limited knowledge of names. So Tommy became my cat, living with us in the flat, coming for food in his bowl. I remember one day seeing him crouching under a bush in the rain. We opened our window and called; he streaked across the garden and in through the window. That was the moment he seemed to realise his home was with us.

Aged four, I learnt a lot about cats: that he liked milk in his saucer in the kitchen (no awareness then that lactose wasn't good for cats: everyone gave them milk), his fur stroked the right way not ruffled backwards, that cats rather strange greenish eyes can see in the dark, that when he kneaded his paws up and down he was "making hay", that cats wash themselves with pink raspy tongues, to recognise purring as a happy sound, that sharp claws meant he could climb trees easily, the name "Pussy" which didn't have the connotations it does now, that Auntie Kay called him a "Poosa!" an intriguing new word for my infant vocabulary. I heard that cats don't like

Dark Cupboards, Dusty Skeletons

changes: if moving house you put butter on their paws (then in short supply). By the time they'd licked it off they would be settled.
But change was endemic in our lives. At the end of the summer term in Headington we went back to Roehampton by train, Tommy in a cardboard box tied with string. Air holes had been punched. Halfway through the journey Mother suddenly became agitated:
"Oh, he *hasn't, has* he?"
She decided he hadn't but this could have been a disaster – watertight plastic boxes weren't available then, or plastic bags with which to line a cardboard box.
So he stayed with us at Roehampton over the summer. Auntie Gladys, the most tolerant of landladies, raised no objection. Then in September, still aged four, I was sent to boarding school near Oxford, Mother later teaching at High Wycombe. Eventually, when we were back at Auntie Gladys's, the three of us sitting round the kitchen table having lunch, I asked what had happened to Tommy. They went vague, didn't seem to know, he'd apparently just 'disappeared'. When we'd left, he'd also drifted. Auntie Gladys tentatively suggested her neighbour, Mrs Chaloner, might have found somewhere for him. People, places – all came and went at that time. I still don't know what happened to Tommy but hope he found a more settled home than we were able to give him.

*

A total non-entity, my father just didn't exist in my infant world, I wasn't told of the letters reproduced here, or shown a photo. I wouldn't have recognised him, never wondered what he might be like. Mother never mentioned him. Sensing he was a taboo subject, I didn't ask.
Why? She didn't talk about stressful situations. Communication about feelings was simply not on the agenda, not stiff upper-lipped. Or perhaps so painful they had to be denied. There was a general feeling that childhood was an innocent world of happiness not to be burdened with tragedy. It was quite usual not to talk to children about family heartaches. Even a death might be glossed over.
Fathers who were absent for no obvious acceptable reason, such as military service or work commitments, just weren't mentionable. She may have worried I'd indiscreetly repeat something sensitive.

Moves and Changes: Snapshot Memories

Auntie Kay, less worried by gossip, once laughingly told me, that Vanessa and I must have been a great embarrassment to our mothers. Apparently one of us had announced over lunch at a rare family gathering:
"My Daddy's gone away."
To which the other added:
"My Daddy's gone away too and Mummy says he's not coming back!" followed by an awkward silence and change of conversation.

During her last illness in hospital Mother talked about her lack of a relationship with *her* father, how he must have been very disappointed she wasn't a boy. She felt this hadn't made things any easier for me.

Although her letters indicate she wanted to get a relationship going, when the question of whether I should see my father did come up in my late teens, she wasn't so keen. I eventually arranged things myself. But that's another story. If I asked, while nothing derogatory was overtly said, she portrayed a rather uninteresting depressed character. Not someone I would really want to know. When I finally caught up with him he seemed surprisingly positive and ongoing.

*

Below is Ruth's draft of a letter to Bill. As a four-year-old expected to be unemotional and stiff upper-lipped I had no idea she was aware boarding school might be in any way traumatic. The mention of this in the following came as a complete surprise decades later, read after she'd passed away. A human side to her she didn't show at the time.

17 Stephen Road, Headington, Oxford.
March 24th, 1949.
Dear Bill,
We have managed this term far better than I had expected, and have gone through since January without a break. The mild, dry weather has been a great help, and I have given Elizabeth sunlight treatment two or three times a week.
Very soon now she will have to go away to boarding school. [She doesn't say why!] Her health has improved during these last months more than I had dared to hope. Whether at this age she will be able to cope with being a weekly boarder, I don't know, even if I can provide a home for her. If not, it will mean a very big change. I have tried during these early years to give her the sense of security which as a child she needs, and which up to this age can come mainly from the mother. The problem has been to do

Dark Cupboards, Dusty Skeletons

this without making her too dependent on me and without too much frustration for myself. How far I have succeeded can only be a matter of opinion. I think that her physique is better than it would have been in any other circumstances, and that she has been happy. But the lack of a normal home has made difficulties for her and me, and it would be no use going on like this much longer, apart from the financial situation.

I am looking round for a school for her. If you hear of anyone who has sent a child of four or five to boarding school and can recommend it, I should be very glad to know, as a personal recommendation would be a great advantage.

Is it possible to carry on through the summer? I can manage it if you can. The best arrangement, since we had to move last autumn, would be to complete the year here, and for Elizabeth to start at a new school next autumn in the term in which she will be five. If the change has to be made now, six months after the move here, it would put a strain on her which is to be avoided if possible. How finances are going to work out later on is another problem. My only answer to that at present is that I have been able to use my savings very sparingly, and have so far kept enough to pay for a school for one year if necessary.

During the Easter holidays I shall go to Hindhead for a few days, but shall be at Roehampton most of the time, leaving here on April 1st and returning April 23rd. Will you write to me there?

Yours,

45, Gower St.   [handwritten]
1/4/49.
Dear Ruth,
Herewith £9 for April. Thanks for your letter. Take it that all will be well now until the end of September. I am very much out of work at the moment, and expect I will have to move soon, but I have a little put by, and something is sure to come along in a month or so by way of regular income. So do not worry.
Sincerely, Bill.

3rd May 1949.   [typewritten except signature]
Dear Ruth,
Herewith £9 for May. Would you acknowledge receipt with the enclosed envelope? Things are a little chaotic for the moment (I have had to relinquish Gower Street), but I expect to let you have my new address when I write next.   Sincerely, Bill.

Moves and Changes: Snapshot Memories

Why did Mother choose to go back to Roehampton in the holidays? I think she later mentioned paying Auntie Gladys a retaining fee, less than full rent, while Janet probably paid for the Headington flat.

Much later Mother told me that one of the difficulties with living with Auntie Janet was sharing a kitchen. Excessively fastidious, Janet needed everything immaculately *clean*. She'd done very little science at St Paul's but had heard of germs. A little knowledge can be a dangerous thing: she became phobic. And she saw ultra cleanliness as vital amongst the upper class circles in which she taught and desperately needed acceptance. She felt there was a 'right' way of carrying out every detail of one's life. Mother later said that in photos of her with her sister she looked limp, washed out, unable to be a person.

Over the next three years we would continue to live a transient existence between Oxford and London, briefly with Auntie Janet at weekends in term time when I boarded, and with Auntie Gladys in the holidays. Why? As mentioned rent may have been cheaper. Then there was the gossip which followed us everywhere particularly, perhaps, as Mother was so secretive. Did she need to escape that?

Looking back I remember being vaguely aware of gossip and hostility among local mothers in Headington but not at the time feeling much bothered by it. I realise now Mother was; she'd always had trouble as a single parent coping with gossip, with insinuations that I might be illegitimate – a huge disgrace then – especially for someone from her background. Grandmother's aspiring Thomson family had always been very conscious of their social standing. Then perhaps, as Mother appeared to be upper middle class, a 'lady' from an Oxbridge background, this made for more juicy gossip. And also, as a single parent she was perceived as vulnerable, an easy victim, liberties might be taken with a fatherless child having no strong parent to stand up for them

If we'd stayed put the local community might have known what the situation was – that she'd married but separated. As it was, with so many moves, we were relative strangers and gossip prevailed. There was a lot of prejudice in the '40s and '50s in British society. Mother, too distressed by her situation to be able to talk about it, left plenty of room for gossip. Much later she said when she first moved to Letchworth she'd told the neighbours,

"I'm not with my husband".

Dark Cupboards, Dusty Skeletons

They were instantly sympathetic.
Strong prejudice also existed against only children who must inevitably be 'spoilt', perhaps rooted in unconscious jealousy from those who had unresolved problems with their own sibling rivalries, seeing only children as being in a situation they imagined they would have liked. Then there was criticism of her more liberal approach to bringing up children: feeling stymied by her own shyness she tried to bring up a more confident child.
Further embarrassment blew up. Deborah's elder brother Yonna, aged six, wanted to play at seeing each other.
"Let's play 'bottoms'," he'd say.
This, of course, was rapidly discovered by horrified adults and stopped. Soon after Mary Utin told me to stay in the playroom with Archie – just me. The others all went outside to play. This promised to be interesting. He sat at the end of the long wooden table at the far end of the playroom whilst I stood next to him; then talked . . . and talked . . . and talked . . . I struggled to make sense of the jumble of sounds, stared at the little pencil sketches that he, an artist, drew on scraps of paper. Suddenly I thought I recognised buttocks. This seemed terribly rude. Shocked, I must have gasped slightly because he said emphatically,
"*Yes!*" as though he felt the penny had dropped, then went off into another spate of incomprehensible . . . blah . . . blah . . . blah's. The promise offered by this novel situation was fading rapidly. I stared longingly through the window at the others playing in the sunshine.
Years later Mother said Archie Utin had told her he'd told me the facts of life – he might have discussed it with her first – if there'd been a father around he might not have taken such a liberty. She must have been horrified: in common with many other parents at the time she hadn't wanted me to know yet.
"You won't tell anyone, will you?" she said that evening, visions of gossip and scandal leap-frogging round should I know anything I shouldn't and tell other children from 'nice' families.
"No," I replied obediently, not knowing what she was talking about. She needn't have worried; Archie Utin wasn't good at explaining the facts of life to a young child and I hadn't understood a thing.
After we'd been interviewed at St Christopher's, the co-ed, progressive, boarding school I went to in my teens, Mother told me she'd been asked by the headmaster if I knew the facts of life.

Moves and Changes: Snapshot Memories

"Well," she told me, "I said 'Yes', but I couldn't really say you knew when you were *four!*"
Warily, I maintained my usual cautious silence while digesting this piece of information, casting my mind back, picturing the session with Archie Utin. Could this have contributed to her decision to send me away, aged four, to boarding school? Had she been afraid I would tell, causing shock and social embarrassment? That we would become social pariahs?
Then criticism obviously arose over her decision to send me to boarding school at such a young age. One can only guess at the rest of this conversation from the note in Mother's diary of Mary Utin saying,
"I could never say *any* child was better away from their mother."

*

We spent the summer of '49 in Roehampton with Auntie Gladys (and black poosa Tommy) also staying briefly at Hindhead with Grannie. People didn't have summer holidays much in those post-war years – instead we just moved around.
Early on at Roehampton Auntie Gladys had a live-in maid, Kitty, one of those unmarried women of whom there were many who needed to earn a living. Kitty cooked and did various household chores, including watering the garden with a hosepipe. Kind Auntie Gladys let Kitty keep her green parrot, Polly. Kitty and Polly spent much of the day in the kitchen. At night Polly was left in the kitchen, her cage covered with a cloth to keep her quiet while Kitty slept upstairs in the small back bedroom behind Auntie Gladys's main front bedroom.
Polly could talk – a little – fascinating to a young child. Fairly standard things like "Pretty Polly", something which sounded like "to-godda, to-godda, to-godda" and sometimes she would screech. I always hoped she'd talk when I happened to be in the kitchen. When Kitty wasn't working she would let Polly out of her cage to sit on her shoulder clicking her beak softly and murmuring in Kitty's ear.
Kitty loved birds putting bread out on the back lawn every day. A large flock of pigeons used to collect on the grey-tiled sloping roof of the house behind to watch for this free bounty, turning the roof white with their droppings. I'm not sure whether anyone actually complained but remember Auntie Gladys commenting, worried they might.
Jumping ahead a few years: when we went back to Roehampton permanently, Kitty had had to leave (perhaps Auntie Gladys couldn't

Dark Cupboards, Dusty Skeletons

afford a maid any longer) and found a job in a large house at the bottom of Roehampton Lane near the entrance to Richmond Park. Her new, less generous employers wouldn't let her keep Polly. Parting must have been quite a wrench. Mother took me to visit once when Kitty's employers were away. A neighbour saw us in the garden and told the owners; Kitty got into trouble. I still have one or two of Polly's green feathers shed from wings and tail.

*

Auntie Gladys's gardener was always referred to just by his surname, "Heard", as male servants were. Never "*Mr* Heard".
He came once a week to cut the lawn, tend the herbaceous borders, prune roses, grow bedding plants in the greenhouse to plant out, lift dahlias in the autumn from the dahlia bed below the terrace, grow runner beans, and prune the apple trees in tiny beds in the lawn. They never produced any fruit. Jumping ahead again: when he eventually retired they weren't pruned producing loads of apples for the first time.
I remember when I must have been about seven, standing chatting to Heard one icy winter's day as he dug over a bare flower bed. He told me about rats, how dreadful they were: if caught in a trap they would gnaw through they own leg to get away. This showed how absolutely awful rats were. I privately thought it quite brave of the rat to be so determined to survive.
More snapshot early memories: I was quite small, perhaps four, when I stood beside Mother in Auntie Gladys's scullery while she mixed flour and margarine in a bowl, one of those old china mixing bowls – white inside, creamy yellow outside, now seen in antique shops – then put the ball of pastry on a wooden board to roll flat with a wooden rolling pin and make jam tarts. It looked enthralling – she seemed to be enjoying it although she normally never liked cooking. I had a go with the rolling pin after the dough was basically rolled, then watched her cut it with a knife. She gave me a tiny piece to eat and another. I loved the taste, wanted more, but she said that was enough. Ever since it's been difficult to understand why anyone should bother to cook pastry, it tastes so much better raw. Mother never felt confident with culinary skills but I think we both enjoyed making pastry that day. Another early cooking experience is of being left next door. Mrs Chaloner was cooking dinner for Mr Chaloner and her grown up family, so she stood me on a chair by her gas stove in the kitchen letting me watch as she stirred saucepans – a new experience.

Moves and Changes: Snapshot Memories

Born into an academic family I probably had more books for young children than most at that time, economy post-war copies but colour illustrated, some of which I still have: a book of nursery rhymes, *Baa Baa Black Sheep* and *Jack and Jill* being two of the first learnt. My favourite had large pages, idyllic illustrations and storyline: *Barbara Lamb by Cam*.

John Lane
The Bodley Head Ltd.
First published 1944,
reprinted 1946.

Below:
Barbara Lamb
is born in the meadow,
in springtime, as the
bluebirds (symbolising
happiness) nest above
and Reuben the
Shepherd
plays his
flute.

Dark Cupboards, Dusty Skeletons

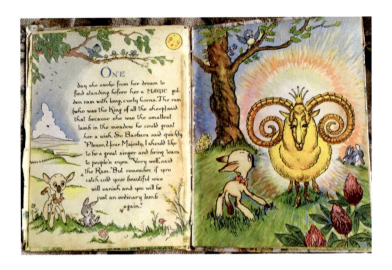

As the first few pages have selotaped tears
I must have preferred this idyllic beginning, where Barbara Lamb
is born, in spring with Reuben the Shepherd, and meets the Golden Ram
who gives her a beautiful singing voice. Pages where she's taken to market,
bought by a wealthy gentleman, sings on the stage until catching a cold which ruins her
voice, are intact, unpatched. This, being a children's story, has to have that vital
ingredient a "happy ever after" ending, So Barbara Lamb is fetched by
Reuben the Shepherd to return to her idyllic life in the
meadow with him and the flock.

Another less welcome flashback memory rears its head: an incident in the general store by the terminus for the number 30 bus at Roehampton. The assistant cut out the little brown squares from Mother's ration book with a pair of scissors, for the few things we'd bought, to show we'd had our allowed quantity. I tried to help Mother pack the shopping bag – got it wrong – put in something displayed on the counter, not paid for. The shop assistant looked scandalised, an angry face scolding. I felt crushed, horrified. But Mother didn't, smiled mischievously going out of the door, said nothing. What *was* going on?

In the small row of shops in the Upper Richmond Road at the bottom of Dover House Road, was a toyshop with a 'dolls' hospital'. Dolls' arms and legs had hooks on the ends; the limbs fitting into holes in the body and

Moves and Changes: Snapshot Memories

hooking on to a thick rubber band inside to hold them in place, while leaving them moveable. I was intrigued by the idea of a hospital for dolls. Mother and I took one of my broken dolls to be 'made better' but discovering this to be horribly expensive brought her home again unrepaired.

We would walk to the top of Dover House Road for walks on "the Common", as we called on Putney Heath, along a well-worn, unmade up path doubling as a riding track, with rough grass stretching away one side and woods the other, then across a road to a small pond we called "the little dirty pond" as mud turned the water dark brown, where I took off shoes and socks to paddle with skirt tucked into knicker elastic to keep it dry. I enjoyed our trips to this pond. From recent maps it seems to have been officially named Scio Pond. Once we went further, taking the pram, to a larger pond, Queensmere, near the cemetery. I had a fishing net on a long stick and felt excited about what I might catch but Mother, presumably afraid I might fall in to the fairly deep water, hid it when we got there saying it had 'disappeared'; a bit of a disappointment.

I liked animals and being outdoors, had definite ideas about what I wanted to be when I grew up: a farmer's wife.

I remember a first trip to the dentist in Putney presumably paid for by the new National Health Service, not feeling apprehensive in the waiting room as I had no idea what was to come. Mother and I both went into the surgery. I was sat in the black dentist's chair.

"This is our little buzzing bee," they said.

Then I did begin to feel frightened and make a fuss. One of them turned and nodded to Mother who obediently left the room. Without her I was too frightened to protest – as they knew children would be. Afterwards I stood at the open door looking across the waiting room to where she sat on the other side, hesitating, not wanting to go to her but having to, feeling betrayed, deserted. In the late '40s it was very common for parents to be sent out when a child had medical treatment believed to be best as an abandoned child would be less confident, cause less trouble.

*

I remember at Auntie Gladys's house, crying, saying,
"You never hug me now," before going to boarding school. Being 'trained' for the change ahead, perhaps? We didn't hug or kiss after I left home aged four – too silly, babyish. Mother seeming irritable, tired, said impatiently,

Dark Cupboards, Dusty Skeletons

"I didn't know you wanted it."
I was still crying. She took me on her lap quickly, without warmth, just to satisfy. She didn't really want to – it was a nuisance. At bedtime I asked for a kiss but she would only give me what she called a "Butterfly Kiss". This meant holding her face close to mine and fluttering her eyelid against my cheek. A compromise between a real kiss and no kiss at all to keep me happy. But it didn't. Was this Truby King again with his advice not to kiss and cuddle the child? "The child": an impersonal entity to be trained to be stiff upper-lipped? Or was it preparation for boarding school? Mother was into mind control. Years later she told me of her interest in Pelmanism popular in the UK in the early twentieth century, marketed through correspondence courses as a means of mind training, advertised to cure 'grasshopper' brain, depression, phobia, forgetfulness, indolence and inefficiency. In fact just about any mental health problem or character defect.

*

It must have rained sometimes but I don't remember. I took my world for granted never aware of the imminent crisis portrayed in Mother's letters, although dimly aware she was looking for a school for me – we visited a convent school in Clarence Lane, sat on a sunny lawn chatting to a lady – but the full implications didn't register. Father, never mentioned, never thought of, remained a complete non-entity. Aunts, Grannie, Auntie Gladys inconsistently appeared, disappeared, Mother the only person consistently there – usually. I was totally unaware of the extent to which life was about to change, that a supposedly secure world would fall apart. Looking back it's now obvious problems mentioned above loomed, besmirching an apparently clear horizon.

Moves and Changes: Snapshot Memories

Probably to help me adjust, Mother produced *Little Miss Pink's School* by Rodney Bennet (1949) which, recently re-read, turns out to be a boarding academy for Little Mouselets. They party, sing, act a play, make paper chains, mince pies and Christmas pudd, kiss under mistletoe, have a riotous time in snow followed by parcels from a Christmas tree. I don't remember the story sinking in at the time or being in any way meaningful. As an introduction to boarding school the book couldn't have got this idyllic scene more wrong.

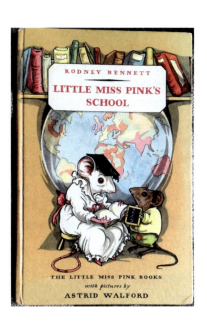

Total Disruption: Catholic Boarding School

I grew up in a family situation in which no one got on with anyone else. You'd have thought that with two maiden aunts living independently and a grandmother alone in a three-bedroom detached house in Surrey they might have come together to provide a home for me as a young child. But no, they couldn't cope with one another. My mother felt Kathleen was very jealous when I was born; in her mid-thirties she must have been coming to terms with being unlikely to have the family she hoped for. Janet, perhaps more adapted to confirmed spinsterhood by life in a world where teaching and marriage weren't allowed – it was thought women couldn't cope with both – was delighted with my arrival, apparently saying:
"I would do anything for Elizabeth."
She helped by letting us share her flat in Headington for a year then, when aged four I boarded at school, for Saturday nights in term-time. My mother said the difficulty with living with her eldest sister was sharing a kitchen. Later I realised Janet had a germ phobia resulting in compulsive cleanliness and tended to snap at and scold her younger sister as she did recalcitrant twelve-year-old, Victorian public school girls. But having us Saturday nights in term time did mean Mother and myself were together more than we might have been.
Mother first searched for a school with a job teaching French for her and a boarding place for me. She liked what was known as freer, "progressive" education, perhaps hoping to remedy family shyness. She looked at various schools: wrote for St Christopher's prospectus (producing it when I was twelve and writing again for an update). I remember visiting a convent school in Clarence Lane. Decades later, she told me that a small, progressive, co-educational boarding school, Long Dene in Kent, now

Total Disruption: Catholic Boarding School

lovingly remembered on the web by its ex-pupils, had offered her a job with a place for me but she felt she couldn't cope with teaching boys. She'd taught briefly at a boys' prep school in Putney, the class got out of control and the headmaster had to come in to re-establish discipline. Her upbringing had given very little experience of men or boys; she very much felt this lack, got on better with women as she knew how they worked. Men she idealised then felt let down by, disillusioned. She later accepted a job at a girls' boarding school, Wycombe Court Garden School taking girls from eight. I was only four.

Mother's childhood world had been a convent day school just across Barnes Green from her family home at 23 The Crescent, a cosy, sheltered world. In finding a school for me she turned towards the secure world she thought she knew. Catholics were people who could be trusted with children, who knew how to bring children up, who treated them well. It's now well known what went on in some Catholic boarding schools.

We visited St Nicholas's School at Tubney House in Berkshire (now in Oxfordshire) one sunny, blue skied, summer's day. Only one short afternoon visit for Mother to take, for me, a life-changing decision. The ancient, stone-coloured, castle-like, building with crenellations, gothic windows and double-door front entrance, surrounded by spacious, tree bordered lawns, couldn't fail to impress parents especially those ground down by war-torn, bombed-out London. It was certainly a beautiful place, Mother was right about that. But small children need close relationships more than a beautiful physical environment and the toxic ethos would be incredibly damaging. The school was charmingly named after St Nicholas, the patron saint of children.

The head, Miss Gisborne, about fortyish but looking older, wore a pale-blue, plain, linen dress, with grey hair pulled back into a tight bun. Charismatic, she had charm, confidence and vitally important in the post-war 'forties – a middle-class accent. And she was Catholic – a convert. With her prospective fee-paying customer she was nothing but affability and tolerance. Shown round the youngest children's classroom on the ground floor I happily climbed through a low window onto the driveway. Mother, of course, wasn't told this was something Miss Gisborne would normally have spanked a child for, pulling clothes off and using the back of a brush or a cane. Instead, Miss Gisborne merely smiled and sweetly suggested they follow me.

Dark Cupboards, Dusty Skeletons

Mother negotiated lower fees as I would be coming home at weekends; told that Anglican children would be taken to their own church; that children's wartime ration books wouldn't be required. She no doubt thought she'd found the perfect place to leave her child. So why should a four-year-old have had misgivings, told her I didn't want to go there? Reminded her when taken back, powerless to decide for myself?
The house and estate lay about eight miles from Oxford, bounded by the A420, the A338 and a golf course. Bus routes ran between Oxford, Farringdon and Abingdon, passing through Tubney. At the beginning of the autumn term '49 Mother and I got off a single-decker green country bus and walked down the long stony drive. For the first time in my life I was dressed in school uniform: dull grey skirt, cardigan, shirt and navy tie. I later learnt Mother had spent her last few shillings on a pair of wellington boots for me but have no memory of ever being told to wear them. Tubney House hidden away in Berkshire countryside by lawns and bordering Scotch pines wasn't visible from any road. Far from war-torn London it seemed at first sight to have eternity on its side. A few small children also just arrived lingered uncertainly with Miss Gisborne by the huge double-doored front entrance. I knew no one but linked up with non-identical twins Vikki and Toni who would be part of my life for the next three years. We each held a carrier bag with a few of our own small toys. Toni took out a tiny doll from hers and dropped it into mine.
"Don't tell anyone," she whispered.
A friendly gesture but already premonition was telling us anything might be disastrously 'wrong'.
A little boy arrived in a black Ford Popular sitting beside his father gazing out enjoying the drive, his world intact, predictable, safe. They got out of the car and stood around for a minute or two. He saw a group of small children standing on the driveway by the huge arched door. Where were their parents? Miss Gisborne sent two older boys to the post box at the end of the long drive with a letter. The father tried to persuade his little boy to go with them. The boy, now apprehensive, clung:
"If I go, you'll leave."
His father kept re-assuring him earnestly that he wouldn't. Eventually the boy, convinced, trustingly walked off with the others. When he was a few yards up the drive his father leapt into the car and drove off past him. The

Total Disruption: Catholic Boarding School

boy, screaming, tried hopelessly to run after the car as it tore round the bend out of sight.
Mother and I watched this little saga of betrayal in silence then she turned to me and said,
"I think I'll go now."
She walked off up the drive – no goodbye kiss – kisses weren't stiff upper-lipped, not Truby King style. Having long since learned the futility of crying – no one would take any notice – I turned towards the open double doors to be taken in with the other children.

The front of Tubney house before restoration. Photo undated but colour so probably 1960s. The driveway in front was where we were all left that fateful first day. Now a Grade II listed building the east section of Tubney House (right) is thought to have been constructed as a hunting lodge, Gollds, at some point before 1521. It was acquired by Magdalen College in 1537/8 and owned by them with alterations until the early '60s. Miss Gisborne took on the lease about 1946/7.

Put to bed that night with four other girls including the twins, in a stark dormitory with bare floorboards, plain, blue-covered, utility metal bedsteads – no pillows: better for "straight backs" Miss Gisborne categorically stated – cuddly toys never allowed, no comforting hot water

Dark Cupboards, Dusty Skeletons

bottles or eiderdowns, no picture books to look at in bed. We all settled without obvious distress perhaps too tired and frightened to protest. I knew I was going home for the weekend; Vikki, Toni and their elder sister Fay were together. After the light had been put out I did cry a few hard, dry tears in the darkness, tears which brought no relief. For more than a decade the luxury of crying wouldn't be an option. We were trained not to have emotions: feelings were a nuisance they got in the way.

Separating children from their families was still strongly ingrained in British culture: at the top end of the social scale middle-class boys were sent away to boarding school at a young age, at the lower end if a family fell on hard times and had to resort to the workhouse children would be separated from parents. John Bowlby's book *Child Care and the Growth of Love* emphasising the importance of the mother-child bond and influencing later social policy wouldn't be published until 1952. Too late for us.

In 2009 meeting my half-sister Claire, seventeen years older than me, she talked of her childhood at a convent boarding school, the nuns so charming, reassuring whilst a parent was there,

"Don't worry. We'll look after your child for you."

But when the parent left and the door shut behind them it was completely different. I understood perfectly what she meant.

"Miss Gisborne" as we had to call her (we never knew her Christian name) was a Catholic convert, a masculine woman whom children wouldn't go to. I've since realised there are many different interpretations of Catholicism: converts can be extremely rigid. She ran the school on extremely harsh, unsympathetic lines with the help of a friend we had to call "Nurse", which may have impressed parents but I doubt she had any nursing qualifications. Nurse was Swiss, looked younger with her short dark wavy hair, was the gentler, more feminine of the pair, and owned a black Labrador called Barry who spent the day in the kitchen with her. She did most of the necessary humdrum chores: growing vegetables in the walled kitchen garden, preparing meals for themselves and twelve or so young boarders aged four to seven, washing up.

Miss Gisborne taught the youngest four and five-year-olds. In the 1940s she wouldn't have needed any professional teaching qualifications to set up a school. She'd started with wartime evacuees, Mother later told me. Mother and Auntie Janet, both spent much of their working lives teaching

Total Disruption: Catholic Boarding School

in good private secondary schools without any teaching qualifications other than Oxbridge college educations, Auntie Janet in some very academic, upmarket girls' public schools.

Mrs Baring Gould taught the girls and older boys. She was quieter, less frightening but uninspiring, and lived in the small gatehouse at the end of the drive with her husband and young son, David, a day pupil taught in the younger class by Miss Gisborne. Mrs Baring Gould's lessons were quiet, no one talked, I never saw her hit anyone or heard her shout, on the whole didn't find mornings with her traumatic apart from struggles with number work. These three grown ups: Miss Gisborne, Nurse and Mrs Baring Gould, ruled our lives.

Other adults at Tubney House were two of Miss Gisborne's sisters we were taught to call "Miss Margaret"– unsmiling, always working on the farm in jodhpurs who looked at us grumpily but never spoke – and "Miss Mary" whom we rarely saw, who – in neat suit and stockings – took the bus each day into Oxford to work. This form of address was in imitation of aristocratic families where, to servants, the eldest daughter would be known as "Miss" followed by the family surname, younger daughters also known as "Miss" followed by their Christian names. The Gisborne family wasn't at all aristocratic; Miss Gisborne wanted to ape the upper classes. The 1911 census shows she was born in Nottingham about 1909, her father's occupation being given as "Silk & Cotton Yarn Merchant", from which he may have made a lot of money elevating the family to *nouveau riche* status, but not aristocratic. Mother said a fourth sister was married with four children and living in Nigeria. One of her children, Janet, Miss Gisborne's niece, lived with her at the school including during school holidays. An unhappy child.

To begin with a very elderly man in a wheel chair lived upstairs whom the 1911 census return shows to have been their father, confirmed by 1940s electoral registers for Tubney House. In my first term Miss Gisborne once took a group of four of us girls up the main staircase, normally strictly "out-of-bounds", to meet him on the landing where we stood round his wheelchair for a couple of minutes. I never saw him again. She never said who he was. Otherwise no men on the horizon. My all-female existence continued at boarding school. At different times two live-in French girls came briefly as assistants; neither stayed long. One seemed openly disapproving of Miss Gisborne's unkind approach to bringing up children.

Dark Cupboards, Dusty Skeletons

Also recently discovered from the internet: Miss Gisborne had taken on the lease of Tubney House from the owner, Magdalen College, Oxford, which possibly turned into a financial struggle dormitories never being full and why we saw little of our pocket money.

*

In the depths of the countryside not visible from any local road the school became a socially isolated environment. Other young boarders all stayed three months each term without parental visits. Arriving knowing no one I found myself with about twelve boarders mostly bigger, six or seven-year-old rather bullying boys, that September of '49 one of the youngest turning five in late November. The school had several boy boarders, few girls: non-identical twins Vikki and Toni – outgoing Toni had short, straight, light brown hair, shyer quieter Vikki dark brown wavy hair – their elder sister Fay, and Janet. A handful of local day children came in the mornings. All of us were white British – except little darker-skinned Malcolm who may have had some Indian heritage – immigration having not yet begun on any scale, all indisputably middle-class then so important, all spoke good English with middle-class accents.

After the war many such small rural private schools sprang up in response to need from families disrupted by bombing. Anyone could set up a school; with little or no regulation they varied enormously in quality. In post-war years many of these schools closed as life returned to normal, children withdrawn, taken home. Child minders didn't have to be registered until cases of maltreatment a couple of decades later led to public outcry in the media. In the countryside locally grown produce was available easing pressure on city families' ration books making a child's rationed food available for other family members. Tubney House had an old walled kitchen garden and dairy farm, a selling point bound to appeal to blitzed, post-war parents.

*

This is the hardest part of childhood to write about – the most troublesome skeleton to drag out of the pitch black cupboard – owing to the trauma of going back into darkest memories trying to dredge up what's deep down, therefore an incomplete though necessary part of this story. Starting with my first term, aged four and three-quarters, some incidents come back clearly: I know they did happen that term. After that, *what* happened *when* becomes confused, sequence jumbles although incidents are still vivid.

Total Disruption: Catholic Boarding School

*

We were woken each morning by the clanging of a hand bell. That first term Miss Gisborne came into the dormitory to train and supervise a rigid routine. No one dared to deviate, act spontaneously, even chat. We were trained to go down the corridor to the bathroom to wash and use the lavatory, then to go back to the dormitory, dress ourselves in grey school uniforms (we had no other clothes). Girls' winter uniform was a white short-sleeved vest and thick navy-blue knickers often with too-tight elastic round the inside leg; a grey, wool, knee-length skirt; a light blue, long or short-sleeved blouse with navy tie we learnt to tie ourselves; a grey wool cardigan with buttons; grey knee-length socks held up by elastic garters but always slipping to runkle round ankles; brown leather sandals for indoors and lace-ups for the playground. I went back one term with the toes of my sandals cut out; I'd grown out of them and Mother couldn't afford another pair. In summer girls wore blue gingham dresses. Boys' wore short, grey trousers in all weathers and grey pullovers with shirt and tie.

Before breakfast we were taught how to fold pyjamas, the precise way to make beds, tuck in sheets and blankets. Hair, we were told, should be brushed a hundred times "to make it shine" but we couldn't yet count that far. Then it was downstairs to the dining room by the back servants' stairs: we were never allowed on the grander front staircase. There were set times to go to the lavatory, rules for every move round the house – none of us dared deviate from the procedure, be in the wrong place at the wrong time. No spontaneous movement was allowed. She taught us in such an unpleasant atmosphere of fear and sexual kinkiness that I for one rejected this training after leaving the school. Early on I learned never to draw attention to myself, it would result in being snapped at, letting go in an unguarded moment with any spontaneous movement would lead to being hit.

*

I wasn't a good eater; every mealtime was an ordeal and there were three of them every day. We had to eat set amounts, the same for everyone, finishing everything on our plates. To say British post-war food was unappetising is a massive understatement. Twelve of us sat, mostly in silence, round a large, rectangular wooden table covered by a plain white tablecloth, six down each side on long benches – younger children nearer

Dark Cupboards, Dusty Skeletons

Miss Gisborne and Nurse who sat on wooden chairs at the head of the table – in the dull-cream, bare-walled dining room. Miss Gisborne and Nurse spoke French to each other which none of us understood, breaking off occasionally to instruct, snap and scold in English. Early on that first term sitting down at table, realising there was a rule for everything, we girls wondered what to do with our skirts. Sharp instruction wasn't slow in coming:
"Tuck your skirts under you! Ladies don't sit on their knickers!"
We were taught to say grace before each meal sitting at table, eyes shut, hands held palms together in front of bowed faces. I don't remember the words – something to do with thanking God for the food we were about to eat – finishing with,
"In the name of the Father, the Son and the Holy Ghost. Amen" and the sign of the cross: right forefinger to forehead, down to waist, to left then right shoulders.
Breakfast was a compulsory one-and-a-half slices of white bread and margarine to be swallowed down somehow without any drink. When we'd finished one half-slice we had to pass up our plate from child to child to the head of the table for the second and third half-slices saying,
"Please may I have . . ." then, "Thank you," when the plate – of hated food! – was passed back. At the end of the meal Miss Gisborne would come round with a jug of milk pouring each of us just three-quarters of a small mug. I was always thirsty, struggled to get down the dry white bread. No one ever dared ask for a drink, even for water would have been like Oliver Twist asking for more. Breakfast was the first major ordeal of the day.
Then it was upstairs again altogether – we did everything in a group – to make beds. Our first term Miss Gisborne came upstairs to instruct: one of us had to be each side of a bed to pull up the top sheet, then blankets, fold the top sheet neatly back over the blankets, each tucking in our side under the mattress in precisely the right way before drawing up the pale blue bedcover over everything.
When sheets had to be changed we were trained to do this again in twos, folding dirty sheets by each taking two corners, bringing them together by walking towards each other, each taking hold of the 'new' corners, bringing these together in the same way; also how to use chins as an extra 'hand' by tucking partly-folded sheets underneath. Many things I rejected

Total Disruption: Catholic Boarding School

when anywhere less frightening having taken nothing to heart in such an unhappy ethos, learnt unpleasantly through fear in a harsh, unloving environment.

Then we'd be regimented downstairs again altogether, to the dull, bare-walled schoolroom where small single, folding wooden desks had been put up for lessons with Mrs Baring Gould, a class of about eight boarders aged five, six and seven. Miss Gisborne taught the few four- and five-year-old boarders herself in a different room with the day children. Until mid-morning break it was Arithmetic. For a short time that first term we rolled brown plasticene worms to shape into numbers, the only play learning. The school had no counting toys to help understand numbers not even an old-fashioned abacus. Early on using fingers was allowed, then arithmetic became entirely rote learning. We sat where we were told in total silence – I don't remember us ever daring to speak to one another – given an exercise book with marked squares on each page, taught precisely how to hold a pencil between right first finger and thumb resting on the second finger, how to practise copying the same number into each square in rows. There was no class teaching; Mrs Baring Gould rarely used the blackboard coming round to each desk very briefly telling us what to do. Then we were left to struggle in silence while she sat at the large teacher's desk in front. When we'd mastered writing numbers we learned to add to ten by counting on fingers, then told not to use fingers, to work things out in our heads. At this stage we'd be given a battered green textbook, *Fundamental Arithmetic* printed in black on white paper, used for the rest of infant schooldays. With no counting blocks getting sums right meant following rote procedures without remotely understanding why, especially when numbers expanded beyond ten.

After a short mid-morning break in the playground the second part of the morning was English. That first term we began by copying letters, in pencil, in rows, on white paper. Then reading and writing were taught from *Fundamental English*, also in a battered grey-green cloth cover. Each new exercise had a black-and-white line drawing at the top of the page – the only pictures. Mrs Baring Gould came round, pointed to the black print on the white page:

"That says c – a – t. Cat. The cat s – a – t on the m – a – t." I was then left to study this page and memorise it. This was no trouble; I picked up reading easily, likewise forming letters in pencil on lines in copybooks,

Dark Cupboards, Dusty Skeletons

sounding out words to write them. Mrs Baring Gould never read stories aloud, the school didn't have story or picture books. When we could read a little we read to ourselves, out of class, from our own few books provided by parents brought to school at the beginning of term. Learning spoken language, practise in talking wasn't considered a necessary part of education in most schools at the time. Only expected to answer when spoken to we weren't verbal children never experienced "Show and Tell", acted short scenes or even nativity plays. For a short while soon after I went to the school a nice lady came in to teach singing. We did have class teaching for this, she used the blackboard, tried to teach us to sing,
"Doh, Ray, Me, Fah, So, La, Te, Doh," in tune, as well as a few songs. A rare attempt at music lessons. Early on we were taught to knit egg cosies in plain stitch, in red wool with a blue or green stripe in the centre. After that craft activities faltered, except for drawing and colouring Christmas cards with coloured pencils (nothing so vividly dramatic as felt tips – they hadn't been invented).

Dull bare classroom walls, greyish cream, had no pictures to spark interest, no children's drawings put up or any of the things many infant school classes had. When I moved on to non-fee-paying Roehampton Church School juniors, peeking briefly round a door into an infant classroom I saw a wonderland of toys: sandpit, water, large dolls' house, castle with soldiers, toy cars, wall pictures, abacus, colouring table, picture books, a home corner with Wendy House, nature table, to mention but a few. I began to realise what I'd missed, that what I'd experienced perhaps wasn't the norm.

*

From the beginning of that first term Miss Gisborne used various sudden, unpredictable punishments: pulling us round by hair or ears; unexpectedly grabbing two of us by our hair and banging heads together,
"To knock some sense into them", so she said.
You couldn't see it coming. Once, in the corridor walking out of the classroom in a perfectly quiet orderly way after a morning with Mrs Baring Gould, Miss Gisborne, standing outside the door, completely out of the blue grabbed hold of two of us by the hair, and knocked heads together. We didn't want to be naughty. She was totally unpredictable.
The next ordeal came when lessons ended. Dinner would be boiled, sliced red meat with boiled vegetables, usually potato and cabbage, probably

Total Disruption: Catholic Boarding School

from the walled kitchen garden we weren't allowed into, and organic and healthy, but tastelessly and unappetisingly cooked as was much British post-war food. Food would be passed through the hatch from kitchen to dining room. In summer we might occasionally be given salad from the kitchen garden: I remember a lot of cucumber never eaten before and not much liked, celery (not then known to be an allergen), some chopped raw veg or lettuce, boiled red meat cold and sliced, occasionally squares of fatty sliced ham. Not easy to eat. Having swallowed whole a lump of solid fat then struggled hard not to throw up, I took the nerve-racking risk of throwing another piece on the floor knowing I couldn't keep a second one down. I don't remember ever having eggs, fish, cheese or chicken (a rare post-war luxury) or imported fruits such as bananas or oranges.

We were given precise orders as to how to hold a knife and fork, where to put fingers – no one dared do it any other way – how to push food onto the fork with the knife, to eat with our mouths shut, not to put elbows on the table, to put our knives and forks neatly together on the plate when we'd finished. Pudding was stewed plums, apples or prunes sometimes covered with a layer of thick yellow custard, served in plain white china bowls. Having had it instilled in me that I must clean my plate I once swallowed all the fruit stones as well. Again, we had only a small cup of milk to finish; no water allowed between meals.

Early on, usually at mealtimes, I learned new, negative phrases: Miss Gisborne frequently used the words: "Not allowed".

Everything, it seemed, was: "Not allowed".

She would announce, "It won't hurt her/ him", when handing out some punishment. But, of course, damage *was* done.

Another frequent phrase,

"You ought to be ashamed of yourself, my girl."

I wasn't "her girl" and certainly didn't want to be!

And at mealtimes rules would be laid down to the older boys about exactly what was: "Out of Bounds": most of the building and grounds It seemed. No doors were locked but fear kept us within a specified room at a specified time, or the playground when sent out.

About one older boy: "He's got his head screwed on properly."

What did having your head screwed on properly mean? How did you have your head screwed on properly? And I remember that first term Miss Gisborne snapping at another child,

Dark Cupboards, Dusty Skeletons

"Use your common sense,"
This stuck in my mind proving quite useful. Common sense can be helpful dealing with life's little setbacks hopefully turning them to one's advantage.
What happened if we didn't eat quickly enough? Motivation was allowing the child who finished first to call out,
"I'm the first of the little ones!" and hand their sweets round afterwards when we were told to get down from the table and line up against the wall. Sweets were kept in round unpainted metal tins on a low sideboard. Too slow an eater ever to be first I never knew what happened to mine, they never got handed round. Sweets' pocket money came from parents. One weekend near the beginning of term Miss Gisborne laid out a selection on the kitchen table as a 'sweet shop'. We were allowed to choose a few which went into our sweet tins. In the kitchen she kept a pile of small identical, metal moneyboxes, black with thin red-and-gold stripes, with our names scratched through the paint. I chose from the sweet shop once in my first term. What happened the next eight terms to the pocket money Mother forked out for me?
Shaming was another technique to get us to eat. Struggling to get food down I was labelled "bad and slow", the child next to me would be ordered to feed me with a spoon, "like a baby". Cold uneaten food might be brought back at the next meal to be finished before the set amount for that meal had also to be eaten. Or we might be sent up to bed for the rest of the day without food which meant getting into pyjamas and right into bed.
Miss Gisborne once announced to the table in general:
"Isn't it a shame? Mrs Wallace's only child and look at her."
I remember feeling indignantly, silently,
"Mummy *doesn't* think that."
A child's spirit is resilient! Or still was that first term.
If she thought someone slouched at table, she would put a walking stick down the back of their clothes to force them sit straight. I was one of those she said slouched as I leant over my plate struggling to eat. The walking stick felt cold and hard against my skin. Very Victorian.
I remember once hearing Miss Gisborne tell Nurse she'd washed a boy's mouth out with soap – he'd said a bad word, quite possibly just something

Total Disruption: Catholic Boarding School

he'd heard his father say. I'd fortunately never heard any bad language so never repeated anything unsavoury. Another very Victorian punishment.
One dinnertime sitting in a bit of a stupor maybe slightly unwell, struggling to swallow down food I didn't see her coming, She suddenly pounced on me from behind, dragged me off the wooden bench, slapped me across the face and stood me in the corner. No explanation. Nothing said. I must have not been eating quickly enough. She then sat down again to eat her own meal. Blood began to pour from my nose. Standing silently facing the wall I tried to wipe it away with the back of my hand. In my first term I'd already learned not to draw attention to myself in any way, so said nothing. Blood streamed, running in red rivulets down the greyish cream wall, down clothes, covering face and hands. My world in the corner turned redder and redder. She must have eventually glanced round. Standing up she took me to the door where she turned to say to Nurse, "We'll have to smack them on their bottoms in future."
She couldn't let herself be seen to lose face, that would have been bad for discipline. In the cloakroom she silently washed my face and hands while I stood by the basin, dull, wooden, still stupefied. My clothes weren't changed. She told me to sit there and wait until the others came out to go out into the playground for the afternoon. My semi-eaten lunch was produced at teatime to finish before the compulsory two slices of white bread, whilst she glowered at me. She was obviously taken aback by my nosebleed, knew she'd overstepped the mark. It was the only time I felt I held my own in any way, otherwise I felt completely crushed. Another time after struggling to force stuff down too slowly and having been sent to bed in disgrace as punishment, I was very sick, bringing up everything in the bed. I dreaded mealtimes, all of them, three ordeals everyday.

*

After dinner we had to go up to our dormitory to sleep on our beds wrapped in our own check rugs provided by parents. Mine was noticeably cheap and thin compared to other girls'. We stood, arms straight down by sides, whilst Miss Gisborne wound our rugs tightly round. Thus imprisoned we were lifted onto our beds and left to go to sleep.
There were never any afternoon lessons or activities, just an occasional crocodile walk at weekends. Afternoons became mind-numbingly dull – the boredom of boarding school. Told to get up from our rest we'd be taken downstairs to the cloakroom to put on coats and outdoor shoes, then

Dark Cupboards, Dusty Skeletons

turned out into the small playground for the afternoon on the north, mostly sunless side of Tubney House. We were never allowed to play on the spacious, beautifully cut lawns at front and side, which must have appealed to parents but were all "Out of Bounds". Playground apparatus paled although the one thing the school was well-equipped with, there were limits to what you could do with it hour after hour, day in, day out: two swings at different levels, a rope ladder hanging from one swing frame, a trapeze from the other, a see-saw, and long metal gymnasts' bar.

The rear, north side of Tubney House before restoration, as we saw it from the playground but probably later than 1949 to '52 colour photography becoming more available in the 1960s. The flat area contained a fenced playground where, despite swings, rope ladder, trapeze, seesaw, and gymnast's bar, we spent endless afternoons drifting aimlessly. The two ground floor windows either side of the orange creeper were the dining room (left) and kitchen. Above on the first floor were the two girls' dormitories with three and four beds (never all filled). The first floor window in shadow (left) was the bathroom. Despite spending three years there second floor rooms remained a total mystery never seen.

Total Disruption: Catholic Boarding School

I remember one sunny day that first term Toni asking me to go on the seesaw with her, briefly having fun pushing up so she went down, teaching ourselves about balance: that two on one end didn't work, neither did one moving nearer the centre, how to get off carefully holding my end down, letting it up slowly so Toni didn't come down with a bump. The seesaw later vanished, removed for some unexplained reason. We had no balls or beanbags, didn't know how to play tag. Mostly we listlessly milled around in the afternoons in two's, three's, or one lone boy on his own, waiting to be called in for the third ordeal of the day: tea. Miss Gisborne and Nurse sat in the kitchen watching through the closed window. If someone put a toe out of line the window would shoot up. One young boy had a small blue cardboard disc from one of his own toys. He put it in his mouth, took it out, popped it in another boy's mouth like a sweet. The window shot up:
"Christopher, if I see you do that again I'll give you the cane," (kept in the bathroom cupboard). He was lucky to get a warning, normally we didn't.
We were on our own in the playground. She rarely came out to speak to us; only scolded from the window, then shut it again. We couldn't see her inside. If someone fell over or off the trapeze and bled, they could go and knock at the back door where they might be given a plaster and spoken to sharply. I never did. Afternoons seemed long, dreary, dull, and in winter, cold.
The surface of the playground was loose gravel covering bare earth; we weren't allowed to dig holes. Someone had dug a small one. Charles, an older boy, was told to go round asking each of us if we'd done it. He came to me last, decided it must have been me. Denial was futile I would be thought to be lying. I was called into the kitchen. She produced a wooden pencil box lid to cane my hands. I suddenly felt terrified: would I survive? I remember this happening my first term, so I must have still been quite young, five at most, probably still only four. But I already knew if you were accused of something you hadn't done trying to stand up for yourself only made things worse. Lying would be added to your crimes. My half-sister, Claire, when I caught up with her decades later, told of a similar experience at a convent boarding school with nuns. A box of matches had disappeared and she'd been in the vicinity at the time. The more she felt unjustly accused and denied it, the worse it became as they assumed she

Dark Cupboards, Dusty Skeletons

was lying. She was beaten so badly by a nun the doctor was called. He said it was "just bruising"! In that type of school a child had no rights.

*

Summoned in for tea, the third main ordeal of the day, we went from the playground through the door into the cloakroom to hang coats on pegs, change shoes. We all had to eat the same, two rounds of white bread, and had to finish everything on our plates. At teatime the first half slice of bread would be just bread and marge. Jam was allowed on the other three half slices or, that first term, lemon curd or sandwich spread, strong flavours neither of which I liked much but had to eat. Nurse probably made the jam herself from local produce. Glass pots stood near her at the head of the table. Occasionally we were allowed to choose which flavour. This didn't make any difference, I still struggled. Passing our plates up along the line on the bench we had to say,
"Please may I have some gooseberry jam?"
If we didn't eat quickly enough the plate would be ordered back, passed from hand to hand up the table, the jam scraped off, the plate passed back. As punishment the bread had to be eaten without jam. Then again, at the end of the meal, just three-quarters of a small mug of milk to drink. I was always thirsty.
The last short play between tea and bedtime was in the schoolroom, turned into playroom with folding desks stacked away, when we were allowed to get out our own few toys kept on our shelves in cupboards. Post-war scarcity meant no one had many. There were no toys belonging to the school, no wireless we could listen to and, of course, no television. As in the playground we were left on our own. We could draw – coloured pencils and paper were provided by parents – the school had none. Any picture books, easy-reading books, story books were provided by parents. The windows had no curtains to hide the pitch-black squares of windowpane on dark winter evenings; the floor had the dark wooden floorboards of much of the rest of the house. We were on our own until told to go upstairs to bed – the only time of day we weren't sharply watched to be corrected – then we had to tidy our toys into the cupboards. We went up the back stairs to our dormitories to follow the precise routine of getting into pyjamas and dressing gowns, folding back bedspreads, folding clothes, placing them at the end of the bed. Once – but only once – when at home I folded my clothes as taught at school. Mother was clearly

Total Disruption: Catholic Boarding School

amazed; how had Miss Gisborne got me to do that? Didn't she know, I wondered, what would happen if I didn't? Apparently not. I became completely different people to fit either home or school life, both equally artificial, identity changing radically. It would be many years before I even began to find myself, my own identity, as a person. Once in dressing gowns we had to go along the corridor to the bathroom. Routine was everything. First: wash hands and face, then clean teeth, sit on the lavatory before going back to the dormitory.

We never went into the boys' dormitory, only daringly peeping round the door from the end bathroom. They were never allowed in our dormitories, although they had to pass the open doors to get to their own.

The main girls' dormitory had four, occasionally five, beds, grey metal-framed, with white sheets folded back over blankets covered with pale blue bedspreads, all the same – no individuality – a chest of drawers, a cupboard for hairbrushes; the window looked out over the playground. We knelt on the dark bare wooden floorboards with Miss Gisborne to say prayers: "Our Father", and one "Hail Mary". Obediently I mimicked the jumble of sounds I thought I heard and was supposed to make. It would be years before I interpreted them as words, even longer before I understood what the words meant. Yet one more time to a different lavatory in the end bathroom then Miss Gisborne put the light out and left. Unless we talked, which brought punishment, we wouldn't see any adult again until morning. No one ever dared go to Miss Gisborne and Nurse's bedroom in the night for any reason. We were on our own from dusk till dawn. Sleeplessness, nightmares, illness, one coped with alone, in the dark. So ended the rigid daily routine of fear and boredom.

Our dormitory was above the kitchen where they sat. If we did talk or make any sound she would hear. The first time she "spanked" three of us, as she called it, was for talking after she'd turned the light out. It happened suddenly without warning. She marched up the corridor into the dormitory, took a large wooden hairbrush from the cupboard, ripped back bedding, pulled down pyjamas. Mother had sometimes given just a slight smack on the arm, an indication of extreme disapproval, but nothing so sexually overt.

Dark Cupboards, Dusty Skeletons

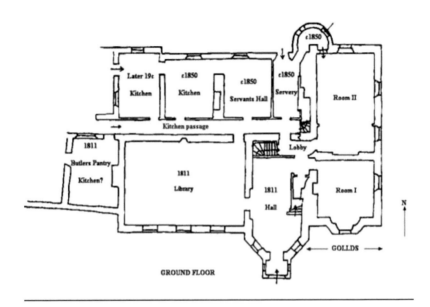

Ground floor plan of Tubney House – room uses late 1940s, early '50s All mostly "Out-of-Bounds". For rooms used times rigidly were controlled no child daring be in the wrong place at the wrong time. Parts of First and all Second floors never seen, despite terms being longer than holidays so more time spent at Tubney House than home.

Gollds hunting lodge:
Room I younger children's classroom.
Room II mornings older children's classroom; evenings/ wet weather
    boarders' playroom, only entrance via Lobby.
1811 additions:
Hall: main entrance south; main staircase east; staircase to cellar north (all
    "out-of bounds").
Library: converted to Catholic chapel, alter west end. We were taken in
    for evening "Our Fathers" and "Hail Marys" with rosaries, also
    Sunday services with Catholic priest.
    First floor room above: large boys' dormitory; girls not allowed.

Total Disruption: Catholic Boarding School

Butler's Pantry: briefly a girls' playroom; door to staircase SW corner; open fireplace east wall.
    First floor: small bathroom & lavatory; doors to Miss Gisborne & Nurse's bedroom & boys' dormitory.

1850 additions:
Kitchen passage: servants' stairs east, leading to staircase to second floor.
    First floor: passage to access bathrooms and girls' dormitories.
Servery: children's cloakroom, child-sized lavatory where arrow shows entrance, exit to playground via circular tower.
Servants' Hall: dining room, only access via Kitchen passage, serving hatch from Kitchen near window.
    First floor: bathroom with two baths, basin, lavatory, cupboards; access from first floor passage.
Kitchen: black solid-fuel kitchen range against east wall near window, heating water and radiators?
    First floor: girls' dormitory, 4 beds; "the Blue Room" to former occupiers of Tubney Ho.

Late 19th C Kitchen (Scullery): where cooking took place; gas stove, sink, wall cupboards; only indoor access from kitchen, exit to outdoor paved yard with entrance to walled kitchen garden.
    First floor: additional girls' dormitory, 3 beds, mostly unused.

*

Children should be trained in the proper habits. One day Miss Gisborne took three of us upstairs, showed us where the second-floor lavatory was. Later she ordered me to,
"Go to the lavatory and don't pull the chain."
Obediently I trotted up the two flights of stairs, sat on the old wooden lavatory seat, did a number one and came down again without pulling the chain.
"Did you go to the lavatory?" she demanded.
"Yes," I said, truthfully, as I thought.
Later she rounded on me, apparently horrified:
"You said you'd been to the lavatory. You hadn't. You told a lie!"
She went on and on, seemingly scandalised:
"You told a lie! You told a lie!"

Dark Cupboards, Dusty Skeletons

Silently bewildered, I said nothing. I'd been snapped at sharply before, "Don't answer back!" when trying to stand up for myself. Best not to argue. Better to keep one's head down, say nothing.
I was four. At home it was called "your number two", "your big job" or, less formally, "your bigs". Fortunately, being bright, I did cotton on afterwards to what Miss Gisborne must mean by the euphemism: "Go to the lavatory."
Another worry! Would I be able to? I felt I had no control over this bodily function. But now I was labelled a liar. My end-of-term school report said I told lies, read out by Mother in an atmosphere of shame who accepted it as gospel never thinking to question, help me talk through, what actually happened. Miss Gisborne followed this up on the next term's report with: "A little better about lying," indicating that, at her school, I was 'improving'.
Other children could tell tales about me. Toni did. Denial made things worse: I must be telling a lie. I never did tell lies about this or anything else, felt this must be a misunderstanding. But was it? With hindsight I wonder? Had I had the confidence to complain to Mother about physical and emotional abuse, particularly about the heavy nosebleed after being hit across the face, having set me up as a liar might Miss Gisborne have covered herself with something like:
"Well she does tell lies, you know."
But whose lies were they? Only this one day that first term was I told to go to the lavatory. If she'd felt it necessary to check, why not on other days? Was it a set up?
In the 1940s and '50s adults assumed that if there was any discrepancy between the word of adult and child, it must be the child who was lying. That, and the taboo around talking about sex, was what gave paedophiles and child abusers such an easy time. With hindsight it seems obvious Miss Gisborne knew this. Also that lavatory matters weren't freely spoken about. Confusion could reign unchallenged.
After minor injuries instead of pulling us around by hair or ears she resorted to pulling knickers down and beating naked bottoms with the back of a wooden brush. Toni told me the boys knew when they were going to be spanked as they were told to take their braces off. For the girls it happened completely out of the blue without warning; she was so totally erratic, unpredictable. We weren't allowed to cry. Anyone who cried was

Total Disruption: Catholic Boarding School

threatened with being spanked again as punishment for crying. I only heard of one child who did, Miss Gisborne's niece. She did get spanked again. I became unable to cry.

Spanking could happen without warning and without explanation on the slightest pretext. She watched us all the time seemingly for opportunities. This was the only form of physical contact we had, an extremely unhealthy ethos to grow up in of fear and sexual kinkiness: no cuddles, kisses or lap to sit on. Always EYES – watching – *watching* – for any slight lapse. I went home at weekends but didn't want to sit on Mother's lap anymore. I'd changed; our relationship had changed.

*

The first couple of weekends Mother fetched me from school, after that I travelled by myself. On Saturday mornings at the age of four and three-quarters I would be given a bus ticket, then sent off to walk alone up the long drive out of sight of the school to where the single-decker, green, country bus stopped on the unmade-up gravel roadside by Tubney House Gatehouse; there was no marked stop. I stood, in nondescript round grey hat above navy gabardine raincoat and knee length grey socks, amidst a universe of towering trees bordering the deserted road vanishing between overgrown grass verges into some unknown distance.

The first time I waited alone for several minutes before the bus roared along – then flashed past, tyres spitting dust. Probably I looked too small to be worth stopping for. After waiting to see if another bus would come, then considering for a moment, I went back down the drive. Mother must have telephoned when the bus arrived at Gloucester Green without me. Thinking the all-competent grown-ups would make some other arrangement the rest of the weekend passed in gnawing disappointment as I realised that was it. Maybe there was only the one country bus on Saturday mornings in 1949.

The following Saturday morning saw the same small isolated figure standing near the edge of the road. Perhaps someone had spoken to the driver because this time the bus lumbered along and pulled up a few feet away. Knowing this was my route to Mother I pushed my small legs forward, pulled my knee up to my chin and struggled up the step. Crawling up onto the lengthways seat behind the driver I sat, feet dangling. The bus moved off on the ten-mile journey into Oxford. The conductor inspected my ticket and punched a hole in it. No one said

Dark Cupboards, Dusty Skeletons

anything. For the first time I was alone in a bus full of strangers on a journey I didn't recognise as the bus twisted through Oxfordshire villages. I sat quietly waiting for the bus to arrive and link me up with Mother. She was waiting at the bus station, Gloucester Green. Another short bus journey through the City of Oxford took us to Auntie Janet's flat in Headington where we spent the weekend. Arriving, Mother sat down looking tired and cross. I remember being really upset at finding only one low camp bed in the small room we normally shared – Mother's. Mine hadn't been put up. Determined to do it myself I struggled futilely for some time pulling the mattress this way and that refusing to give up, let her help. Then, wanting her to know which bed I slept in at school, I tried to explain. Did she remember the bed with a pile of folded blankets in the dormitory we were shown round when we visited? That was my bed. But, "Oh no! I don't remember."
She didn't even seem to *want* to know.
Then, smiling confidently over lunch she stated:
"So they put you on the bus."
Instinctively I maintained a cautious silence; it seemed wiser. On Sunday afternoon I was taken back to the bus station for the return journey to Tubney. The conductor was told where to put me off. Kisses, not expected, were not missed. Goodbyes not said.
Again I was alone on the deserted country road at the end of the long driveway, the bus pulling away, the school not visible. But I had done it. The weekend pattern established there would be no looking back. Although the bus stopped by the Gatehouse there was never any sign of Mrs Baring Gould, who lived there. Effectively I was totally unsupervised but never minded this, wouldn't have given up the opportunity to get away, get 'home', for anything. This set the routine for regular weekend honeymoon visits in spite of impassioned requests by Miss Gisborne who, apparently, tried hard to renege on the original agreement,
"Please, Mrs Wallace, for your child's sake . . ."
Lower fees had been negotiated as I was not there at weekends. I was the only weekly boarder. To Mother's credit she steadfastly resisted appeals to leave me boarding at weekends. Advice for a single mother with her first and only child has never been in short supply from those jealously sure only children – with mother all to themselves – *must* be spoilt.

Total Disruption: Catholic Boarding School

Against this Mrs Chaloner, our psychologist neighbour in Roehampton, was convinced these visits were vital:
"I know it's very difficult for you, dear, but she does need you. She'll become very *dead* without you."
Why didn't I tell Mother what was going on at school? Children are easily shamed, convinced they're bad, evil, worthless: why they're being treated badly. Miss Gisborne knew this, generating guilt, shame and humiliation. I didn't want Mother to know how bad I was. Supposing she knew? She might turn away from me. Detach herself. Other people mustn't know. I sensed she and her family were very susceptible to what other people thought. And this, apparently, was what school was like: I had no previous school experiences to compare it with. (St Christopher's would later change all that, show me a different way of life, a totally non-kinky ethos in which fear was absent.) Also the intense sexual connotations made punishment difficult to talk about sex being something of a taboo subject. Worst of all, supposing Mother knew and went along with it, didn't do anything, accepted how we were treated? That would be worse. As long as I thought she didn't know I could imagine she would do something if she did. I could still believe in her. Pretend.

One weekend, unusually, Mother came to the school to see Miss Gisborne and take me back to Oxford. Whenever together they'd chat charmingly, getting on well. We walked away down the gravel drive past empty lawns and silent pines. Plucking up courage I decided to tell Mother about the naked spankings. Nerves steeled, cautiously, tentatively, I ventured,
"I don't like it there."
Mother appeared to have her answer pat. She turned, leaning over me.
"You like it there *sometimes*, don't you. You like it there *really!*"
I shut up – as intended. I could still pretend our relationship.
We never communicated well.
I don't think she ever had any idea of what it was really like, tended to live in her own dream world in which what she imagined was true: us all playing, happily carefree, in beautiful surroundings.

One evening at bath time, at Auntie Gladys's, the last before the beginning of a new term, it suddenly came over me that I was going back the next day. I found I couldn't speak. Mother had arranged a nice day with Vanessa to play. She understood I was unable to say anything but thought it was because I was so happy.

Dark Cupboards, Dusty Skeletons

Tubney House not visible from any road, became an isolated community, a world on its own. No boarders' parents collected outside at the end of the school day to chat, exchange information, compare notes. Boarders' parents rarely, if ever, met; had no outside knowledge of how Miss Gisborne ran the school, how she treated us.

*

Aged four, being moved about meant being bathed in different places. To my secret delight Mother once lifted me into Auntie Gladys's large white enamel bath with my socks on.
"I've still got my socks on" I squeaked excitedly.
"No you haven't" Mother said firmly then, the wet socks on my feet being an undeniable fact:
"Well, they needed a wash anyway!"
She passed off this momentous event with disappointing casualness.
The Edwardian bath stood on four ornate feet; one end sported two silver-coloured metal taps out of which hot and cold water gushed, the other end curved roundly. I had a small brownish-red Bakelite boat and three Bakelite ducks, pink, blue and green, to play games with in this vast expanse of water.
Mother taught me to push water from the running hot and cold taps along the side of the bath with outstretched palm mixing it to the right temperature until it wasn't too hot. I discovered that by sliding myself up and down the bath I could make 'waves', create such large ones they slopped over the sloping curved end onto the floor making puddles on the black linoleum. I watched the water spin and disappear as it emptied down the plughole felt momentarily frightened (of disappearing with it?) The lavatory was a tiny separate room just along the landing.
In Auntie Janet's flat in Headington the bath was in the kitchen hidden behind a freestanding, folding screen giving an unrealistic impression of privacy. I remember peeping round to see Auntie Janet sitting in it, her hair tucked into an intriguing pale blue waterproof hat drawn together in elasticated wrinkles round her face, Mother telling me not to look. The bath water was heated by an ancient gas geyser, a green cylinder fixed to the wall above the tap end with a pilot light inside, a small naked flame always alight. When you turned the water knob on the geyser the cylinder seemed to explode with a big "whooomph" into a mass of flame before dying back, supposedly heating the water instantly as it trickled out of a

Total Disruption: Catholic Boarding School

thin pipe and fell into the bath. In practise this took so long that by the time one had enough water what was already in the bath had largely cooled. Sometimes the geyser wouldn't light at all leading to a lot of earnest discussion between Mother and Auntie Janet as they stood and stared at this temperamental contraption.

At boarding school all boarders, boys and girls, were bathed together one evening a week. There was a rigid routine to stick to. Take clothes off in dormitory and fold neatly at end of bed; put dressing gown on; bring pyjamas to bathroom; sit on lavatory (no privacy and no paper); perhaps have hair washed in white porcelain basin; take off dressing gown and queue for bath; get in bath when told sharply; sit, three in a bath, waiting to be told what to do. The bathroom contained two large, white enamel baths side by side. The older six and seven year-old boys went in one, the girls and younger boys in the other. No toys, no playing. One child would be told to get out, another told to get into the space available.

When told to: get out; dry self with own towel; put pyjamas and dressing gown on; clean teeth at basin; queue to have nails cut – Miss Gisborne sat on the wooden lavatory seat to do this – go to the other lavatory once more before bed. No one dared to deviate; no one talked. In the late 1940s children weren't normally bathed more than once a week. Fuel rationing continued after the war and many smaller family homes without bathrooms in poor areas still used galvanised metal tubs in front of an open coal fire.

We girls were lucky enough to have some heating: a small radiator outside the dormitory door in the corridor presumably heated from the black solid fuel boiler in the kitchen. Many schools had no heating in dormitories. At Wycombe Court School where Mother taught she said the doctor, called during a 'flue epidemic, said the feverish girls lying in bed must have some heating. The school had to find coal to get fires going in open fireplaces with unswept chimneys that hadn't been used for years.

If something needed mending we were to put it on the radiator outside the dormitory at bedtime. I don't remember our clothes being washed often, Miss Gisborne decided when to take clean underwear out of the chest of drawers. Winter outer clothes were seldom washed. Nurse probably did all the washing by hand as well as numerous other chores.

*

Dark Cupboards, Dusty Skeletons

That first term Miss Gisborne did organise a few moments of light relief expanding our experiences. There was, of course, no television in the '40s but she had a ciné film projector. For a short while that first term on Friday mornings before lunch she would set this up in the schoolroom and show a (probably hired) black-and-white, silent, ciné film. We looked forward to this treat. The whirring projector wheels and grey shapes on the screen were fascinating if incomprehensible. One film seemed to have people grouped together in front of a rough corrugated iron building. Miss Gisborne said it was about a mission school in a hot country. Another was possibly a Marx Brothers' comedy. Then there was the one where a man seemed to be jumping in and out of a volcano; supposed to be funny but I held my breath. Basically adult viewing unexplained but we but we enjoyed them nonetheless, looked forward to these moving pictures. Of course this meant the treat could be used as yet another punishment, someone being suddenly sent out for some inexplicable reason apparently on a whim, a huge disappointment.

One weekend early in that first term on a fine afternoon, Miss Gisborne packed all five girls into her tiny, black, four-seater and took us to a small airfield. We climbed onto the rough wooden boundary fence by a quiet country road and watched parachuting from barrage balloons, the first I'd seen. Light aircraft took off roaring into the air just over our heads, making us duck in alarm. The older boys looked angry when we got back and told them where we'd been. They'd spent the usual dull afternoon in the playground. I enjoyed this outing, one of my few positive memories of the school.

Once, but only once, we were all taken out to eat our bread and margarine teas on the normally out-of-bounds front lawn. It wasn't a happy picnic, a tense atmosphere despite sunshine: Toni was scolded for some slight unexplained lapse and sent indoors. As she walked away across the grass towards the house, a small lonely figure, her hand went up to her eyes rubbing tears away. The one interesting thing was Miss Gisborne showing us a white puffball growing in the lawn near where we were sitting, another new experience.

That first term we were once walked to a summer fete nearby across the road from the end of the drive by the golf course, given some of our pocket money to spend. This was another enjoyable afternoon although I was a bit upset when I thought I'd dropped some of my money and lost it.

Total Disruption: Catholic Boarding School

"You spent it," said Nurse firmly and convincingly, trying to console. But I didn't think I had. She lent down, picked something up from the grass.

*

My fifth birthday fell in late November towards the end of that first term. At Miss Gisborne's school birthdays weren't celebrated usually passing unnoticed. Some of the younger children might not even know how old they were. Not noticing birthdays was normal in day schools in the '40s but parents would see their children every day so probably told them. I did know when my birthday was, that I was turning five, as Mother had told me when we met for the weekend. At school a small parcel arrived wrapped in brown paper. Mrs Chaloner had sent me some tiny painted, metal farm animals: little pink piglets and mother pig with teats lying down to feed them, grey woolly-looking sheep and a farmer in brown tweeds holding a walking stick. Otherwise nothing happened that day to mark this milestone. Discovering the farm animals among my toys when term ended, Mother seemed slightly horrified:
"Where did these come from?"
"Mrs Chaloner sent them for my birthday." Mother looked taken aback.
"Oh! Well! I must ask her not to!" Had she jumped to the conclusion I'd added stealing as well as lying to the list of undesirable qualities assumed inherited from my father? Seven decades on I still have those little metal animals. Needless to say no parcel arrived on my sixth birthday. Memories above of my first term at boarding school are clear, Below are traumas of the next eight terms, incidents still clear but sequence tending to jumble, remembering exactly what happened when.

*

I've since tried to understand Catholic ideology. Many believed children were born with Original Sin (presumably from the sexual act) and needed to have this evil crushed, beaten out of them. Catholics believed suffering and humiliation were 'purifying' for the soul which seemed to justify a lot of maltreatment: they were carrying out 'God's will'. And a child's mind needed constant control to prevent the Devil entering. As in Victorian times fear was often still confused with respect: to respect a teacher children needed to be frightened. We were very frightened of Miss Gisborne.

Dark Cupboards, Dusty Skeletons

Aged five.

In the '40s and '50s a teacher having sex outside marriage would be viewed with horror and loss of job, they would be a 'bad' influence on the young. No one with dubious 'morality' would be allowed to teach. During and after the war there was a population imbalance of women over men; many women never finding the husbands and families they longed for. Taught from early childhood never to "touch yourself *there*" sexual frustration became rife leading to female jealousy and spite not always consciously realised. Beating little children's naked bottoms became a sexual outlet acceptable in the interests of discipline, as an excuse for abuse. Despite sexual repression or perhaps because of it, sex was everywhere. It seemed there was always someone wanting to use my body for their own purposes. As far as I know Miss Gisborne never did anything technically against the law as it stood then although what she did do might have raised a few eyebrows even in the '40s. But as a veil of secrecy and guilt surrounded such punishment no one knew what went on. One girl, who came to the school later, my best friend known as "Wixie", must have made a fuss about coming back telling us at the beginning of one term that her parents had said she wasn't to be spanked or sent to bed, she was to have a pillow and a drink of water when she wanted one. Miss Gisborne placed the pillow on top of the chest of drawers in the dormitory, telling Wixie to take it if she wanted it. After the light had been put out Wixie told us she *did* want the pillow but, knowing Miss

Total Disruption: Catholic Boarding School

Gisborne didn't want her to have it, didn't dare take it. Did she ever dare ask for a drink of water?
Another common punishment meant being sent to bed for the rest of the day without food, getting right into pyjamas.
"You send them to bed and they just go to sleep," said Miss Gisborne to Nurse in exasperation. The punishment was supposed to be lying awake, perhaps hungry, hour after hour. What we mostly got spanked for was any sound after she'd turned the light out at night; any child who wet themselves or wet the bed – I was lucky never having any problem there – or not doing well enough in lessons. And the bathroom cupboard contained a cane, presumably for the older boys, aged only six or seven. I never got the cane, didn't know it was there until Toni showed me. Outgoing, resilient Toni talked more about punishments, otherwise there was a veil of secrecy. And shame. None of us spoke about anything or even knew what went on. Miss Gisborne told our parents we told lies, safe in the knowledge that, at that time, if it was a child's word against an adult's it would be the adult who would be believed. Like myself, my half-sister, Claire, could never bear being watched and felt it dated from her time at a convent boarding school.
I thought I was bad, evil and worthless, didn't develop any real conscience, just learning to keep out of trouble with no proper sense of right and wrong. I looked forward to being grown up, having power so I could treat little children like that. I can't have been a very nice child!
Some religious education was given at mealtimes. When Miss Gisborne wasn't talking to Nurse in French, scolding or snapping out orders, we were taught Catholicism. We learnt about Heaven, Hell and Purgatory. If you weren't good, when you died the Devil took you to the torment of the fires of Hell for evermore. Most people went to Purgatory before getting into Heaven to be purged of their sins and repent. How long you spent in Purgatory depended how bad you'd been. That we were bad, we never doubted. That was absolutely clear. Then there was a place called Limbo for the souls of people who'd never heard of God so couldn't suffer eternal torment in Hell for not following His teachings. She told us we each had a guardian angel looking after us. Sitting on the hard wooden bench trying desperately to swallow down a plateful of tasteless boiled vegetables, I struggled to imagine a white, winged, benevolent figure

Dark Cupboards, Dusty Skeletons

standing behind me, felt he wasn't doing a very good job, couldn't believe in him.
Little darker-skinned Malcolm volunteered that he had a book with a picture of the Devil he'd scribbled over, thinking he'd done the right thing. But no, she said you should never do that in a book. Once, when Malcolm had done something mildly wrong he had to stand with his back to the room, plate on the windowsill to eat. One or two tufts of his jet-black hair stood up; she teased he had horns like the Devil. Being like the Devil was really terrible.
Only once were we walked to the nearby local Anglican church – where Mother had been led to believe I would be regularly taken – to a formal adult morning service where we obediently knelt silently in wooden pews in the dim light, confused, not understanding a word. We were never taken to any Sunday school geared up to four- and five-year-old children. After a couple of terms Miss Gisborne set up a Catholic chapel in the large, front, downstairs room under the boys' dormitory, with alter and facing chairs. We knelt on the floor. A young Catholic priest came on Sunday mornings to conduct a formal, ritualised service. We would be lined up and taken in to kneel down. A couple of the older boys, six or seven year-old Paul and Leo, were trained as alter boys to stand behind the priest dressed in white robes handing things to him. They had to learn the entire order of the service whereas we, in the front row, had only to stand or kneel, as required. The mumbo jumbo meant nothing. The priest stayed to have dinner sitting at the head of the table between Miss Gisborne and Nurse. He said we didn't talk enough she told us, she wanted us to talk more, but I don't think any of us were up to it.
Pain and humiliation were considered purifying for soul. We were all sinners, all bad. We knew that.
To begin with we said evening prayers in our dormitory kneeling on the wooden floorboards. After the chapel had been set up we were lined up to be marched in every evening before bed to kneel in pews facing the alter, holding rosaries, counting the beads: one bead for an "Our Father", interspersed with groups of ten for "Hail Mary's". Dull, meaningless, incomprehensible. Never any hymns, Christmas carols, or lively religious sing-alongs which might have engaged us more.
Other children had their own rosaries; mine was a spare belonging to Miss Gisborne. She wanted me to have my own, said I was to buy one next

Total Disruption: Catholic Boarding School

weekend when I went home. I told Mother. Mother, not surprisingly, refused. Arriving back at school Miss Gisborne immediately asked if I had a rosary. When I told her Mother wouldn't buy me one she said, "Well couldn't you have got the money and gone down into Oxford and got one?"

Apparently stealing money from Mother would be justifiable for such a Godly purpose. But in any case it was totally impractical: Oxford City Centre was a big place to a small child; Auntie Janet's flat where we stayed at weekends was out at Headington; I was seven at most, had no idea which of the large red double decker buses to take, or where to go to buy a rosary.

Then one weekend Mother gave me a flower from Miss Woods' garden to take back for the Chapel. Miss Gisborne was pleased, demanded I bring more flowers the next weekend. Mother, again quite reasonably, said no, because it wasn't our garden and she couldn't pick any more. I went back to school without any, afraid of being spanked. Miss Gisborne confronted me as soon as I arrived:

"Have you got flowers?"

Anxiously looking at the floor I had to say I hadn't. She liked us to look frightened. But she wouldn't let this lack of flowers go unpunished. It's easy to remember events, less easy to remember their sequence: what happened when. I think it was after this I was called into the kitchen (Miss Gisborne and Nurse's private area) where Miss Gisborne sat smugly powerful – and told to stand by the door. Turning, she picked up one of our small money boxes stacked near her, oblong, black with red and gold stripes round the hinged lid and small keys tied to the silver handles. All the same, except that each had a name scratched in the black paint on top. I was too far away to see whose name was on the one picked up. Looking pleased with herself she opened it, took out a ten shilling note, a whole term's pocket money, and handed it to Nurse in the scullery. (When I was in junior school my mother earned two pounds, ten shillings a week as part time medical secretary.) She said sweetly to Nurse,

"Is that someone at the door collecting for charity?"

Nurse smiled as though knowing what was going on, took the ten-shilling note and disappeared into the scullery where the outside door was. Then I was told to go. That was all. Puzzled, I left. I do remember the next time

Dark Cupboards, Dusty Skeletons

we were taken into the Chapel it was full of flowers, wondering why she wanted me to bring more when she had so many.
Miss Gisborne was highly unpredictable and we were a listless unimaginative lot never quite sure what we might be allowed to do, afraid of doing anything spontaneous in case it might be 'wrong'. It was me that thought, one long dreary winter's afternoon in fading playground light, of collecting prettier bits of twig and stones lying around and arranging them to make tiny 'chapels'. Surely she couldn't object to that? So we enjoyed ourselves for a while doing something mildly creative. She came out looking doubtful as we hopefully showed her our little 'chapels' thinking she would be pleased. Looking at them without comment as though unsure whether to approve or not, there wasn't the positive response we'd hoped for. So we did this only once.
Auntie Kay, who'd also converted to Catholicism, gave me two colourful children's religious pictures, one had four angels with the quote:
"Matthew, Mark, Luke and John, Bless the bed that I lie on."
The other was a nativity scene with the Baby Jesus. I felt reasonably safe mentioning these to Miss Gisborne; she would be pleased. This time she did approve and insisted I bring them to school where she produced hammer and nails and hung them above my bed. Miss Gisborne was a Catholic convert; later, when I learned the word "fanatical", I immediately thought of her.
Tubney House was a beautiful place very upmarket and distinguished, a gentleman's country seat in wonderfully peaceful country surroundings, but many children living in city slums playing on the streets among their own families, friends and communities, although living in poverty, may have been a lot happier.

*

For minor illnesses we were sent to bed on our own in the dormitory to lie awake with nothing to do. I suppose as this wasn't a punishment one of the older boys, Charles, was once sent up to talk to me, briefly. They'd been allowed in the shrubbery:
"We're digging a hole to Australia," he told me, and various other exciting things I seemed to be missing.
Isolated from the outside world, we weren't prone to the usual childhood epidemics not catching many of the usual childhood diseases. I didn't have chicken pox until my teens at St Christopher's and German measles

Total Disruption: Catholic Boarding School

even later. At Miss Gisborne's school there was, however, a mumps epidemic. Feeling desperately tired although not aware of any pain from mumps-type lumps I decided not to eat at dinnertime, for once actually hoping to be sent to bed. I was. Later, Miss Gisborne said, quite kindly, "Why didn't you tell me you were feeling ill?"
But I was too frightened of her to start a conversation for any reason even when feeling so ill.
To begin with we were put to bed separately from the healthy children in the smaller girls' dormitory and given thin exercise books and pencils to draw with. Beginning to feel livelier mine was filled all too soon. Then a day or so later we were taken downstairs in pyjamas and dressing gowns to a waiting passenger ambulance on the front driveway and driven to a hospital which, with hindsight, must have been an isolation hospital. As we were all together I didn't feel alarmed. One older boy Anthony, who seemed more seriously ill than the rest of us, never came back to school. Could he have had something worse? Antibiotics weren't generally available then for infections such as much-feared scarlet fever.
I was put in a small ward on the ground floor with french windows with three other children, Vikki, Toni and Anthony, cared for by young uniformed nurses. The only time I remember being frightened was when told to lie flat and helpless as two nurses, one on each side, held up a heavy looking wall of sheets and blankets to bring down over me. Four boys from the school were in the next ward.
Mother came to visit once but wasn't allowed in, so stood outside the french windows trying to chat. She spotted a small open window high up in the wall by my bed from where I might hear better, came round to try to talk to me through that. A nurse, discovering this reacted with alarm and shut it, presumably as it was an isolation hospital.
We were allowed our own toys. I instantly fell in love with a new cuddly toy duck Mother brought. We girls, knowing each other well, sat up in our beds playing and chatting fairly contentedly. Better than being at school with its harsh discipline. But one day a nurse said I had a dirty face, asked what had caused it. By now convinced by school experiences that what I loved most must be bad, that anything which made me happy must be bad, I pointed unhappily to my much-loved cuddly toy duck. The nurse picked it up and took it away. I never saw it again. After she'd gone Toni pointed

Dark Cupboards, Dusty Skeletons

out it wasn't the duck that had made my face dirty but a piece of black carbon paper for duplicating drawings, also from Mother.

One day for some unknown reason I was taken out of the ward, bathed, hair washed, then dried in front of an electric fire. In those days no one ever told children anything.

"Am I going home?" I asked the nurse.

"Well . . . I don't know. We'll see . . . If you're good!"

All our toys had to be left at the hospital to avoid spreading infection. One girl had a tiny model sewing machine which really worked. A nurse said, "I'll enjoy playing with that when you've gone."

Why were we admitted to what must have been an isolation hospital? Mother said later she thought Miss Gisborne just couldn't cope.

Eventually after a long wait, when my hair had dried, I was put in a black taxi with some of the other children. I think it was the driver who let out that we were being taken to our homes to convalesce. I was the first to be dropped off in Headington at the end of Miss Woods' drive in Stephen Road. I ran happily through the garden and burst in at the sunroom door. Disappointingly Mother, not expecting me, wasn't nearly so happy or pleased,

"Ooooh! You'll have to go back to school. I'm not supposed to be here, anyway."

I never discovered what she meant by that. Convalescence forgotten she took me straight down into Oxford to Gloucester Green and put me on the bus to Tubney where convalescence also seemed to have been forgotten. It may have been after the mumps episode that at breakfast some of us had to line up and open our mouths for a dessertspoon of cod-liver-oil or the iron tonic, Minadex.

*

We spent a lot of time lying awake in bed sent there when we weren't tired or ill as punishment for the rest of the day, without tea. Alone, or forbidden to talk, we stared vacantly at the bare walls and ceiling; picked noses or bottoms; examined the tiny weave on the white sheet looking for patterns. I learned to bite bits of skin off the insides of my lips and cheeks, a bad habit that continued into later life, bent my middle toe until a hammertoe formed. Every night the dull rigid bedtime routine had to be followed before Miss Gisborne switched off the light. Then came lying awake watching shadows on the wall, counting days to the weekend,

Total Disruption: Catholic Boarding School

making it seem nearer by missing out one day, pretending four days to Saturday instead of five. The week needed to be 'shortened'. No comforting pillows allowed – for straight backs she'd told Mother – no cuddly toys or teddies. Children shouldn't be brought up to be 'soft'. No picture books to look at in bed; no bedtime stories; no hot water bottles or eiderdowns in cold weather. Discipline and routine were everything.

*

Occasionally allowed to play in the shrubbery beyond the playground, we once gathered round a fallen tree daring each other to search underneath for snakes. I moved a pile of dry grass; a long, dark brown, snake tail disappeared rapidly.

One night I had a snake nightmare, woke in pitch dark in a state of terror, staring into blackness. There were snakes at the bottom of my bed. Mum had provided bedsocks. I believed if these stayed on the snakes couldn't bite my feet. But one foot had lost its bedsock. I couldn't find it. Paralysed with fright I pulled my bare foot up level with my neck away from the serpents under the sheets, lay uncomfortably awake not daring to sleep, at last falling asleep awkwardly twisted. Seventy years later I still have a snake phobia. Miss Gisborne and Nurse slept only a short distance away but no one dared venture into their room in the night. They only ever appeared after putting out lights to spank naked bottoms. One of the older boys, Charles, was rumoured to have once gone into Miss Gisborne and Nurse's bedroom when they were in bed. The rest of us were astounded, disbelieving, thought this very brave. As far as I know, no on else ever dared. I certainly never did.

Crush, crush, crush. Deep inside. Don't do anything spontaneous, don't draw attention to yourself in any way, don't feel anything, be numb – the only way to survive.

Another night I had a vivid dream, now slipped from memory. Waking, lying staring into darkness, images still floated in my head, intriguing, entertaining. Suddenly I realised I could make my own dreams, have my own dream world, invent people, family so much longed for. Relationships as and how I needed them. I could do what I liked, have whom I liked. Miss Gisborne couldn't know, couldn't control, as with every other detail of our lives. Complete freedom inside my own head, a chance to survive as myself. And another advantage: I couldn't be separated from this inner world. Wherever I went it went too, inside my

Dark Cupboards, Dusty Skeletons

head. I became dreamy, detached, another habit I've never unfortunately been able to break. This might sound mentally unhealthy but became a lifesaver for my own individuality, getting me through a lot in life. The dream was the start of an imaginary world which sustained me until teenage years. Somewhere I could always retreat to for comfort. At first it contained imaginary older brothers; oddly enough I never had an imaginary father. The problem was where to put my mother in this inner world. I couldn't quite kill her off, imagine her dead, so she'd just gone away, wasn't there, as indeed she had but my dream world advanced this process. My inner world was a private space that was mine and mine only. Once, eating dinner in the dining room at Hindhead, daydreaming happily, I smiled to myself. Mother noticed, tried hard to persuade me to reveal all: "Oh! TELL me, *TELL* me!"

She was very persuasive, wanted to get right inside my head, influence, possess my mind. But I couldn't tell her, needed to keep the freedom of my inner world intact.

Another time in a rare moment of talkativeness about the boarding school world, the other life, I described sleeping arrangements. After telling Mother where all our beds were in the dormitory, I went on to say,

"Miss Gisborne and Nurse sleep together in a room by the bathroom, next to the boys' dormitory."

"Do they?" she said. "Ooooh!" She seemed taken aback. "In the same room?"

"Yes!" I didn't understand her reaction. Seeing my surprise she quickly changed the subject.

One little boy got up one night to go to the lavatory in the pitch black of the boys' dormitory, the large first floor room at the front of the house with about ten beds. In the darkness he couldn't find his own bed again. Wandering blindly, he found another boy's bed, tried to get in. How long did he wander? Feeling his way he eventually came across a spare unmade-up bed with just a thin blue bedcover over the mattress, no blankets. He'd spent the rest of the night in that. He must have got very cold. I'd had the same experience getting up for the lavatory, trying to find my own bed, not knowing where I was in the dark, feeling momentarily panicky. But in the smaller girls' dormitory did manage to find my bed again.

*

Total Disruption: Catholic Boarding School

The weekend bus journey to and from Oxford turned into a time of being neither in one world nor the other; not the rigid routine of a Catholic boarding school where any spontaneous move might result in disaster, or the laid back approach of Mother too tired to bother. A hiatus when I need be neither the ultra-controlled person inside the battlemented walls of the forbidding grey stone house, nor the child my mother invented, imagined she knew. Full of anticipation on the outward journey; heavy with the thought of the week ahead on the way back. None of my school friends were so lucky. They all stayed three months at a time. Without visits.

The journey didn't always go smoothly. Once, Mother wasn't at the bus station. Everyone disappeared; the bus drove away. I stood by the shelter where I'd got off in the now totally deserted bus station. Waiting. Wondering what would happen if she didn't come. She eventually appeared, late that time.

Then there was the time when, twisting the paper ticket with my fingers, it somehow parted in two. I agonised over whether the conductor would accept the pieces, holding them out nervously for her to inspect. She passed them looking displeased.

A trickier situation arose when I'd been given eight pennies for the fare. The conductress said the fare had gone up to nine, stood in front of me angrily insisting I pay the extra penny. I explained I'd only been given eight. Her face set in hard lines. She stood rigid in navy uniform, pushing her outstretched palm towards me, voice rising, words pounding. Helplessly I stared at her. Eventually a motherly middle-aged lady opened the bag on her lap and produced the penny. The conductress took it, moved on down the bus. Seeing the lady again on a bus back to Tubney I pointed her out to Mother who returned he penny.

One Saturday I was told by Miss Gisborne to tell Mother the return bus had been re-routed and I should get a different one. But Mother, smiling, blithely asserted,

"Oh, No! It's still the same bus," and wouldn't take my protests seriously: I was too young to know. She did, however, check briefly with the conductor when she put me on the bus stating,

"You *do* go to Tubney, *don't* you."

Perhaps he'd temporarily forgotten, as he said the bus did. Or perhaps it was another part of Tubney, a village straggling along country lanes. It was high summer and the cottage gardens were bright with colour as the

Dark Cupboards, Dusty Skeletons

bus trundled through the countryside. Oxfordshire villages with their grey Cotswold stone and low hedgerows tend to look alike but I had an uneasy feeling the world outside didn't seem quite right. The conductor began a rapid, intense conversation with two lady passengers. Feeling, uncomfortably, that it was about me, I tried unsuccessfully to make sense of the jumble of words. Eventually the bus stopped, the ladies got up to get off, the conductor turned to me and said,
"You go with them."
These were the days when children were taught to do as they were told. They weren't taught to be wary of strangers; I was always being left with strangers. So I silently followed them off the bus. We walked along the road to their house without saying anything where I was taken into an empty basement room with a billiard table, sat in a corner and left alone. Sometime later I was brought a cup of hot milk. Sipping it I wondered what would happen next. Eventually Miss Gisborne arrived in her small black car. I sat next to her in the passenger seat afraid she would accuse me of not telling Mother about the buses being changed and scold, but she seemed in a good mood and said nothing. I'd missed school tea. Having discovered I'd had some milk she didn't seem to think it necessary I should have anything more to eat before bed. Meals always being such ordeals, I was totally unworried about missing tea. When Mother later asked me she took a different view.
Late on Sunday afternoons in winter I made the journey in the pitch darkness that exists only on unlit country roads. The dim yellow light from the bus windows didn't penetrate enough to reveal anything of the world outside. Getting off I would cross the road and walk between tall ghostly pines casting deep black shadows, for a short distance alone with them and whatever they hid, the road behind out of sight, the hulking great shape of the fortress-like house not yet visible. Once, when the bus stopped, I stepped down as usual into the darkness and stood on the grass verge as its lights faded into the distance. Only then did I realise I wasn't at the end of the school drive. In the utter blackness the dim shapes of brooding trees swaying in the cold wind and the ubiquitous dry stone walls gave no clue as to where I might be. I decided I'd better try to walk somewhere. In the intense blackness, dark as the Catholic demon hell we learnt about in school, there didn't seem any reason to go one way rather than another. About to turn back along the way the bus had come, I saw

Total Disruption: Catholic Boarding School

what looked like the silhouette of a roof ahead in the opposite direction. It seemed better to walk towards that. Getting closer, outbuildings seemed familiar, then a house became recognisable and the driveway back to school. Turning the other way I might have wandered endlessly along icy, pitch-black, country roads. But it hadn't happened, so best not dwelt on.

*

Miss Gisborne didn't like us to be sent presents although she gave presents to her God-children, Vikki and Toni. One Sunday afternoon walking with Mother down North Parade in Oxford (Auntie Janet had moved to Rawlinson Road) to catch the bus to Gloucester Green and thence back to boarding school, I saw a toy parrot in a shop. Inside a cage about six inches high, it had a rubber pad at the bottom you could press to make the parrot squawk. Not in the habit of asking for toys, I desperately wanted this one. Perhaps it reminded me of Kitty's Polly and Auntie Gladys's house. But Mother said firmly,

"No! Not now!" and hurried me on. Perhaps she didn't have the money or, as it would have been a Sunday, the shop was shut anyway.

At school, two or three days later, Miss Gisborne appeared suddenly; made a pretext of saying I was doing something wrong. I hadn't realised but had come to expect inconsistent condemnation, sudden punishment out of the blue. She waved a small parcel wrapped in brown paper and said she wouldn't give it to me yet, as punishment. Another couple of days passed, then I was summoned into the kitchen given the parcel and told to unwrap it. She watched as the toy parrot emerged, then commented caustically,

"What a silly present to give a child. You can't do anything with it."

Trying to stand up for Mother I pressed the base making the parrot squawk, said timidly,

"You can do this."

She glowered, told me to go.

That wasn't the end of the story. One of Malcolm's toys got broken. Someone said I'd done it or perhaps Miss Gisborne decided I'd done it. I had to give Malcolm one of my toys in return. He was to be allowed to choose whatever he wanted. I had to put all my toys out on a table in the schoolroom-cum-playroom. Upset, I wondered which of my favourite toys I would lose. We didn't have many in the post-war years. The others gathered round the table to watch, speculating interestedly on this unusual

Dark Cupboards, Dusty Skeletons

event. What should he choose? Charles who, as eldest, had dubbed himself head boy said he thought the doll's cot for a girl, the mosaic kit with hammer and nails for a boy. Miss Gisborne arrived. Malcolm quickly chose the parrot. I stacked the rest of my toys back on my shelf in the toy cupboard. Later he told me she'd said he had to choose the parrot. At the beginning of the holidays when Mother asked, too guilty to admit I'd been in any trouble feeling, as always, it was somehow my fault, I said I'd given it away. She looked surprised, disapproving, but didn't pursue it. Malcolm brought the parrot back next term with his initials inked on the bottom. At some stage he gave it back to me, sympathetically, as though he felt there'd been some injustice. Its appeal had gone.

*

One mealtime little Anthony announced,
"I'm four and three-quarters."
Probably what his parents had told him before the beginning of term. Miss Gisborne corrected him,
"No you're not. You're five."
His birthday had passed without him knowing.
A young French assistant sat at the end of the dining table. One day Miss Gisborne told us it was her birthday. There was some slight celebration, small pieces of cake just for her, Miss Gisborne and Nurse. One of the older children's birthdays fell on the same day; we did know it was their birthday. The French girl protested indignantly,
"But it's the child's birthday!"
Miss Gisborne brushed this aside,
"Oh no, we don't do anything about that."
Birthdays just weren't on the menu. The French girl didn't stay long.

*

My memories are of endlessly dull afternoons spent hanging around in the playground. But to be fair, Miss Gisborne did make some effort to provide occasional activities, rare diversions which relieved the monotony, mostly earlier on, then fading out. Condensed here they may sound a lot but spread over three years such events were few and far between. Outings outside school grounds, apart from long dreary walks, hardly ever happened as she had no transport apart from the small, black, four-seater into which a few of us were occasionally crammed. Apart from the trip to the airfield four of us girls were once unexpectedly squashed into the car

Total Disruption: Catholic Boarding School

along the back seat, to collect a sack of potatoes from a farm. We were briefly allowed to get out of the car. An unexpected diversion.

One baking hot summer, probably my first year there, brought an occasional treat. There was nowhere to swim so a hose was fixed upright on the front lawn – normally Out-of-Bounds – to run under in just knickers or pants. One weekend I took back a pair of knitted grey cotton shorts I really liked but Miss Gisborne scolded angrily they were too difficult to dry – probably true as they were rather thick – so that was wrong too.

Early on there were one or two visits to places on the estate: we were once taken to a farm outbuilding near the playground to see a cow, told a calf had been born during the night. I don't remember seeing any chickens as at the Utin's nursery school or being given eggs or chicken on our dinner plates. We rarely saw any animals.

The kitchen garden had "Out of Bounds" written in white paint on its wooden door in the brick wall across the yard from the scullery, but once, also early on during my time at the school, Miss Gisborne walked us round showing where our food came from: gooseberry and currant bushes, potato plants and cabbages. I remember another time going into the kitchen garden with Toni who'd asked me to come with her to look for Nurse, finding her kneeling, working round some vegetables. She probably did a lot of growing as well as cooking, generally holding the situation together on a practical level. In the scullery a few of us were occasionally put to work 'topping and tailing' bowls of gooseberries or black currants. Once I remember being taken blackberrying with empty glass jam jars to fill in the grounds of the estate, all of us being scolded for not picking fast enough. Nurse probably made jam from these for our teas. Once, Miss Gisborne took us to some small flowerbeds at the edge of the lawn next to the playground, saying we were to have our own gardens there. That sounded interesting but came to nothing, never happened again, the small beds becoming covered in weeds. A lot of things happened only once.

One weekend when I hadn't gone home for some reason Miss Gisborne took us for a walk. We seemed to trudge endlessly along rough earth paths through dreary nondescript woods, a Saturday 'crocodile' of two's in round grey hats, belted navy gabardine raincoats, itchy grey woollen, knee-length socks and heavy brown leather lace-up shoes. Subdued – no

Dark Cupboards, Dusty Skeletons

one dared deviate from the crocodile – we marched obediently in line beneath a dull grey sky. Tired and bored I watched Barry, Nurse's big black Labrador, as he enthusiastically chased imaginary rabbits, burrowed under tree roots, leapt up and down small hillocks, bounded through puddles, crossed a small bridge over a brown sluggish stream, doubled back nose to the ground as the whim took him. The crocodile struggled on no one daring to put a foot out of line. The dog was having fun. I longed to join him.

One autumn Miss Gisborne organised a tall blazing bonfire and fireworks after dark on a patch of rough ground to the left of the shrubbery. Sparks, fizzles and bangs surprisingly frightening to someone not normally panicky.

At the end of one term there was a puppet show with string puppets, performed in the large front room, perhaps before it became a chapel, by two ladies hired from outside the school. We watched with interest, enjoying, I had never seen string puppets before, but didn't understand much of the story line or what it was about; nothing was explained.

I had coloured pencils of my own to draw pictures with during evening play sessions, rarely used during lesson times. Once, over a two-day half-term when Mother couldn't have me, Miss Gisborne told a French assistant to organise a painting session, a competition with a prize. I painted a green hill, blue sky with large round red sun above children playing dressed in red and blue. The assistant judged,

"Oh yes, I like that. The red and blue [children] matching red and blue [sky]."

I won the prize. And waited.

"I won't give you one if you keep asking," she said.

Eventually she handed me a tiny metal statue of the Virgin Mary. Delighted with this unprecedented prize I treasured it for decades. Otherwise art and craft activities were virtually non-existent.

*

Early on I'd learned the new phrase: "Out-of-Bounds". I never saw the whole of Tubney House despite spending three years boarding – more time there than anywhere else – never knew how many rooms it actually had. We were restricted to confined areas, a dull, unstimulating environment, all having to be in certain rooms at certain times, all together. No one dared drift into any room at the wrong time for fear of

Total Disruption: Catholic Boarding School

having knickers (or short trousers and pants) violently ripped off to be spanked. Our world consisted, during the day, downstairs of only the morning schoolroom / evening playroom along the east, oldest side of the house, believed to have been the original hunting lodge; at mealtimes the dining room facing north over the playground; in the afternoons the cloakroom but only in transit to change shoes, put coats on or go to the lavatory (no loitering); and the small gravelled playground fenced round with wire-netting with a high swing, rope ladder, lower swing, trapeze, seesaw (until taken away) and metal bar. We spent hours every afternoon here, on dry summer days only occasionally allowed to play in the small overgrown shrubbery beyond. Of course, Miss Gisborne couldn't have young children roaming loose and out of sight all over the house and grounds; children in day schools would also be kept track of in defined areas. But day children have an outlet when they get home after school and at weekends; were able to let off steam in school playgrounds, run around, shout, make more noise, behave like normal children.

*

At night we went up the back stairs, never the front stairs, to the girls' two small dormitories and the two bathrooms. We were too disciplined, too frightened, to wander anywhere other than where we were told to be at any one time of day or night. I got out of it at weekends which relieved the boredom; all the others spent three months there at a time, mostly confined to this small area of house and grounds.

Other areas, all "Out of Bounds", but occasionally glimpsed when summoned and permitted, were the kitchen and scullery; the yard outside the scullery; the walled kitchen garden; the sweeping south-facing, front lawns; the spacious hall inside the front entrance and grand staircase leading to unknown, unseen rooms. Miss Gisborne and Nurse spent a lot of time in the kitchen overlooking the playground – *watching*. We only went in there when summoned. Upstairs was the larger boys' dormitory overlooking the front lawns, which girls weren't allowed in, a smaller room next to this where Miss Gisborne and Nurse slept in two single beds. From the small second bathroom I once daringly peeked round the doors of these rooms.

Above the first floor was a second floor I never saw, I would look up from the playground at the row of mysterious windows, wonder what secrets they hid. Toni said there was an attic in which a boy had once been locked

Dark Cupboards, Dusty Skeletons

without food; he ate the apples stored there. I wasn't aware of the cellar until my last year at the school, although the door leading down to it was opposite the classroom/ playroom. Dark and ghostly, this had also had a boy shut down there as punishment. Paul was a nice boy; Miss Gisborne had no reason to treat him like that.

For a short while we were separated from the boys for indoor play, sent to a small room near the kitchen overlooking the back yard, marked on the early plan above as the Butler's Pantry. No explanation. This had another door on the far side of the room, always shut. No one would have dared open it to look beyond. But one day it opened from the other side. A strange, youngish woman stood there holding a baby, a staircase winding up behind her. She looked at us in silence for a minute or two. We stopped playing, kept still, and silently looked at her. Then she closed the door and disappeared. I never saw her, the baby, or that part of the building again. Where did the stairs lead? What was at the top?

*

Boredom reigned: endless afternoons in the playground, time spent awake in bed, no pictures on the walls or picture books apart from our own, very few craft activities, no sports. On dry days in summer, but only on a few dry days, we were allowed to play in the shrubbery just beyond the playground. I have no memory of ever feeling mind-numbingly bored in the shrubbery. Here we could let go a little, run along small paths, dodge round bushes, behave more like normal children although, as ever, in school uniform. We had no other clothes. A fallen down tree stark, white and hollow in the centre, became a ship, castle or den; whatever we wanted. We knew every cranny, crevice and stubby broken off branch, peepholes in and out. The upended root of the tree, the highest part, would be the ship's prow, the other end hollow enough to wriggle up inside. We pulled up long grass to make dens, or trampled some down to hide in on the far side by the rusting brown bars of a fence. We found a birds' nest with one abandoned pale blue egg. We learned to avoid stinging nettles; where to find dock leaves if we did get stung, to recognise dead nettles that didn't sting. We watched insects, kept snails in matchboxes, treasured spent gun cartridges unexpectedly found lying on the ground: small orange cylinders of thick papery stuff, a brass cap at one end, hollow inside, smelling of gunpowder. Little Anthony found half a transparent,

Total Disruption: Catholic Boarding School

scaly, snake's skin, which I filled with tiny pebbles until it disappointingly fell apart.

Wixie, my best friend and taller, discovered how to climb a tree we hadn't climbed before. Soon I'd also found the secret handholds and footholds under the ivy. We sat together astride wide branches where they grew outwards, happy in our new hideout, unable to be seen from below. Anthony, too small to climb up but wanting to join in, found sticks, grass and anything we might need to make our roost more interesting, passing them up.

Another upright tree was discovered one day, with great excitement, to be largely hollow, the inside accessible through a small gap between huge roots. We spent a happy afternoon squeezing in and out. This was stopped after Miss Gisborne found we had dirty hair, thick with tiny particles of dead leaves and decaying bark. To be fair, she did produce a huge man-size saw, one with handles at both ends, and got two of the older boys to try to saw through outer bark to make the entrance larger. But they couldn't manage such a heavy man's task, so we were forbidden to go inside. It was fun while it lasted. Apart from this one time we had dirty hair no one seemed to worry. Cleanliness, apparently, was not next to Godliness in Miss Gisborne's book. Of course, she sometimes used the shrubbery as summary inexplicable punishment, making one of us stay in the playground alone.

The shrubbery was where we could briefly be ourselves, without feeling that anything spontaneous, anything enjoyable, anything we liked, must be bad, would be pounced on and stopped. I don't remember ever feeling mind-numbingly bored when allowed to play in the shrubbery as in endlessly long afternoons in the playground, could forget, briefly, deeper pain below the surface. But we were only allowed there on dry days in the summer term.

*

Spankings were very unpredictable, carried out in silence. Neither Miss Gisborne nor Nurse ever gave any warning or explanation. To this day there are some instances where I still don't know why. You felt if you did anything spontaneous it would result in punishment, so watched every move. Even then it seemed unavoidable. If she felt like spanking, she would invent some pretext.

Dark Cupboards, Dusty Skeletons

What we mostly got spanked for was any sound after she'd turned the light out at night; any child who wet themselves or wet the bed (I was lucky never having a problem there); any sex play; not doing well enough in lessons; not keeping to every detail of rigidly prescribed routines, doing everything as precisely laid down; letting go for a moment, moving spontaneously. The way to survive was to keep your head down, not draw attention to yourself in any way, not to let go in an unguarded moment, not do anything spontaneous that would end in disaster. Even then punishment seemed unavoidable, discipline an excuse for abuse. We were watched all the time, lived with the feeling that *eyes* were always *watching,* waiting for you to let go for a minute, make some small mistake that could be punished. I developed a lifelong dislike of being watched as did my half-sister, Claire, whom I met late in life. She felt her dislike of being watched dated from her early years at a convent boarding school.

I was very frightened of Miss Gisborne. She was totally in control. The school she'd set up consisted of few children, in remote countryside, unregulated, run with no teaching qualifications, with parents far away, so no checks and balances. She'd started with wartime evacuees, Mother later told me. The atmosphere was one of fear and sexual kinkiness: a very emotionally unhealthy atmosphere in which to spend three years of early life. Young children need a lap to sit on. The only physical contact we had was violent, sexual, frightening. She made us feel bad, shamed, guilty, secretive, told parents we told lies. We were a dull, unemotional lot, never laughed, cried, got excited, shouted, sang, danced, or ran around except occasionally in the shrubbery in summer. I don't remember any quarrelling, although there was a spate of tale-telling to get others into trouble. Tightly controlled as we were we got unpredictably spanked on the rare occasions we let our guard down. The most consistent reason was making any noise at night. Once, coming into the dormitory, she asked who'd been talking. I knew she'd know anyway, realised there was just a chance I might get off more lightly if I 'owned up'. So Toni got spanked and I didn't. No doubt Miss Gisborne thought she was training me to own up to wrong-doing, but this was a purely calculated act on my part without conscience. The other girls, already asleep, must have been more disturbed by the commotion than us talking quietly.

One morning Mrs Baring Gould came up to my desk and said quite quietly,

Total Disruption: Catholic Boarding School

"Go to Nurse." Nothing more.
Walking up the stone-flagged corridor I wondered whether I was to help with something in the kitchen. Nurse told me to go up to the dormitory. After sometime she walked in with a slight smirk, without speaking, picked me up under her arm, pulled clothes off and beat my bare bottom with the back of a brush. Then left the room still without speaking. I remember clearly the feeling of sexually abuse. I suppose I must not have been working properly, but if not, I was too young to be conscious that I wasn't. Punishment, as usual, seemed unpredictable, unavoidable, and all the more feared. Schoolwork went through a bad patch when Mother was in hospital with T.B. and I didn't see her at weekends.

By ourselves in the bathroom two of us, Toni and myself, played at throwing our towels in the air and catching them in a rare, unguarded moment. Daringly spontaneous and good fun until mine caught on the top of a cupboard with one corner hanging down. Horrified, I discovered it was just out of reach. If the towel were discovered it would lead to a spanking without clothes. Panic welled – a swamping wave – paralysing. I jumped – still it was just out of reach. Now desperate I jumped and jumped for the corner, only managing to touch it. Then suddenly, miraculously, my hand grasped the corner, the towel was in my hands. A moment later Miss Gisborne walked into the bathroom. Nothing was amiss.

Walking out of the chapel in line one evening after prayers I saw rough tears in a thick, paper-like substance covering the wall. Walls were normally hard. Suddenly I felt uncontrollably curious to know what this soft stuff was. Momentarily letting go I ran spontaneously two or three steps out of line, lightly touched the papery substance, then dashed back to the same place, terrified by what this huge risk might bring. But all Miss Gisborne said afterwards was, quite mildly,
"Don't do that again."
Another time this might have resulted in the usual spanking. She was so unpredictable. One could never tell.

In the smaller girls' dormitory there was a little faded picture hung on the wall above a bed. I don't remember why I was in bed in the room, by myself, in daytime. Probably as punishment. With nothing to do I stood on the bed and lifted the picture, discovered it could be taken down, how it hung by a cord on a hook. A momentary diversion. Putting it back I

Dark Cupboards, Dusty Skeletons

couldn't get it to hang straight, tried again and again. It still wouldn't hang straight. I knew the crooked picture would be instantly noticed as soon as Miss Gisborne walked into the room. Fear and panic began to well up. Standing on the bed I went on and on trying, moving the picture this way and that, unable to get it to hang straight. Eventually after much anxiety and perseverance it just seemed to happen. I got back into bed and waited. Toni wasn't so lucky. She also moved the picture but couldn't get it straight again and was spanked as usual, with the back of a brush without clothes.

Once, getting ready for bed, in the corridor after the routine visit to the end lavatory, I noticed a shiny patch on the polished floorboards. No one was around. Taking a quick run of three or four steps I tried to slide on it. Miss Gisborne suddenly appeared through the door at the other end of the corridor, marched down in silence, grabbed my arm, dragged me into the dormitory where she pulled down pyjama bottoms slapping me several times, then left, still without a word. I only did it once but had deviated from the rigid bedtime routine, done something lively, spontaneous.

An unemotional lot, no one laughed, cried, ran around, got excited, quarrelled or had temper tantrums. Certainly not temper tantrums! Except once. For a short while a few day-children stayed to dinner including Mrs Baring Gould's son, David. Miss Gisborne told him where to sit; he wanted to sit somewhere else. Then the unheard-of happened: he had a temper tantrum. She apparently didn't dare hit him and seemed to actually back off – another first – while he calmed down. We boarders, cowering over dinner plates, watched nervously from under lowered lids, over-awed, too terrible to imagine what she would have done if one of us had had a tantrum. No boarder, over whom she had total control, had ever dared let go that far. But with David, Mrs Baring Gould's son and a day child, she apparently didn't dare inflict violence. Soon after during another dinnertime she announced loudly to Nurse that she was stopping dinners for day-children. They came just for morning lessons, as before.

One weekend while I was away the other girls were involved in some sex play on the bar in the playground looking at each other's private parts. I was told by Toni they'd all got spanked. Janet had cried, was threatened with being spanked again if she didn't stop, wouldn't or couldn't stop, and did get spanked again as punishment for crying.

*

Total Disruption: Catholic Boarding School

Toni and I were alone in the bathroom; she said, "The cane's in there! In that cupboard! Look!" She put her head round the door, beckoning. I saw a stick about two feet long, half an inch thick, dark brown, knobbled. Whether anyone *was* caned I don't know, there was so much secrecy and shame surrounding such acts no one knew what went on. Only outgoing Toni talked. I didn't get the worst of it, mostly managed to keep my head down, not draw attention to myself or do anything spontaneous, so was never locked in the cellar or the attic, the cane never used on me. Presumably it was for the older boys although the eldest couldn't have been more than seven.

We weren't allowed to cry, perhaps this spoilt the moment for Miss Gisborne. The act would be carried out in silence without warning or explanation. Unpredictability generated fear. It seemed Miss Gisborne and Nurse enjoyed this sexually kinky act reminiscent of the sleazy adverts one sees today pinned up in phone booths around Soho.

Miss Gisborne apparently told Mother she couldn't control us when we came back at the beginning of term, especially the older boys. The school notice board at the end of the drive said the school took boys only to a younger age, something like:

"Boys to 6 ½, Girls to 7 ½".

What could she have meant? There was so much control!

*

Little dark-skinned Malcolm couldn't do his sums, kept doing the sensible thing by going up to Mrs Baring Gould's desk to ask for help. One day she produced a piece of rope and tied him to his chair for the morning. She obviously thought this would solve the problem, he would do his sums on his own, seemed surprised and annoyed to find he'd done nothing at break time.

Outgoing, resilient Toni talked more about what happened, otherwise there was a veil of secrecy. And shame. None of us spoke about anything or even knew what went on. Miss Gisborne told our parents we told lies safe in the knowledge that, in the post-war era, if it was a child's word against an adult's it would be the adult who would be believed.

Going back after one weekend Toni rather gleefully pointed out a boy with a plaster over his ear.

"Miss Gisborne pulled that boy by his ear and it bled. Look, he's got a plaster on it."

Dark Cupboards, Dusty Skeletons

I looked. The boy stared woodenly back, eyes dull. A sticking plaster taped his ear to his head. Miss Gisborne had torn it. Toni knew she'd overstepped the mark.

*

We'd sit in the dining room in set places eating mostly in silence, younger ones near Miss Gisborne and Nurse, older boys at the other end, girls in the middle. Looking round the table new faces occasionally appeared, some familiar ones would have disappeared. Children appeared or disappeared without warning or explanation. We weren't told if someone was leaving, weren't taught to say goodbye. They just weren't there anymore. One mealtime another girl who looked slightly older than me, slim and graceful, with long dark pigtails, appeared. We were told she was "Elizabeth". Another Elizabeth. Nurse' kindly suggested that perhaps they should give me a nickname.
"NO!" snapped Miss Gisborne, "She'll be called by her surname: WALLACE!"
That sunk its popularity with me for all time; heard in so many derogatory contexts became associated with trouble and self-dislike. To be fair, the other Elizabeth was also called by her surname, "Wixie" (possibly from "Wicks"). We got on well and became best friends known as "Wixie and Wallace".
Boarding at the same time, two Richards of different sizes became "Big Richard" and "Little Richard". All the other children were known by their christian names.
The school had middle class children – I don't remember any child with any sort of accent – and about twice as many boys as girls. At mealtimes three younger four-year-olds sat near Miss Gisborne and Nurse: little Anthony who seemed fairly confident, Murray with an older brother at the prestigious Dragon School in Oxford, and Richard Eardley, "Little Richard", who virtually never spoke except to repeat what others had said. Another older Anthony never reappeared after the mumps epidemic. Older boys I remember, sitting at the far end of the table, were Charles who was a bit of a bully, Paul McDevite and Leo Green. Malcolm appeared to be aged between the older and younger boys. I was usually put in the middle of a side with Vikki, Toni, Janet and Wixie, all boarders like myself for most of the three academic years '49 to '52. Other children whom I remember briefly at the table were a girl called Susan, and

Total Disruption: Catholic Boarding School

another girl whose baby brother sat in a highchair – their mother was in hospital. Miss Gisborne announced one mealtime that she hadn't wanted to take the baby – the mother had wanted them to stay together. The baby began to cry, she roughly turned the highchair away from the table: "We don't want to hear your noise!"

The baby disappeared although his sister still ate with us. I remember a boy, Alan, whom Miss Gisborne constantly labelled 'bad', and another younger boy, David (abandoned running after his father's car when he first arrived). For a short while a few day children stayed to dinner. Robin Wilcox who lived opposite the end of Tubney House drive had a tough little brother who'd put a garden fork through his foot and laughed – Robin would proudly relate this story – the family emigrated to Australia. And there was David Baring Gould.

*

Malcolm came back at the beginning of one term talking enthusiastically about a wonderful holiday he'd had with his family in Swansea. He kept chatting away at mealtimes until Miss Gisborne shouted:

"WE DON"T WANT TO HEAR ABOUT IT," after which he lapsed into silence. But she couldn't stop him reliving it inside his head. Hopefully he did.

When I first went to the school there had been two little kittens. The following term they were gone. Someone asked about them. One was lost, we were told; the other "fell into the water tank in the greenhouse". I tried to imagine the kitten near the tank, how it could have fallen in, couldn't quite see how that happened.

One bitter winter's afternoon snow lay in the playground. At tea Miss Gisborne started a brief, rare conversation with us. Usually she and Nurse talked in French. We weren't to know what they said.

"What did you do in the snow?"

"I tried to make a small snowman," ventured someone, "but the head wouldn't stay on."

"You didn't make it properly then."

"I made a tiny snowball," offered someone else.

She turned to Nurse saying disparagingly, in English,

"We [she and her sisters] used to build ships and things out of snow. But these children have *NO* imagination."

Dark Cupboards, Dusty Skeletons

She didn't think much of us; dull, subdued, we hadn't known we were *allowed* to. None of us talked much at mealtimes (or at other times). After the Catholic chapel had been set up the priest who came to take the Sunday services stayed for dinner, sitting at the head of the table between Miss Gisborne and Nurse. He apparently told her we didn't talk enough. She told us this, wanted us to talk more. But none of us were up to it.

*

Christmas celebrations were almost non-existent. The only story I ever heard Miss Gisborne tell (she never read to us) one mealtime as we all sat round the table apathetically chewing white bread and marge, was of St Nicholas, the patron saint of children the school was named after. Ancient fairy tales were originally full of cannibalism and incest. Invited to dine with a wealthy man, St Nicholas had been given unusually tender meat with a delicate flavour. Suspicions aroused he went down into his host's cellar to investigate. First, he came upon a barrel with joints of the fresh meat. Going deeper into the cellar he found another barrel. Lifting the lid he discovered terrified small children cowering inside, whom the wealthy man had kidnapped to kill and eat one by one. St Nicholas of course rescued them so the story did have a happy ending, at least for those not already slaughtered. We absorbed the story in silence. This was not a sanitized version of a fairy tale as rewritten by Louis Perrault in the eighteenth century for children of the French court, but an older, darker story full of cannibalism, now told to small children the youngest only four or five. For Miss Gisborne this seemed very much in character. I don't remember her ever telling gentler Christmas stories of the nativity, shepherds, or wise men, or being shown pictures of Baby Jesus in the manger.

*

The rigid routine continued soul-destroyingly, any deviation would have meant a spanking or being sent to bed without food. Early on I learnt to keep my head down, never to attract attention – bound to be unpleasant – never do anything spontaneous that would end in disaster.
One bitter winter's morning Miss Gisborne, having taken Susan's clothes for washing the night before, had forgotten to put clean ones out for her. We weren't allowed to get anything from the small chest of drawers where our clean clothes were kept. Susan knelt by her bed, waiting, shivering with nothing on until Miss Gisborne came into the dormitory and found

Total Disruption: Catholic Boarding School

her. Furious the girl might have got chilled, she delivered a resounding slap on her bare back,
"There's something to warm you up."
Totally unpredictable and unfair; Susan had no intention of doing anything wrong. She simply hadn't known what to do.
We had to brush our hair with our own hairbrush kept in a small cupboard. Hair we were told should be brushed a hundred times "to make it shine". Mine was short, easy to manage, but to hold it out of my eyes I had to wear a Kirby grip which continually fell out and got lost. Yet another thing to worry about, be scolded for.
I was in the kitchen one day when Janet's mother, Miss Gisborne's sister, was there, with Janet. Miss Gisborne was saying that Janet didn't brush her long hair properly and it would be better cut short. Janet pleaded desperately,
"No! Please Mummy! No! *Please!*"
Neither her mother nor her aunt took a scrap of notice. Her mother seemed very dominated by her sister, saying,
"Yes, yes! Of course! If you think that's best!"
Janet's long, dark hair was cut off. She was very upset.
In the early days Miss Gisborne came into the dormitory to wake us each morning, train and supervise, later on our day began to the sound of a hand bell. Then we had to do everything on our own, not seeing any adult until we got downstairs. For a short while we had, after bed making, to go downstairs to the cloakroom and put coats on for "Drill" in the icy playground. We stood in rows, Miss Gisborne in front, precisely copying her physical jerks, arms and legs in unison. Rather in the tradition of boys' boarding schools' military training. We never knew any form of more enjoyable exercise with balls, beanbags or sports.

*

In common with many other schools in the post-war period there was never any toilet paper. As baths only happened once a week we must have smelt pretty awful!
I think in my last year there, Mother may have worried I was constipated and spoken to Miss Gisborne who thought children should be "trained in the proper habits". For a while, each day after breakfast, I had to sit on the lavatory until I'd done something, then leave it without flushing for her to see. As far as I know the other children didn't have to. Sitting on the

Dark Cupboards, Dusty Skeletons

lavatory until I'd done something made me late for lessons the first being working through exercises in *Fundamental Arithmetic*. As I'd missed time for this I had to stay in at mid-morning break to catch up, also missing the half apple the other children had. When I couldn't 'go' Miss Gisborne sat me on a white adult porcelain chamber pot next to the lavatory intended as a humiliation:
"Like a baby," she said.
Once, she came into the bathroom, walked across apparently to the cupboard next to where I sat, then suddenly hit me several times, saying: "You haven't done anything."
She was very unpredictable. Punishment seemed unavoidable. Intended to train me to control my body I felt continually anxious, helpless, frightened, unable to control this basic function which just seemed to happen. Or not. A fourth daily ordeal added to the three mealtimes.
Outside the kitchen door Miss Gisborne was telling little Anthony he hadn't been to the lavatory.
"I have," he said tentatively, standing looking up at her in his grey shorts and V-neck pullover.
"No you haven't," she persisted, waiting for the penny to drop. She wasn't going to spell out what he had to do. That would have been undignified. Whether he understood or not I don't know, but she didn't accuse him of lying as she had me. I don't think Mother ever had any idea of what went on. I felt too shamed and guilty to let on.
While boarding I developed eczema behind my ears. Mother got some ointment and told the school about a later patch between the legs. I'd asked her not to, I didn't want them to know about this embarrassing development but, of course, she felt she should. In the kitchen Nurse tried to be understanding, sitting me on the table to apply the ointment to private parts:
"We'll put a chair against the door."
This happened only once. Had mother asked I would, of course, have said the ointment had been put on – and she would have assumed regularly. Uneasy communication blurred knowledge of reality.
Miss Gisborne ordered me not to scratch behind my ears – not easy as the eczema itched terribly. I managed not to during the day but lying in bed at night half asleep, scratched unconsciously without realising. She examined my ears in the morning. Finding the scratches she caned my

Total Disruption: Catholic Boarding School

hands with the back of a hairbrush in front of everyone in the dormitory – the bad hands that had scratched – as I thought then. I learned to ignore physical discomfort, to detach from my body, take no notice of it, in much the same way as learning to detach emotionally from unhappy surroundings, be somewhere else. Fifty or so years later, trying a new diet for slimming including raw celery I discovered I was allergic, developing sores round ears. We'd been forced to eat everything on our plates, mostly kitchen garden vegetables, including raw celery. Little was known then about allergies. For whatever reason the eczema did eventually clear up. Perhaps when celery went out of season?

*

Lessons with Mrs Baring Gould continued; we had the same teacher for three years. Morning lessons weren't stressful or dreaded apart from occasional struggles with Arithmetic. She wasn't an inspiring teacher, sometimes scolded, but I never saw her hit or shout.

Moving on in *Fundamental English* it was:

"Those two letters say 'ch'," then I was left to stare at the page and sound out words. But I only needed to be told once. Even with rather uninspiring teaching I quickly found reading enjoyable. We never had stories read aloud to provide encouragement; when we could read we were expected to read to ourselves from our own books provided by parents at the beginning of term. The school had only basic textbooks. I had a couple of books from home including a large print, hard cover copy of *Peter Pan* beautifully illustrated with coloured plates, a birthday present from cousin Vanessa's mother Audrey, favourite pages becoming known by heart, reread so often.

The alphabet I taught myself during indoor playtimes from the cheap paper alphabet book Mother had bought me, just three or four thin sheets of colour pictures stapled together. She had very little money but was keen to spend on anything educational. 'M' and 'N' the middle letters of the alphabet came where the staples fastened the sheets in the centre.

There was never a nature table. Science consisted of a few brief lessons when Mrs Baring Gould read aloud to the class from a small book.

"Now isn't that interesting?" she enthused, "A spider isn't an insect, it's an animal. Now, Malcolm what is a spider?"

"An insect," he said brightly.

"NO! That's just what I've been saying. It's *NOT* an insect."

Dark Cupboards, Dusty Skeletons

She soon gave up in exasperation. Sitting at desks listening to a rather dry book being read aloud didn't help absorb information.
Mother, however, was amused one day when looking out of her bedroom window in Roehampton she said imaginatively,
"Look at those little fluffy white clouds. Wouldn't it be fun to catch one and tie it to your wrist."
And I'd replied, "Silly! They're only water vapour!"
There were no music or singing lessons apart from the nice lady who came in the first term. Very briefly Mrs Baring Gould tried a schools' radio music programme:
"Come on! Sing!" she commanded.
We weren't used to hearing our own voices, sat and looked at each other in blank nervous silence. She didn't try again.
Lessons focusing on *Fundamental English* and *Fundamental Arithmetic* gave little scope for drawing or colouring. No pictures adorned the bare classroom walls. I had coloured pencils of my own to draw with during indoor evening play, rarely used in lessons. To begin with Miss Gisborne lent me a wooden pencil box, then said she needed it for another child, I must get my own at the weekend. The shop Mother took me to didn't have one large enough. She took me back to school to explain perhaps hoping to smooth things over. But Miss Gisborne's response was:
"Well it won't hurt her to go without her pencils for a week."
But it did hurt: one of very few emotional outlets lost. By the following weekend Mother had bought a suitable pencil box.
There were no sports or sports days, a couple of times a man came to kick a football around with us, really for the older boys but we were all sent out there. Toni announced at dinnertime she'd scored eleven goals; she meant eleven kicks of the ball. The rules hadn't been explained, younger ones left in the dark as to what to do. But most of us managed to get in a few kicks, a rare fun diversion from crushing routine.

*

One later term on a Saturday morning instead of being given a bus ticket to go home I was handed a small white, fat envelope to open unsupervised in the playroom. Inside was a letter from Mother written in capitals – I couldn't read joined-up – and a pair of little pink doll's shorts knitted, apparently, from the remains of my pink twin-set chewed up on a clothes line at Wycombe Court School where Mother taught, by the headmistress

Total Disruption: Catholic Boarding School

Miss Robinson's, black dog, Simon. Evidently I wasn't to go home that weekend. When the same happened the following Saturday morning, I sensed something must be seriously wrong.

Back with Mother some weeks later she told me:

"I had to go into hospital. I asked Miss Gisborne to explain it to you."

Didn't she know how Miss Gisborne operated? She would never have explained anything. Nothing had been said about why I wasn't going home for the weekends. I was left not knowing.

Fifty years later I found the following in Mother's effects:

211 Keyes House,
7th June 1951.
Dear Ruth,
I am indeed sorry to hear that you have had to go into hospital for observation, and do hope that it is nothing serious. Patches on lungs are always a cause of anxiety, but it is something that with present-day Xray technique, diagnosis can be early and certain.
The job is still with me (or I am still with the job) and so am able to keep going. I look like being able to get some additional (free-lance) work during the autumn, which will help a lot. The paper situation certainly is the devil – and it is the outside man who suffers first.
I shall be glad to hear the result of the observation.
Sincerely, Bill.   [Handwritten]

Claremont, Highdown Road, Roehampton S.W.15.   Sept. 14th, 1951.
Dear Bill,
It was not easy to know what arrangement to make for this winter, but finally I decided to stay on at the same school, and that Elizabeth should remain at her school for the winter. I had given notice at my job when I returned to it at the end of June, but luckily I was able to cancel this before it was too late. I feel that full-time teaching, with the child in the holidays & difficult home conditions is too exhausting, but I must do it for another year, then, if it is in any way possible, I will try to make a home for her, & send her to a day school.
Elizabeth often asks about you now [untrue, she discouraged asking] and wants to write to you. She needs more than I can give now, and I should be very glad for the contact to be made, as it can now be done independently of me.   [Handwritten draft or copy]

Dark Cupboards, Dusty Skeletons

I remember asking about my father only once after leaving Tubney when she briefly opened her blue trunk and produced a couple of faded black and white photos. My father just didn't exist, was a complete non-entity. I had no visual memory, no picture of him in my mind. By saying I often asked about him did she hope to establish regular visits through me? I was completely unaware of this correspondence or of any contact.

Claremont, Highdown Road, Roehampton, S.W.15.   Jan. 20, 1952.
Dear Bill,
About the end of October I had a letter from the hospital at Oxford to say that while I was there last June, a specimen had been taken to be cultured (I did not know this at the time) and had produced a positive reaction, proving that there had been in June, an active T.B. [tuberculosis] lesion, which had not been detected by other tests. I then went to the specialist at Wycombe, & he said the condition was quiescent, so it had presumably healed some time between June & October.
However, because of this the Ministry of Education won't accept me for the Pension Scheme for at least six months, after receiving another medical report. [handwritten draft]

A new drug cure had recently become available on the new N.H.S. Before this T.B, often fatal, had been much feared so not talked about; a taboo subject as cancer became later. Mother never said much, something else she didn't talk about, another skeleton in the cupboard.
The speech awarding Professor Waksman the 1952 Nobel Prize for Physiology or Medicine said it was for: "your ingenious, systematic and successful studies of the soil microbes that have led to the discovery of streptomycin, the first antibiotic remedy against tuberculosis".

*

During my last year morning lessons with Mrs Baring Gould continued. When we'd finished an exercise in *Fundamental Arithmetic* we had to take our exercise books to Mrs Baring Gould at her desk be marked. So we largely taught ourselves. Apart from very simple sums counted on fingers I learnt by rote, not understanding numbers at all. Moving tens in adding and subtraction sums was an operation learned by heart following instructions. I had no idea what it meant. I just did what I'd been told and

Total Disruption: Catholic Boarding School

the answer often came out right. Any sum with a wrong answer had to be repeated until right.

Teaching me multiplication Mrs Baring Gould pointed to the two times table in *Fundamental Arithmetic*:

"That says two times two equals four"; then, pointing to "3 x 2 = 6":

"That says three times two equals six. Now learn it."

That was all. No explanation of meaning. No counting apparatus.

I learnt the rest on my own, by rote, up to 12 x 7 before moving on to junior school (and eventually up to 12 x 12, needed as twelve pence made one shilling) then learnt how to do short multiplication by rote using tables to get the right answers. As there were never any bricks or abacus to enlighten, I would be adult, helping my own children, before understanding the concept that three groups of five objects made fifteen items.

I remember feeling slightly daunted by being expected, out of the blue one morning, to write a "composition" – a whole page – but managed somehow and soon found it wasn't a problem. As time went on and I could read more, I romped through exercises in *Fundamental English* without any explanation from Mrs Baring Gould, reading and understanding instructions and teaching myself: sentences with punctuation, 'nouns', 'doing words'. When I left the school aged seven-and-a-half, Mother said I was a year ahead of my age group in English, a year behind in Arithmetic – no doubt partly due to all those mornings sitting on the lavatory, but she didn't know about that. I spent all three infant school years with Mrs Baring Gould. As she wasn't good at explaining Arithmetic I tended to struggle, but never saw her hit a child. She was never frightening or traumatizing.

*

One Saturday morning Miss Gisborne came into the playroom and announced she had a parent coming to see the school. She told Paul to rig up his green suspension bridge kit between two small tables. His bridge was an unusually educational toy; there weren't many construction kits around in post-war Britain. Paul spent the morning struggling alone with the multitude of small green metal shapes – whilst we played. It was half built when she came to see if he'd done it - made him take pieces apart - then issued verbal instructions to get him to construct it properly. Later

Dark Cupboards, Dusty Skeletons

the visiting mother with small daughter was brought into the schoolroom-cum-playroom.

"Now this is the sort of thing they do, you see," Miss Gisborne announced, stopping by the green bridge spanning two small tables. This mother wasn't so easily taken in, asked quickly,

"This is the school's?"

Miss Gisborne had to admit it belonged to a pupil. (The school hadn't actually any toys; they came with the boarders. A rocking horse that had belonged to her family was kept in another room. I was once allowed on it, only to be told almost immediately to get off: someone else's brief turn.) They talked together. Miss Gisborne looked down at me:

"Run off and play."

This parent didn't send her child to the school; the little girl never appeared at the dining table. Only this once did I see a parent being shown round. There weren't many takers. Janet was her niece, the twins Vicky, Toni and their elder sister Fay, her godchildren.

Although an unstimulating environment I did learn to ride a bicycle. I think it was Mother who suggested I should. She visited briefly and we were taken to a shed by the playground where Miss Gisborne said she had a child's bicycle. It must have been autumn as I remember a hard spiky conker hitting my head from the horse chestnut above.

So in the afternoons, while the others stood around in the playground, I was told to take the bicycle from the shed onto the lawn next to the playground and learn to ride it – every afternoon – until I could.

With no one to hold the saddle and help me get my balance this wasn't easy. I was given no tips or instructions. After sitting astride it, getting the feel, trying to push the pedals and falling over many times, I worked out the best pedal position for my right foot to get started. High up so as to get the most push down while I got my balance. I had to learn simultaneously to start off as well as keep going. Each afternoon I struggled.

Suddenly it just happened. I was off – pushing the pedals round, balancing – for a few feet across the lawn.

The lawn wasn't very big, rapidly became boringly small. After a few days I ventured onto the larger lawn at the front. Miss Gisborne appeared at the front door, shouted at me to put the bike away. Never told to ride it again I had to stay in the playground.

Mother cottoned on:

Total Disruption: Catholic Boarding School

"Oh! Don't you ride it? Couldn't you ask?"
"NO!" Didn't she know one never asked for anything? Any attention was bound to be unpleasant?
But it was a skill never forgotten. Equally useful I'd discovered what I could do all by myself if I persevered. That was never forgotten either.

*

Mother once asked if I could stay on for a couple of days after the end of term as her term finished after mine. She'd explained this to me when I'd seen her at the weekend. I wasn't worried.
Janet, Miss Gisborne's niece, stayed with her aunt during school holidays; just the two of us left in the dormitory. Early morning Miss Gisborne walked in and pulled Janet out of bed. Janet's pyjamas and sheets were soaking wet, a smell of urine rose from the bedclothes. Probably it had happened before, and why Miss Gisborne had come upstairs. Taking a hairbrush from the cupboard she pulled Janet's pyjama bottoms down and spanked her several times, quite cheerfully in a matter-of-fact way, not even seeming annoyed. The child had wet the bed and must be punished. She simply couldn't identify with her niece's feelings. The child had done something wrong. It wouldn't hurt her. She'd get over it. Any problem with a child could be solved by more discipline.
Walking towards she door she turned, said mildly to Janet,
"Don't forget to wash."
After she'd gone downstairs I realised why: Janet, intensely distressed, crying, and confused, went a bit ga-ga. I had to help her through washing, dressing and getting down to breakfast. Unable to cope she seemed completely unaware of what she was doing. I think the wet bed and confusion may have been due to emotional disturbance as all the others had gone home and she hadn't. Hence the wet bed. But child psychology had a long way to go before reaching remote rural Berkshire.
As it was holiday time breakfast was a more relaxed meal round the kitchen table with Miss Gisborne and Nurse, not the dining room where boarders ate. After breakfast Janet seemed herself again and I discovered that during school holidays she had the free run of the estate: we were allowed to roam the grounds unsupervised, the only time this ever happened. Not confined to the playground we wandered off together for the morning. She showed me sapling woods, small outbuildings, tombstones for family dogs I'd never seen before. She seemed all right.

Dark Cupboards, Dusty Skeletons

Outwardly she'd got over it. Deep down trouble grew; no one saw it coming, knew how distressed she was. Looking back, I think a number of children must have been building up mental health problems, Janet was almost certainly one of them. How many other children developed mental health problems as I did in my teens. There were signs that some children weren't as calm below the surface as they seemed. I didn't know any of them before the day Mother took me there, never saw any of my friends out of school, or after the day I walked up the school drive for the last time to catch the bus. We moved back to Roehampton. All very different from many children's early experiences growing up in local communities. The kitchen window shot up one afternoon when we were all out in the playground:
"Why don't you play with him?" she shouted at us, waving her hand towards Little Richard, aged four, who stood alone as always, saying nothing, lost in his own world. We moved obediently towards him, trying to relate, knowing it was hopeless: there was, of course, no response. Occasionally he would repeat something he'd heard one of us say in an echolaliac way. Otherwise he just did what he was supposed to, silently, in his own world. Of the three younger boys, little Anthony and Murray were friends, Little Richard isolated.
An elderly man appeared one day on a rare visit to see Paul, a grandfather perhaps, grey-haired, round, gentle-looking, like Paul. He chatted with Paul then stayed indoors to talk to Miss Gisborne while Paul came out to the playground where we all had to be. Coming in again at the end of the afternoon Paul, running into his grandfather unexpectedly in the cloakroom, broke down sobbing completely uncontrollably, while his grandfather tried vainly to comfort him saying again and again,
"Now, Paul! Paul! Be brave! Be brave!"
Paul usually seemed a relatively happy boy who appeared to cope, an alter boy at Sunday services. Underneath, it seemed, were disturbed feelings he didn't usually show. This was the kind of incident which made adults say: best for the child not to have visits that might upset them. Better to leave such feelings deep down where they wouldn't bother anyone, bring children up to be unemotional.
Miss Gisborne often seemed relatively benign on bath nights. Once, the telephone rang distantly. She was towelling Malcolm who stood in the bath, said chattily,

Total Disruption: Catholic Boarding School

"Perhaps that's your parents ringing to see how many spankings you've had. How many spankings have you had?"
She seemed to think she was being jokey, friendly. Perhaps she thought we'd come to enjoy being spanked. He went very quiet, looked upset, didn't speak.
Toni, more outgoing than her twin sister, Vicky, seemed to be playing Miss Gisborne and Nurse at their own game, provoking spankings, possibly having learnt to enjoy them. She'd definitely seemed excited by the cane in the bathroom cupboard when she'd showed it to me. In our last term Nurse said rather regretfully one mealtime in her faintly foreign accent:
"Oh . . . She is bored. That is why she is so naughty!"
I became more and more dependent on my own inner world daydreaming inside my head which no one could control, no one could see. I could be where I wanted, have whom I wanted; some characters might appear while others faded. They did what I wanted them to do. I felt safe and comfortable in this world and best of all, it went everywhere with me. I couldn't be separated from it.
We each had our own ways of coping.

*

How old was I? Six? Seven? I remember the death of King George VI – us all being made to sit round the table in the dining room to listen to the King's funeral on the wireless, told the jabber of sounds was the King's funeral, not understanding a word, looking round at a row of solemn, lifeless, non-comprehending faces of the other young children similarly bemused and at a loss – all sitting round the large dining table, normally laid with plates, cutlery and food we had to eat – now completely bare, as bare as our comprehension, bare as the looks on our faces, all as utterly devoid of life as the dead King, as coldly unemotional as his corpse, totally silent, without even a crackle issuing from the ancient pre-war wireless.
If, before television, we had a concept of the King at all, it was a picture book character with crown and throne.
"What's 'King' ?" asked little Anthony.
"Well, you know, the KING !" Miss Gisborne told him.
He didn't.

Dark Cupboards, Dusty Skeletons

What on earth did she think we might get out of this experience? The occasion was totally inappropriate.

*

Most walks happened in long tiring crocodiles under grey skies through damp, wet countryside. But one hot day in the height of summer we were taken through the stubble of a wheat field men were harvesting with machines, grain and stalks magically separating. Drifting along in blue gingham summer dresses we didn't have to conform to the customary crocodile. The corn was being cut first round the field edges, gradually moving inwards leaving a clump at the centre where rabbits hid. A man with a gun waited to shoot as they made a dash for the woods; rabbits eating crops were a nuisance. An unusually relaxed, interesting walk.

*

On the last day of the summer term 1952, aged seven and three-quarters, I stood at the end of the driveway for the last time knowing I was going home for good. It was full summer. Every quivering leaf and fat seeding grass head reached towards the limitless blue. The country road melted into the far distance, shimmering. I'd been given my bus fare, taken my grey blazer from the peg and slipped out through the back door as usual. Having schemed a dash into the shrubbery to fetch two pet snails hidden in a matchbox, I feared hard eyes might be watching from one of the many windows in the grey stone walls and lost my nerve.
As we ate dinner Mother asked confidently,
"And did you all say goodbye?"
"No," I said, surprised she thought anyone might have. "Nobody said goodbye," and anxiously hoped one of the others would find my matchbox and set free the hidden snails.
By then an inveterate traveller, I have always enjoyed travelling. Being between two worlds, cocooned from the tragedies of either, while a changing scene dreams by outside. A world removed. Belonging neither to the one left behind nor the one not yet reached. Where it's all right not to belong, to be oneself.

*

Several other children also left at the same time. Vicky and Toni had been suddenly collected one day near the end of term, leaving just myself, Wixie and Janet in the girls' dormitory. Relationships with the other children ended but by then I never expected them to last, had never seen

Total Disruption: Catholic Boarding School

any friends away from the school or ever heard what became of them. Perhaps a year or so later Mother told me the school had closed. When life had settled down after the post-war years and food rationing ended there was no longer much demand for small private country boarding schools. I remember wondering how Miss Gisborne would cope without being able to spank little children's naked bottoms – which she probably couldn't if teaching in a day school – feeling she somehow needed to.

When I was ten Auntie Janet discovered Miss Gisborne had left Tubney House and, still with her companion friend 'Nurse', had moved to a large house in the Banbury Road in Oxford at the junction with Rawlinson Road, where Auntie Janet rented rooms in the Boving family's home. Auntie Janet said she'd take me to visit Miss Gisborne.

We knocked on the front door and were ushered in. Miss Gisborne spoke mainly to Auntie Janet with the odd remark thrown out to me. I remember standing beside them in a lounge while she showed Auntie Janet a black, rectangular box with dials and wires, spending sometime forcefully explaining it. Mostly I couldn't follow, but do remember her saying:

"One can use blood or hair, but I prefer blood."

It seemed entirely in character that she should want blood drawn. Auntie Janet listened, asked questions, seemed slightly worried, disapproving.

Nurse, in what seemed an unprecedented act of generosity from one of those two, gave me a sixpenny piece. Her black labrador, Barry, was still with her wandering around. I was then sent to wait in the hall while they discussed me privately. Apparently Miss Gisborne came out with the classic schoolteacher pleasantry:

"We're always pleased to see our old scholars."

Nothing to reveal what it had really been like.

Afterwards I asked Auntie Janet about the black box. She smiled, shrugged her shoulders, said she didn't know. Looking back, remembering the way she'd questioned Miss Gisborne, the expression on her face, I think she knew the box was fraudulent medical equipment but thinking "the child" should always respect authority wasn't prepared to admit it.

Decades later I recognised this bogus 'machine' from its description in a book. Radionics, the book said, used a complex looking black box to both diagnose and cure. The practioner might never meet the patient, a drop of blood or hair sent by post the only contact. Inside the box beneath the

Dark Cupboards, Dusty Skeletons

dials there was no workable circuit, merely wires linking. A piece of fraudulent, pseudo-scientific medical equipment later banned in the U.S. (but not the U.K), obtaining money from the desperate for whom conventional medicine could do nothing. There's no problem with distance healing that's what prayer is, but prayer is what it says it is. This black box deceived claiming scientific know-how to make money. When Miss Gisborne found us on her doorstep she must have seen another potential customer offering themselves up – why she'd talked so forcibly to Auntie Janet.

This was the last time I saw those two women who'd had such a negative influence on my early life.

*

A little older, with experience of Roehampton Church School,
"Why did I go there?" I asked Mother in more confident moments when the trauma of memory didn't stop me from mentioning it at all.
The first time of asking a swift sharp reply came:
"For your health!"
I shut up, as intended.
Another time: "Well, things were very difficult for *me*."
I should understand her feelings. But empathy had never been a strong feature of family life.
Then later, in my teens:
"Well it wasn't as though you were a baby. I could have put you in a children's home."
Once again I was unable to continue for fear of further hurt, the knife being turned.
Then once, more sympathetically,
"A Catholic convert! I should have known" – that Miss Gisborne would be so harsh – and,
"It was only supposed to be for a year."
She told me she'd been offered promotion at Wycombe Court School, felt she had to accept, had cried in morning assembly, trying to pretend it was a cold.
Talking about emotional problems was always enormously difficult in our family, communication blocked by my feelings of shame and guilt about being so bad, as I believed, and Mother not wanting to believe wrong decisions had happened on her watch.

A Precarious 'Normality': Roehampton 1

The plan had been for me to join Mother, boarding at Wycombe Court School where she taught French, already familiar through having stayed odd nights in her room, meeting some of the teachers and having been taken to see Matron to try on second-hand uniform who had the shaggiest-haired dog I'd ever seen.
"He hasn't any eyes," I blurted out in surprise.
"*Of course* he's got eyes," she retorted indignantly.
I remember a spreading cedar tree on the lawn outside Miss Boyle and Miss Robinson's, the headmistresses', spacious lounge; watching races on sports' day, a girl managing to swim underwater the full length of a fair-sized pool picking up a series of plates from the bottom without coming up for air; an afternoon with Mother of absorbing indoor games, quizzes and a treasure hunt in the school hall, the whole school taking part; going to a pottery lesson, moulding wet clay for the first time. But I never saw any of the chosen items of second-hand uniform again. When at Roehampton during the summer I mentioned going to Wycombe Court, Mother responded with: well ... no ... we weren't going back there ...
She'd changed her mind. Why?
Our GP in Roehampton, Dr Barnes, at some stage signed her on for another term's sick benefit after she'd been ill with lung trouble. Dr Barnes was sympathetic to Mother's plight, said she'd read some of Bill's crime novels.
Auntie Gladys, now widowed, wanted someone to live with her in the four-bedroom house she loved so much, set up with her husband, Jack, too large for one person. Perhaps she wasn't happy with us only being there part-time in school holidays? She offered us rent-free accommodation.
"We share a house," Mother would tell people. So, as always, money must have been a major factor in her decision.

Dark Cupboards, Dusty Skeletons

Then there were the tensions with her own family: she wouldn't turn to them for support. She was tired of full-time teaching, one of her letters indicates this; with me boarding at the same school there would have been no excuse to escape at weekends. In any case she had to give up teaching until deemed no longer infectious by the powers that be. But this is all guesswork. She never really said why she'd changed her mind. I was happy living in Auntie Gladys's lovely house which came to feel like "home", although as we'd continually moved I also came to expect change at any time never really believing anywhere might be permanent. Auntie Gladys was the kindest landlady anyone could hope for. She'd married late in life and no children had come along, so we became her 'family', she an adopted grandmother I came to know much better than the person I was taught to call "Grannie". After Mother had tuberculosis she had to give up teaching; Auntie Gladys was prepared to take us in. There was a lot of fear of T.B. then, an often incurable disease, so this was quite strong-minded of her. But I never knew when Mother might decide to uproot and change our lives again.

A rather meaningless, artificial approach to religion still played a large part in my life. When we came back to Roehampton Mother began bedtime prayers, wanting us both to kneel by the side of my bed, palms together in front of faces, heads bowed. To begin with she would say a longish prayer. Shortly after, one night when we must both have been tired, she knelt as usual whilst I lay in bed and gabbled a little made-up prayer: "Dear-Lord-Jesus-I-love-you-Amen". That was it. This became the regular bedtime ritual. Artificiality can be stressful; I felt relieved she was so easily satisfied, that I didn't have to go through a longer rigmarole of pretense, able to just lie in bed gabbling this very short line. A meaningless appeasement which kept her happy. She felt she was bringing me up properly as a good Christian, how "the child" *should* be brought up. She told me years later she thought this so sweet, my own little prayer. Unfortunately it meant nothing spiritually.

*

Aged about seven, on one of our sporadic visits to Hindhead, a one-off moment of closeness with Grannie occurred whom, Mother later told me, had said she hadn't wanted a grandchild. Grannie and I were alone in her sitting room. She actually took me on her lap saying I was her "little fairy". I liked being her little fairy. Then, as soft footsteps were heard outside the door, Grannie suddenly, quickly, pushed me off. Bewildered, I stood

A Precarious 'Normality': Roehampton 1

silently. Mother appeared laughing, something had amused her. Grannie looked annoyed as though caught out, the brief moment of warmth shattered, never to be repeated. What *was* going on between them?

Grannie's back garden, Brambletye circa 1951,
wearing the favourite grey shorts and
holding "Baby Honey" named
by Auntie Kay!

Not long after Grannie said I was too big to be her little fairy, I would have to be her little "flibberty gibbet" – then that she could never remember the name. I disliked this, later wondering if it had something to do with the ghost of an executed criminal flitting around a gibbet. Mostly, when we

Dark Cupboards, Dusty Skeletons

visited Hindhead, Grannie would be sitting in another room not seeming too pleased when we poked heads round her door.

It was family minded Audrey who arranged a cottage holiday, our first proper summer holiday, in '51 or '52, inviting Mother and myself. Vanessa and I may have both been seven, perhaps only six, but dates and ages are hazy. Fares were cheap and affordable: the two of us, Mother and I, travelled by train then country bus with just one small brown suitcase packed with all we needed for the week – which Mother carried. The only place-name connected with this holiday I remember, which stuck, was of the small, country, circular close the cottage was in called "The Frying Pan": the round bit being 'the pan', the track across the centre 'the handle'. I have a vague memory it was somewhere to the west of England. This always stuck in my mind as: "The Frying Pan Holiday".

I liked being with Vanessa; we played happily together for hours. Mother wasn't so keen as the cottage was very primitive, the only 'privy' being a trek to the end of the garden inside a shed with wooden seat revealing a dark smelly hole beneath. Cooking was done on an ancient black kitchen range which had to have a solid fuel fire lit below. I remember Mother, who hated cooking, standing beside Audrey next to this out-of-the-ark contraption, preparing hot meals. Vanessa and I would be sent off round the Frying Pan to a couple of smallholdings to buy homegrown vegetables. I remember at one helping to pick bright green pea pods, weaving hands round tall twiggy stakes the plants clung to; at another the elderly couple openly commented on how shy I was compared to Vanessa who had no trouble chatting away. She'd had a settled home with her mother and grandmother.

Downstairs the cottage consisted of a fairly large dining-cum-sitting room with open fireplace and large wooden table we sat round for meals – a rare family group of four – and the small kitchen. Up narrow stairs were a couple of bedrooms; the one I slept in had two single beds but I don't remember whether this was shared with Mother or Vanessa, or both at different times. There may also have been a small bathroom at the back. I think the cottage had fresh running water although no indoor lavatory so presumably no sewage outlet.

Vanessa and I spent most of our time playing: there are photos of us with a pram found in the cottage; she's put me in as the (reluctant) 'baby'. We explored the thick Frying Pan hedgerows discovering a fascinatingly vast number of grey garden snails. Taking from the kitchen a galvanised metal

A Precarious 'Normality': Roehampton 1

bucket we picked a huge collection up by their shells until bored, then showed our booty to the grown ups expecting suitably impressed comments. What happened to the contents of the bucket? We'd lost interest. Its slimy occupants were probably surreptitiously disposed of, tipped back into the hedgerow or open field beyond the privy.

Auntie Kay visited just for one day so there were – very unusually – *five* of us round the dinner table. Years later she later reminisced, laughing, that we must have been a great embarrassment to our mothers, as one of us had said, "My Daddy's gone away!"

To which the other replied,

"My Daddy's gone away too and Mummy says he's not coming back!"

Neither of us remembered our fathers. In those days families without fathers elicited a good deal of rather juicy gossip. Outgoing Auntie Kay and Audrey took this more in their stride; Mother became terribly upset this being one of the largest of many terrifying skeletons to be eternally locked away in the deepest, darkest, of cupboards.

I think it was on this holiday that Vanessa and I were taken to the seaside, photos taken of us having donkey rides but the pictures may have been of some other trip. Mother never wrote dates or place names.

Searching Google for "the Frying Pan" brings up "Frying Pan Farmhouse" in a Wiltshire village but this seems to be some distance from the coast, although roughly in the area where I believe we stayed. Perhaps we took one of those single-decker Greenline buses to the beach.

Mother told me Audrey had invited us again the following summer but she didn't want to go, so Audrey and Vanessa went with friends instead. I would have liked to have spent another holiday with Vanessa, The Frying Pan holiday being the only one ever spent with relatives. In my teens I once went with Auntie Janet when she visited teacher friends from St Leonard's School in St Andrews where she'd taught Classics. Otherwise, until I was sixteen it was just the two of us, Mother and myself for holidays, after which I organised my own alone or with friends.

Dark Cupboards, Dusty Skeletons

The Frying Pan
holiday, summer '51 or '52.
Top: myself, left, in pram, with Vanessa,
playing outside the front door of our holiday cottage.
Below: donkey rides on a beach, myself left,
Vanessa centre.
*

Mother's decision to live in Roehampton raised the problem of getting me into a *good* school, education being a top priority for an Oxbridge educated family. Roehampton Church School was in the Village, its two parts on a hill

A Precarious 'Normality': Roehampton 1

either end of Holy Trinity Church. It was the best non-fee-paying, primary school in the local area having a well-established reputation for getting a high percentage through that all-important eleven-plus exam, that is: important from the point of view of maintaining social class, grammar schools then taking mostly brighter middle-class children. But, oversubscribed, Roehampton Church School wasn't easy to get into.

Mother had already established a relationship with Holy Trinity Church having had me baptised there the year before. Ever resourceful she circumnavigated the usual channel of going to see the headmaster, Mr Whitaker, taking me instead to see the vicar, Canon Campling. We were ushered into a front room in the Vicarage where Canon Campling, tall, saintly looking, and white-haired, in black clerical suit, interviewed his parishioners. I remember standing quietly beside Mother whilst they talked, not following the conversation as they spoke too quickly, the way grown-ups did. I'm not sure whether I knew at the time *why* we were there but distinctly remember the occasion. Probably Mother, obviously of good social background, presented the reverend gentleman with her plight: a middle class lady fallen on hard times; bringing up a child on her own in financially straightened circumstances ruling out the usual middle class private school option; perhaps mentioning her own serious health problems although TB also tended to be one of those taboo subjects – yet a another skeleton. It was quite acceptable at that time for an obviously middle class lady to wish to stay in that social milieu. Later, to claim middle class status was definitely not compatible with the ideal of the classless society.

In the early '50s Roehampton Church School, although socially mixed, had a higher percentage of brighter middle class children than the average state school, presumably selected by Mr Whitaker. Canon Campling must have agreed to speak to Mr Whitaker, and the school being under the auspices of the Church Mr. Whitaker probably felt obliged to agree to the Vicar's request. But the only place available was in the class above my age group, so to begin with I skipped a year and joined the second-year juniors: Mrs Clack's class.

Roehampton Church School stood at the edge of the Village about half-a-mile from Auntie Gladys's house. I think Mother must have walked me there the first couple of days along Dover House Road and across the small stretch of open Common past the war memorial. Turning eight later that term I was soon expected to take myself. Oddly enough, although I remember starting

Dark Cupboards, Dusty Skeletons

at the day nursery in Putney, arriving at Auntie Janet's flat in Headington, meeting Miss Woods and Deborah crying, then being left that first day at Miss Gisborne's school, I remember nothing of my first day at Roehampton Church School. Perhaps, being non-traumatic, it doesn't stand out in memory.
So to begin with I was put in Mrs Clack's class, the year above my age group, with about forty children, in the part of the school at the top of Ponsonby Road hill, and placed in one of the light-coloured, wooden, double-desks with horizontal tops to work on, next to a nice older girl, Diana. Mrs Clack was nice too, neatly dressed in skirt and stockings, fair hair tidily pinned back, a good teacher able to keep order without inducing fear. Her ultimate sanction if the class got a little rowdy was:
"Hands on your heads".
Instantly all forty children would put hands on tops of heads and go perfectly silent. I don't think she ever shouted, never saw her hit a child. She used positive encouragement: each of us had a row of stickers on the wall for good work. The classroom was light and cheerful with pictures on the walls. Later I learned she had a young daughter also called Elizabeth, who spent weekdays with her grandparents while Mrs Clack and her husband both worked full-time. It was clear from the start this school was a great deal happier, less kinky and intensely frightening than what I'd come to accept as 'normal'.

*

Roehampton Church School had just one class for each year, forty children in double desks facing a blackboard at the front – near the teacher's larger desk – on which sums would be written in white chalk; then gone through again and again to be sure even the slowest in mixed ability classes had grasped – by rote – how to get answers right. Even so, as I didn't yet know all my multiplication tables, Arithmetic turned into a series of mysterious white squiggles called Long Multiplication. Writing compositions, having only ever written in pencil and separated letters, I struggled for the first time with a split nib pen dipped in dark blue ink in a white porcelain inkwell sunk in the desktop. The others had learned joined-up writing in the first year juniors. Then the playground was a mass of children who all knew each other having started school together aged five. To begin with I felt rather isolated at break times.

A Precarious 'Normality': Roehampton 1

One thing I was good at was cutting out with scissors having been allowed to experiment at home. During a joint craft activity with Diana involving cutting paper she produced a very jagged edge; my edge being neat and straight. Mrs Clack, glancing our way, suggested I leave the cutting to Diana. I explained I had. She gave poor Diana a very disapproving look.
Another craft activity was sewing small scissor holders from felt, decorated with coloured embroidery thread in cross-stitch, loops and 'knots'. Allowed to take these home at the end of term, I kept mine for years, although never actually using it for scissors. Mrs Clack's class also had an interesting nature table with a variety of leaves and autumn seeds.
Given a composition topic of "My School". I ended with:
"The children there are very nice".
For "My Mother" I wrote:
"She has a big blue trunk and in the winter she puts all her summer clothes in it, and in the summer all her winter clothes."
Mother let out a shriek when I told her of this embarrassing revelation.
Before morning break we had to stay sitting at our desks and drink milk from third-pint glass bottles carried into the classroom in a large metal milk crate and distributed by child milk monitors, then drunk by pushing paper straws through silver foil tops. This being provided by the government (to prevent rickets?) wasn't charged for; for school dinners we had to take dinner money into class, in coins, at the beginning of each week: silver sixpences and shillings, brown three-penny (or "thru'penny") bits, large old pennies and half-pennies.

*

Mother now tried to tackle my problems with Arithmetic. She arranged for a private tutor, a Mr Moore, to come to Auntie Gladys's house; he and I sat in her dining room. When he discovered I'd only got three out of six homework sums right he wanted to administer corporal punishment. Mother said no, she didn't agree with that sort of thing. After she'd left the room he wanted me to stand up and bend over,
"To show you how I do it."
Another pervert. But with Mother nearby I felt confident enough to offer passive resistance; half stood then sat down again. He didn't push it further. Soon after this incident Mother told him she felt I didn't need more coaching. It was Audrey who found a lovely young lady to coach Vanessa and we began lessons together at her house, chatting and giggling, taking our

Dark Cupboards, Dusty Skeletons

new glove puppets to show her; we both had furry black cat puppets, mine was "Sooty". This worked well and I continued with her on my own taking myself on the bus after Vanessa stopped coming. Audrey got on well with people; she was a good judge of personality.

I'd never imagined for one minute that I would miss Miss Gisborne's awful school but did miss my friends. On several afternoons, getting home after school, I'd have a temper tantrum, no doubt convincing Mother I was less happy at my new school than at Miss Gisborne's. But I remember actually feeling grateful, even at the young age of seven, for being able to *have* tantrums, get upset, let anger out, something I'd been too frightened to do for years, feeling too unsafe to protest.

I'm still half asleep. I hear Mum opening the door, slipping quietly in. She is already dressed, hair still in curlers.
"Time to get up now."
I don't want to get up, don't feel settled in my new school, don't want to go. I huddle under the faded eiderdown, filled with duck feathers which poke out at the corner, pull an end, extract a tiny white curled feather. Stroke my lip with the softness.
"You *must* get up now!"
She pulls back the eiderdown and I resign myself, rolling off the mattress over brown wooden frame spanned by coiled metal springs. More bouncy than I feel. Much more. I begin to pull on thick navy school knickers, white vest, blue-green polo-neck jersey with pleated navy gym tunic on top, the school badge showing red and brash. Identified as a school pupil, I'm no longer *me*.

Mother, realising I was stressed, went to see the headmaster, Mr Whitaker and managed to get me moved down to the class below, the first year juniors, the right year for my age. Perhaps one of the brighter ones was moved up to create a space. She also asked if I could sit next to someone from Roehampton. In Mr Frazer's class I was sat in a double desk with Andrew who lived in Roehampton. We became best friends, unusual at an age when girls wanted to be friends with other girls, boys with boys; we were the only boy-girl best friends in the class. Andrew's parents weren't so keen his father being a retired naval officer felt his son's friendship with a *girl* wasn't *manly*, although they were nice to me and I wasn't aware of this until later.

A Precarious 'Normality': Roehampton 1

Mr Frazer's class, also with about forty children, was down the hill at the other end of the Church, in the lower part of the school. It still had antiquated Victorian, dark wooden desks for two with sloping tops to write on. The sloping part lifted on hinges; our books were kept in the space beneath. If either of us needed to get out a book the other had to stop writing while the top was lifted. A fixed horizontal strip contained the ubiquitous white porcelain inkwells – one each. The attached flat wooden bench seat for two also lifted on hinges. Old-fashioned, Victorian, only a few years later this style of desk could be seen in museums.

With good formal class teaching on the blackboard in a mixed ability class where a sum would be gone through again and again until even the slowest had got it, my Arithmetic soon picked up to the point where I could comfortably cope.

Mr Frazer, having first drawn carefully spaced lines on the blackboard with a large wooden blackboard ruler, would very slowly form joined-up letters while we watched. We then dipped pens in inkwells and carefully copied the letters into lined exercise books. We mustn't dip too far: only the lower, split part of the nib should have ink on it so as to avoid inkblots – Mr Frazer made surprise inspections. Nevertheless we all went home with inky fingers. These metal nibs slotted into long wooden orange holders, some of which became so well-chewed at the non-nib end they looked like paintbrushes. I don't think anyone was ever told off for chewing, the ethos, even with blustery, sometimes short-tempered Mr Frazer, infinitely more easy going than at Miss Gisborne's school.

Mother went to call on Andrew's mother at their large, detached, middle-class house in Dover House Road, and arranged for us to play out of school. Being obviously middle-class herself, with the right accent, she could do this and be accepted. So began our two-year friendship until Andrew was sent away to board at an upmarket boys' prep school.

*

Mother never liked the Church School. Was it these early difficulties, too working class, or did she feel a non fee-paying school was a come down? Always a "lady's lady", did she find Miss Gisborne easier to get on with than Mr Whitaker and Mr Frazer? Once settled I found the Church School a vast improvement on Miss Gisborne's set up, more relaxed, humane and child-orientated – less kinky, frightening and much more fun. Even so, when asked by a kindly adult,

Dark Cupboards, Dusty Skeletons

"Do you like school?" I'd politely give what I thought was the expected answer:
"Yes," while really preferring the freedom of *not* being in school!

*

Roehampton Church School was a mixed, non-fee-paying day school for primary age children aged 5 to 11, I attended for the four junior years from 7 to 11. The school was situated on a hill, Ponsonby Road, in two parts at either end of the Church. The top three junior classes for children turning nine, ten and eleven were at the top of the hill; the second and third year juniors in the main building. This also housed a small room with hand basins and running cold water, a cloakroom with pegs, and the main hall used for assembly, hymn practice, singing, plays, and school dinners for all including infants, who walked up Ponsonby Road each day. The hall still had gas lighting; the rest of the upper building had electricity by 1952. The playground had outside lavatories behind the hall with no inside access – when raining you ran quickly so as not to get too horribly wet – and no washbasins or lavatory paper. On the other side of the playground from the main building stood the headmaster, Mr Whitaker's house, with the top junior eleven-plus classroom underneath entered through a separate door from the playground and tiny cloakroom.

Holy Trinity Church was sandwiched halfway down Ponsonby Road between the two parts of the School, the first year juniors' – Mr Frazer's class – and the three infant classes at the bottom of the hill with Mr Whitaker's office and the nurse's room. This lower part of the school had a playground with just a low chain between small concrete pillars separating it from the road which, in those days, had very little traffic. I remember Mr Whitaker in the playground, worried and angry about a boy straying onto the road, but this didn't happen often. The reception class played separately in a rather narrow space bounded by their classroom wall one side and Ponsonby Road wall on the other. As in the upper school the lavatories were separate from the main building open to fresh air to reduce odours, but linked under a roof covering so no risk of getting wet visiting in rain. Another part of the lower school building was Mr Frazer's teacher's cottage overlooking the lower school playground. As you progressed up the school, you also progressed up the hill.

A Precarious 'Normality': Roehampton 1

Behind the upper part of the school and Church was the part of Putney Heath known as "the Common" where we were allowed to play in dry weather greatly enhancing freedom, enjoyment and play possibilities
Each school year had just one class of forty children of mixed ability from families of mixed social backgrounds with one class teacher occasionally helped by a female student from the local Froebel Training College in Roehampton Lane.
School uniform wasn't compulsory – perhaps unaffordable for some parents – although many children wore some version of it. The girls' winter uniform was a red blazer with school badge – a black silhouette of Holy Trinity Church – worn over dark navy tunic with three pleats both front and back and expandable belt round the waist over a white shirt and school tie sporting red and black stripes. To begin with I went to school in the clothes I already had. Then Mother bought me a school tunic. Mostly I only ever had this item of uniform worn over a jumper in winter or T-shirt in summer, an ideally practical grow-with-the-child, ink-stain disguising, garment. The blazer was too expensive. In the top-year juniors, my last year, for hot weather Mother had a red gingham cotton dress tailor-made. From the one class photo I have, there seems to have been no standard design; several girls have red gingham dresses each one a different style. With no local shop selling standard red gingham dresses they were perhaps all homemade, or the fabric purchased and left with a paid seamstress. Seventy years later my granddaughter also had a red gingham dress for school. Life is full of change but some things never change.
The boys had to wear red caps to school every day, thick red fabric, lined, with a peak in front below the school badge. They were expected to raise their cap or at least touch the peak with forefinger if they met anyone they knew, as a mark of respect and good manners. Mostly they did.

*

I'd been baptised aged six on 9th September 1951 at Holy Trinity Church Roehampton before going back to boarding school. With all the early troubles Mother hadn't got round to it before. A girl needed two godmothers and a godfather. This was a problem: we didn't know any men.
"Would you like me to be her godfather?" offered the young curate, adding quickly, "Please don't hesitate to say 'No' ". So that solved that.
Thus unlike most children, normally baptised as babies, I have a clear memory of standing by the font at the end of the church, dim light piercing

Dark Cupboards, Dusty Skeletons

stained glass windows, being blessed with Holy Water, Mother and Auntie Janet also standing by the font as godmothers.
"Are you going to wash now?" asked a boy after the ceremony, when my new godfather had marked a cross on my forehead with Holy Water. At bedtime I washed the rest of my face. Then, suddenly impatient with the whole rigmarole, drew the flannel across my forehead and thought no more of it.

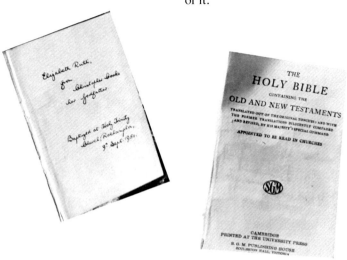

Christening presents to be kept for life: from my Godfather, above, and Godmother, below. Illustration: *Light of the World* by Holman Hunt, English painter, one of the founders, in 1848, of the Pre-Raphaelite Brotherhood.

A Precarious 'Normality': Roehampton 1

After we moved permanently back to Roehampton in '52 my new godfather, The Reverend C. K. Hamel Cooke, would come to tea sitting at Auntie Gladys's polished dining room table, in white dog collar above black clerical suit, chatting to Mother who made cups of tea and carried plates of sandwiches and biscuits in from the kitchen.

We also visited his family, wife Mary and baby son Stephen, on the other side of Roehampton. On one visit soon after settling back in Roehampton Mother was determined I should wear a skirt; I made a fuss, equally determined to wear my much-loved grey shorts. Eventually she gave way but must have worried terribly about the unfemininity and impropriety of shorts all through the lengthy walk to the other side of Roehampton.

We knocked on the front door. When the young curate opened it, beaming a welcome, before even saying "Hello" she blurted out as though the sky had fallen,

"She wanted to wear her *shorts.*"

With exemplary good manners he at once replied with great enthusiasm, "Oh, we LOVE little girls in shorts!"

His elderly mother one afternoon during tea, spilled the beans on the pranks he'd played as a boy: knocking on doors and running away; sticking postage stamps to the pavement and hiding to watch people try and pick them up; tying string across paths to trip people up; climbing trees and mewing like a stranded cat; she went on and on. I listened, fascinated.

At the end he said quite mildly,

"I've never heard you say so many bad things about me in one afternoon!"

So he was human despite the black clerical suit and dog collar.

Illegitimacy being such a scandalous issue, I think their friendship gave Mother some support and respectability at a time when she was trying to cope with Village gossip about her marital status, difficult to prove, and my possible illegitimacy:

"I couldn't really go around waving a marriage certificate," she said later.

Unfortunately my godfather was moved about a year later, as parish curates often were, from Roehampton to Lichfield Cathedral. He wrote when I was about twelve saying I must be a very grown up goddaughter by now. Mother opened, read out, and answered the letter. We saw him once in Oxford with Mary, Stephen and second son, Jonathan, when they visited Sandfield Road. Described as one of the outstanding parish priests of his generation, after a

Dark Cupboards, Dusty Skeletons

spell as Vicar of St Andrew's Bedford he was appointed Rector of St Marylebone Church where he became well known for converting the crypt into a health and spiritual centre. Passing on the coach to Oxford I'd see his name on the board outside but there was no opportunity to get off and catch up.

My godfather, his wife Mary and eldest son Stephen,
in the front porch of Auntie Gladys's house,
Highdown Road, 1952.

A Precarious 'Normality': Roehampton 1

Elderly, small, stout and irritable, in dark grey suit and tie, Mr Frazer or "Sir", the first male class teacher I had, could seem alarming but, underneath the bluster, was conscientious and caring. After struggling in Mrs Clack's class I caught up quickly with his clear formal teaching with white chalk on blackboard. A vast improvement on St Nicholas's School, Tubney, where we were left to struggle on our own with very little help.

He had no scruples about punishing boys. When he'd had enough, visibly losing his cool, he would bend a boy over his desk, pull up a short grey trouser leg and smack a bare thigh with his hand, known amongst children in his class as, "The Slap". It didn't happen often. I was never afraid he might hit *me*.

He once decided there was too much noise, told several boys to stand by the wall with their hands on their heads. Then they all had to line up to be bent over for "The Slap", including Andrew. Talking to the class afterwards, "Sir" grinned slightly at Andrew,

"Yes . . . my hand slipped when it came to you, didn't it?"

Knowing Mr Frazer had a soft spot for Andrew, who was young for that class and should really have been in the year below, I suggested later in the playground that it had 'slipped' on purpose. But Andrew didn't think so.

*

I don't remember what Andrew did at playtime in those early days but don't think we played together much. I spent one winter playtime happily damming a stream, a thin trickle of water along the side of the lower playground, with sodden twigs, mud and gravel. Mrs Herbert, who supervised dinner play, walked past looking disapproving, but kindly said nothing until others joined in, then told us to stop. With hindsight it seems staff were understanding about my difficulties settling.

There was no apparatus in the school playgrounds except what we brought in ourselves: mainly skipping ropes and small rubber balls. As I began to join in more the girls showed me "two-balls": juggling against the outer brick wall of the lower school lavatories.

Most girls could already skip, swinging a rope rhythmically, running in and jumping over as it came down – helping me pick up the technique. Usually we skipped in groups, two girls holding each end of a rope, turning, while the rest queued to run in one by one, skip through a chant sung by all, then run out again without the rope stopping. At first this looked impossible; I'd run in and find my feet tangled in the rope bringing its revolutions to an

Dark Cupboards, Dusty Skeletons

ignominious halt. But once I'd learnt the knack of running in at the right moment and judging the rhythm to jump to, it was surprisingly easy. I can no longer remember any of the rhymes chanted, the same repeated until all the girls in the queue had had their turn.

Expensive skipping ropes had ball bearings inside the wooden handles so the rope revolved more smoothly but we mostly had cheaper ones: just thin fibre rope, ends threaded through holes in the balls of the two handles and knotted. The longer part of the handle screwed into the ball. For individual skipping smaller children could shorten the rope by unscrewing the handle cutting off a bit of rope, re-knotting the end. The cheapest skipping ropes had handles that didn't come apart, the rope shortened by simply tying knots in its centre.

On days when it was too wet and gloomy to play on the Common we took in brightly coloured glass marbles. You had to throw or roll yours to hit your opponent's. If you managed this, their marble became yours. If they hit yours, it became theirs. The flat hard level playground was fine for playing marbles.

Playing 'he', running round the playground or across the Common, brown leather sandals with strap, buckle and crepe soles were easy to run fast in. (We didn't have to change shoes going out or coming in.) Who would be 'it' to start with was decided by rhymes and chants. Someone would take charge, say:

"Right! Put your spuds up!"

Three or four pairs of clenched fists would be produced, held in a circle. One girl would use her own fist to count round, touching each one in turn including both her own:

"One potato, two potato, three potato, four,
Five potato, six potato, seven potato, more.
You are out!"

The fist touched on "out" would be removed from the circle and put behind a back. The rhyme was repeated until only one fist was left in the circle. That person was 'it', chasing until they managed to touch another. The cry would go up, "I 'had' you!" and the person who was 'it' changed to the one touched without any break in running.

*

School dinners, never the ordeal they had been at Miss Gisborne's school, arrived by van each day delivered to the hall in the upper part of the school

A Precarious 'Normality': Roehampton 1

in huge cylindrical bare metal containers. Arranged on tables in a line in a corner of the hall, three or four silent dinner ladies in overalls stood behind to serve. The younger children walked up the hill for a first sitting.
We queued, each picking up a solid white china plate from the pile. Mashed potato would be served with a half ball-like bare metal implement – usually one scoop each, shaped like an ice cream on a cornet but a lot less tasty. Vegetables, often over-boiled soggy pale green cabbage, and lumps of red meat in dark brown gravy came from similarly stark containers. After assembly, while we'd been having morning lessons, long, rectangular folding plain wooden tables and benches had been put up by Mr Brown the caretaker. Holding full plates of dinner we'd find an empty place to sit. There was no system of set places. Still no drink, although as the food was softer and moister than at Tubney this seemed less of a problem, but swallowing it down, especially fatty, gristly, red meat, still a struggle. You were supposed to eat as much as you could then put your hand up. A kind, gentle, grey-haired lady, Mrs Hill, the school nurse who supervised dinnertimes, would come round. If she felt you'd eaten enough you could put the remains in the slops bucket and queue for pudding. Coming to me, she'd look doubtfully at my half-empty plate, say I should eat a little more, seeming genuinely concerned. Once, in a highly conscientious mood, I decided I'd do the *right* thing and clean my plate completely. Getting down a long stringy piece of yellow gristle was quite a challenge: trying to swallow it down whole it slithered, sticking in my throat making me almost throw up but with a supreme effort of will power I managed to send it down. Mrs Hill beamed, seemed so genuinely delighted by my unusually clean plate. I think she really cared. Apart from dinner times she would normally be in the medical room in the lower school next to Mr Whitaker's office ready to care for any minor medical problems such as cut knees. Young children liked her, were happy to go to her; putting arms round she'd give cuddles.
Mrs Robilliard, Ann's mother, said when she asked son Christopher what he'd had for dinner it would inevitably be:
"Cake and custard". Perfectly true, the custard being the standard post-war thick, yellow slightly lumpy stuff, the cake varying a little in colour but never in taste.
School dinners at Roehampton Church School were relaxed, humane, never traumatic, never ordeals in the way they had been at Miss Gisborne's school.

Dark Cupboards, Dusty Skeletons

Even post-war food, still anything but appetising, wasn't dreaded with this kinder approach to eating.
No one took in sweets, crisps or anything to eat at break time. At the start of morning break we all had the compulsory third pint of milk. Wartime rationing of sweets had only recently ended in 1949. I never saw a packet of crisps.

*

I'd met Ann Robilliard in Mrs Clack's class before being moved down. She lived five minutes walk away on the council estate in Crestway and was good at two balls, skipping and hopscotch. Out of school we chalked hopscotch games on the paving stones outside my house and played for hours, throwing a tiny pebble into the numbered squares, hopping through the routine. She always wore skirts, never shorts, had brown shoulder length hair, neatly cut, well brushed and shining.
Her small terraced cottage in a row all identical – with neighbours' front door in an alcove next to hers obliterating privacy and enforcing socialisation – had much smaller rooms, front and back gardens, than Auntie Gladys's house. There wasn't much to do, I thought. But close by a half-moon shaped green surrounded by a low chain easily stepped over, offered space for estate children to play together. I met her friend, Gillian, and other girls, on this green.
Their front room had something possessed by neither Andrew's nor my homes in our larger, wealthier houses: a small black-and-white television, also a radiogram. The first time I watched television was in Ann's tiny front room. Mother and I were invited round to watch Queen Elizabeth II's coronation. Afterwards a film on Guy Fawkes was to be shown. Would we like to stay and see that? I wanted to; Mother thought we should go.
"You don't see him being hanged," smiled Ann's mother. She'd rightly guessed that would be the main attraction. Growing up in a hard, post-war world that was how I was; I can't have been a very nice child, now seems horrifying for a seven-year-old. St Christopher School, allowing emotional life, offering empathy, would change all that.
Disappointed, I left without further protest.
Ann's grandparents lived next door; she was always in and out of their house and garden, a close family situation in total contrast to my own. Her father was a fireman.

A Precarious 'Normality': Roehampton 1

"You don't have to worry about your house catching fire with people like my dad around," she'd say.

I think her mother was at home all day, not out at work. Ann's brother, Christopher, did well in the eleven-plus exam getting into the prestigious Emmanuel School.

They were very well brought up: had to say,

"Yes, Dad," or "Yes, Mum," when spoken to by their parents. If Ann was a little flippant in replying she would be taken into another room where I could hear her being spoken to in quiet, serious tones, her parrying the seriousness with a spate of light-hearted's,

"Yes, Dad! Yes Dad! Yes Dad!" Even when invited round estate children were expected to hesitate on the doorstep and ask,

"May I come in?" before entering.

They had a bus stop a few yards away at the end of Crestway and a public phone box on the corner of Crestway next to a red fire alarm with the notice: "In case of emergency break glass" – to pull the handle inside. I longed to try but there was never a convenient fire.

*

When we moved back to Roehampton I saw more of my second cousin Vanessa, think we started travelling alone on the number 72 red double-decker bus between Roehampton and Barnes, from the age of eight.

I'd walk to the end of Crestway, then between the tall wooden fences of a narrow alleyway (no longer marked on maps); past Queen Mary's Hospital – only a tall brick chimney billowing smoke visible – to the bus stop in Roehampton Lane.

I'd get off at the Boileau Arms – without realising this was a pub; pubs being unknowns not existing in our lives – just before Hammersmith Bridge, and walk up Lonsdale Road to Auntie Daisy's house, number 91, opposite the reservoir.

Vanessa and I being in similar family situations – only children without fathers – it was her mother's, Audrey's, idea we should be brought up as sisters.

Dark Cupboards, Dusty Skeletons

Mrs Chaloner suggested dressing up and taking photos as an activity.
Mother liked the idea and got some old clothes together
to choose from. Ann Robilliard looks very feminine;
I'm a cowboy with hobbyhorse. Auntie
Gladys's front garden, 1953.

A Precarious 'Normality': Roehampton 1

The same dressing-up activity when Vanessa came to play. She's a shepherdess, I'm the "Bird Man", a story book character, wearing my favourite grey shorts.
Vanessa's holding a 'crook', I've a toy bird. Like Ann
she's chosen a more feminine outfit.
Auntie Gladys's front garden,
1953.

Dark Cupboards, Dusty Skeletons

On a freezing winter's night the lighted oil stove would be left standing on the linoleum in my bedroom as I fell asleep, a shiny, black metal cylinder on black metal feet, its warm smell of paraffin wafting to where I lay cosily in bed. As I drifted off to sleep holes in the cylinder cast glowing patterns on walls and ceiling, dots of soft yellow light on shadowy shapes in the room. Nearer the stove the dots would be small, clear, more precise; those further away increasingly large until they became huge, hazy blurs. The oil stove gave more light than the tiny white wax nightlight I'd had when afraid of the dark, a naked flame flickering in a white china saucer on the mantelpiece.

Earlier I'd helped fill the oil stove, unscrewing the cap on the small round tank at the bottom, pouring in paraffin from a metal can through a metal funnel; seeing the round cloth wick which soaked up paraffin dangle down into the rich-smelling liquid; helping trim the top of the wick with a round metal cutter you placed on top and twisted to remove the black singed bits. Finally, the most thrilling part, taking a wooden match out of the tiny box, striking it, holding it to the top of the oil-filled wick. Flames, blue below, orange higher up, would flare, sending curling black smoke to the ceiling until the tall black, hinged cylinder was lifted upright over the flame.

"Turn the wick down," Mother said, with a necessary eye on economy. I wanted to turn it up, make my room really warm, watch it glow, make the round flat black top burning hot, untouchable. I turned the gold metal knob until the flame sunk to a circle of pure blue.

After I'd gone to sleep Mother would creep in and, lifting the stove by its cooler wooden handle, carry it out still lighted, to warm her bedroom before getting into bed after turning it out for the night.

Paraffin had to be fetched from Addison's the ironmonger's in the Village, in a can, brought home on a bus or carried the half-mile. Auntie Gladys said the bus conductors didn't like you taking it on the bus, but it was a long way for her to walk. She'd take a large, old bag to hide the can on her lap.

*

During term-time my main meal of the day was school dinner with a snack at home in the evenings, often a one-egg omelette or bowl of Heinz Tomato Soup. At weekends midday dinner was the main meal of the day, Auntie Gladys, Mother and myself sitting round the kitchen table. We ate mostly red meat; less often white boiled fish, liver, or rabbit. Chicken was a rare Christmas treat, vegetarianism almost unknown, considered cranky and unhealthy. Only the very poor ate little meat. We weren't that poor! People

A Precarious 'Normality': Roehampton 1

took it for granted that much of the meat would have quantities of fat and gristle; bought in small, over-the-counter shops there wasn't much choice. Raw, unwrapped meat would be spread on slabs in the shop window but one couldn't choose, had to take what was offered. Auntie Gladys grumbled at dinnertime about what she'd been sold. Nothing would be wasted, we weren't wealthy enough for that! The lean parts would be eaten hot, sliced; then fat and gristle minced in the meat mincer. I enjoyed this, so it was my job. First came the task of putting together the heavy metal pieces, working out where they went. The funnel, where one put in the roughly cut chunks of meat, went at the top; the large screw to push the meat against the small holes went inside the centre piece; the handle to turn the screw fastened at the side. Then there was a choice of circular grills one could slot in to mince the meat coarsely or finely. Lastly, the vice at the bottom of the assembled contraption had to be tightly screwed to the kitchen table. I needed help with tightening.

The best bit was the feeding in of chunks of meat from the white china plate on the table, half-hearing warnings about not putting fingers in too far. As I turned the handle slowly, looking down the funnel, watching the screw revolve, I could see chunks disappear – then reappear as long thin 'worms' curling out of the grill, twisting, turning, breaking off, dropping onto another plate below. With raw meat the worms would be pink, speckled with white flecks of fat and gristle. Eating them wasn't so enjoyable as mincing as they would usually be stewed into a sort of greasy shepherd's pie with mash and boiled cabbage. I was never a good eater, never thought of meat as dead animals – didn't really make the connection. Meat was . . . well . . . just . . . meat . . .

*

Auntie Gladys's house had electric light and power points to plug in small electric fires and "the Hoover" (never "the vacuum cleaner"). Plugging into light sockets with flexes trailing from ceiling to floor might be resorted to when running out of power points, health and safety not considered a problem. I don't remember any sawn off remains of pipes for gas lighting, so the house must have been built with electricity. Our school hall still had only gas lighting. Grannie in Hindhead had a large electric fridge in her kitchen; in the '50s not many kitchens had anything so fashionably up-to-date.

Dark Cupboards, Dusty Skeletons

1930s state of the art technology: top left paraffin heater similar to the one heating my bedroom on icy winter nights. The knob on the right turned the wick up or down. Top right a mechanical meat mincer. Below the type of telephone I talked on for hours to cousin Vanessa.

A Precarious 'Normality': Roehampton 1

Besides electricity another exciting modern convenience Auntie Gladys had was a telephone. My Vanessa and I would chat for – literally – hours. It stood in the dining room on a table in the bay window at the front of the house. The mouthpiece was on an upright pole, the dial on a circular base. The earpiece, attached by a brown, fabric-covered electric wire, hung on a bracket from the pole. When you lifted the earpiece and held it to your ear the bracket rose and you heard the dialing tone, then dialed your number. A type of ancient telephone now seen in museums along with our antiquated Victorian school desks. Sounds out-of-the-ark but we were the lucky ones: many homes didn't have a telephone. When Mother and I moved into a recently built modern brick semi in Letchworth some years later we managed without a telephone until Mother had one put in, involving having an overhead outside cable linked to the house. At Roehampton for a local call you had to dial the first three letters of the exchange, then the four figure number. In my seventies I still remember Vanessa's number: RIVerside 5713, and ours: PUTney 6353. For a long distance call, perhaps to Auntie Janet in Oxford, Mother had to dial "O" for the Operator (a real, live person!) and ask to be put through. Auntie Gladys probably paid our telephone bill; Auntie Daisy, Vanessa's grandmother, theirs.

Auntie Gladys had a "wireless" (a radio) in her sitting room; later I had one in my bedroom. I think both these were plugged into the mains. On Saturday mornings I would lie in bed listening to requests to *Children's Favourites* with Uncle Mac playing records of songs for children, *The Laughing Policeman* (he seemed unable to stop!) being highly popular.

In Auntie Gladys's dining room which became our sitting room when we moved back permanently, still with the never-to-be scratched polished table, Mother and I had a more primitive type of wireless with large glass, liquid batteries standing behind it. Periodically they had to be carried to Addison's ironmonger's in the Village to be refilled.

Once, when Ann Robilliard's mother sent her with a message to her uncle in the village, I went with her.

"He makes records," Ann told me.

We went to a tiny rough-looking, workshop on an unmade-up earth track between Roehampton High Street and the horse trough in the centre of the Village. Ann's uncle was making large black 78rpm records. I remember going in, waiting while he and Ann chatted, seeing shiny black, grooved discs lying around.

Dark Cupboards, Dusty Skeletons

The coke boiler in the kitchen heated water but the house had no radiators. In the winter the boiler was alight much of the time, having to be fed coke carried in from the coalhole outside, then raked and cleared of ash each day with a metal shovel. Auntie Gladys looked after the boiler. Coke and coal were delivered by an open lorry in sacks carried one-by-one on the shoulders of a soot-covered driver, along the tradesmen's entrance to the coal hole past the kitchen door, part of the house but accessed only by its own external door. When the greedy boiler had consumed an entire hod of coke someone had the unwelcome job of going outside and fetching more – normally a job for the man of the house but we were an all-female household.

In winter, every day, Auntie Gladys would make up an open coal fire in the fireplace in her sitting room and we did the same in ours (her dining room). This was another job I enjoyed. First there were sheets of newspaper to roll into tight balls and place in the empty grate as kindling. On top went small wooden chips of wood to be covered with carefully selected smaller pieces of coal which might 'catch' more easily; larger lumps of coal went on top. Lastly the front part of the grate had to be pulled out to let a draught in underneath to cause small flickering flames to burn larger. Then came the striking of the match, holding it to the newspaper, watching carefully to see whether the coal was beginning to glow as it should. If it was damp and the flames looked sluggish one could intensify the draught underneath by holding a full sheet of newspaper over the whole fireplace opening; firmly so the paper wouldn't be sucked into the fire and the situation get out of control. Grey smoke would begin to curl up the chimney. From time to time Auntie Gladys would employ a chimney sweep to clear the soot, exciting for me watching him kneeling on the floor in front of the fireplace fitting rods together one by one as he pushed the brush to the top, running outside to see if I could see it appearing. The grown ups didn't view the chimney sweep's visit as quite so exhilarating, leaving a black sooty mess indoors to clear up afterwards however careful he'd been to avoid it. Soot managed to get everywhere.

*

Our clothes were hand washed in the bathroom basin; then discretely hung out to dry on a rope line over a corner of the terrace away from Auntie Gladys's sitting room which overlooked the terrace, and where neighbours wouldn't see. Underwear was hung more even more discretely on indoor

A Precarious 'Normality': Roehampton 1

washing lines over the boiler; I'd left junior school before insisting on clean navy blue knickers every day.
Our white cotton sheets, towels and pillowcases were washed and ironed by a laundry service which collected and delivered, spotlessly white and neatly folded. Sheets were always white, never coloured, never fitted. Each week Mother removed the bottom sheet, put the used top sheet to the bottom and a clean sheet on top to be folded back over rough woven blankets and feather-filled eiderdown, fresh against one's face. Only the bottom sheet would be laundered. When sheets got thin and worn in the middle, to make them last longer Mother would cut them lengthways and stitch the less worn outer edges together, making a seam down the centre. She had an old Singer sewing machine of her mother's. Duvets were unheard of and perhaps unobtainable, blankets rarely washed, eiderdowns never. Mother would make the beds each day, after leaving bedclothes pulled back "to air" for a while. Unlike at boarding school I didn't make my own bed, was a teenager before insisting she stopped this and left it to me.

The back garden, professionally laid out, had a raised terrace, steps leading down to a sweeping lawn with apple trees in tiny circular beds planted with petunias. Down each side, against wooden fences, herbaceous borders provided a riot of colour throughout summer. Lupin and delphinium spires, deep blue, pink, purple; daisy-headed pyrethrums magenta and white; trails of golden rod, michaelmas daisies and sweet william with little scarlet geums underneath; backed by dark firs the Chaloner's side, on the other, loganberries trained along the fence. White alyssum self-seeded along the gravel path under standard roses. Under the terrace, blousy pink hydrangeas grew; in the larger bed the gardener, Heard, planted dahlia corms in spring, a mass of colour in late summer: shades of crimson, scarlet, pink, white and yellow.

The lawn, every tiny circular bed round the apple trees always neatly trimmed, seemed calm and focused. Rough grey rocky stones bordered the side beds, separated by an earthy gap from the trimmed lawn edges. At the lawn's end trellised arches of roses climbed above beds of rose bushes. Beyond, either side of the white greenhouse door, striped furry bees hummed endlessly round purple sweet-smelling lavender.

In vegetable patches on each side of the greenhouse red and black currant bushes grew, spiky gooseberries, onions and parsley at the front in sun. On the other side a clump of rhubarb with thick reddish stems and huge green

Dark Cupboards, Dusty Skeletons

leaves came up every year. This bed, freshly dug in spring, once grew green beans climbing tall twiggy stakes, later became largely empty as did the cold frame attached to the greenhouse. Along the back fence were yellow winter jasmine, a laburnum, row upon row of neatly stacked terracotta flowerpots in all sizes; an old, unusable, rusting boiler for heating the greenhouse. Bill Chaloner appeared one day in the back garden clad from head to foot in home-made protective clothing and cautiously approached this rusting boiler to deal with a wasps' nest inside.

I played endlessly and happily in this garden; gathering crinkly everlasting flowers; picking fresh flowers to press under heavy encyclopedias; making dens of sticks propped against the fence and covered with withered remains of plants pruned by Heard; building camp fires to boil kettles for tea; planting seeds; dipping watering cans in the rainwater tank in the greenhouse; finding hedgehogs and putting out bread and milk for them; climbing the laburnum; 'racing' across the lawn placing one foot after the other on upturned flower pots; collecting gnat larvae in jam jars from the greenhouse tank.

I watched Heard sort boxes of greenhouse seedlings to be bedded out, stood by while he planted dahlias; listened while he told me about rats in traps chewing off their own legs to escape. The garden provided for my pets: tortoises, a dog, a rabbit, newts in an old metal bathtub, tadpoles in an aquarium. I tasted sweet red loganberries, sour green gooseberries, sweet-sour pear-shaped crab apples, marvelled at the size of rhubarb leaves.

"In the war," Auntie Gladys said, "people tried eating the leaves because of food shortages, but they're poisonous – it's only the stalks you can eat."

I jumped off the terrace over hydrangeas growing beneath; hid against the fence behind deep blue delphiniums and golden rod in the herbaceous borders; learnt flower names. I picked daisies for daisy chains, white petals tinged with pink, closing in the evening opening again next morning; made pot pourri from the lavender. Rocks bordering the flowerbeds, up turned, uncovered beetles, ants, worms; once even a small brown newt.

Behind the greenhouse was a secret world out of sight of the house. Mud pies could be experimented with; campfires and huts built; a tiny pond made with concrete bought from Addison's ironmonger's. Auntie Gladys didn't seem to mind what happened on this waste patch. The wooden shed had spade, fork, hoe, rakes; wheelbarrow, fruit nets, sieve; long-handled shears for lawn edges, push mower, heavy roller: Heard's domain the day he came each week, explored other days when he wasn't there. Amongst the tools were a huge saw, axe and hammer, necessities for someone like me always 'making things'; nails, useful for mending bits of fence broken when climbed over, the twin boys (who later moved into the Chaloners' house) and I, scrambling over to their garden next door. On hot days the hose would be brought out to water the front garden. I might be allowed to help.

On the lawn I ran races with Jonathan (when Mother's university friend Sheila visited with her children) had dolls' tea parties with Vanessa, played cricket or rough and tumbled with Andrew, romped with Scamp (our mongrel bought when I was ten), played under the hose with friends on hot days, designed practice courses for the school obstacle race, learnt to put up a tent and camp out.

In warm weather Auntie Gladys would be sitting on the terrace; from time to time we would chat. Her silvery grey hair cut short just below her ears with side parting and clip, permanently waved by the hairdresser, framed her round smiling face. Fairly squarely built, wearing a necklace or brooch, her dark blue, grey, or navy dresses belted at the waist came down below-the-knee. In cold weather she'd wear a dark coloured cardigan buttoned down the front. Her brown leather shoes, solid with low wide heel, made a familiar clomp as she moved around the house.

"Auntie Gladys is going into the kitchen."
One always knew where she was.

Looking back she became a surrogate grandmother. Her sense of humour stands out in my memories: she really tried to be cheerful, cracking jokes, telling funny stories, cackling loudly with laughter – the only person I regularly heard laugh in my early years. She told amusing stories of little brother Reg, being awful when she and elder brother Will had to get him dressed for a party, battling to push him into his party clothes and walk him down the road.

"But", she would laugh, "the minute the door opened he would be all smiles and everyone would say,

"What a dear little boy!' "

Sadly Reg had been killed in the First World War.

She told me she'd been good at art and Maths at school, been shy like me. She'd grown up in Barnes, but hadn't known Auntie Daisy, Vanessa's grandmother, until they met at their tennis club. In colder weather she'd sit in her lounge with its sparkling glass chandelier, a folding screen inside the

Dark Cupboards, Dusty Skeletons

door against draughts, elegant china figures of shepherds and shepherdesses on the mantlepiece, sitting on her sofa close to the open coal fire listening to her wireless. She liked classical music but couldn't understand opera saying it seemed "Silly!" We would hear her trying to 'sing' it, her voice rising and falling in a comic croon. "Utterly tuneless", she would say.
Auntie Gladys had friends round to play bridge, had tea with her sisters-in-law Kitty and Nelly who lived round the corner, took number 30 buses into Putney, and went to "the Bank". After maidservant Kitty left she swept floors and dusted, cleaned the silver cutlery and wound the grandfather clock in the hall with its huge key so its twenty-four hour Westminster chimes never failed. She and Mother shared the cooking of main midday meals at the weekends. I remember her with her hands in the kitchen sink washing up. I was never asked to. She organised the redecoration of the house, paid the bills.
She'd moved into the house when she'd married Jack. She told us that at the end of the war, when everyone was celebrating, Jack was dying so she couldn't share the jubilation. I used to visit his unmarried sisters, Kitty and Nellie, once taken round the house and shown their collection of colourful cuckoo clocks in action, whirring, singing, tiny wooden doors opening, tiny figures popping out and in again.
I realise looking back how fond Auntie Gladys was of us, particularly me whom she'd watched grow up and opened her home to. I had free run of the garden, any pets asked for (except mice which she couldn't stand), although my rabbit ate all her pyrethrums down to the roots which she studied rather sadly, never complaining. We had most of the house: her rooms were the front bedroom upstairs and back sitting room downstairs – the only parts of the house I didn't play in, although going in to chat. She said she thought I was prettier than Vanessa who had "such a funny nose". I was unused to this kind of loyalty from my relatives, they didn't seem to think much of me, might have worried about that deadliest of the Seven Deadly Sins – vanity.
Although I was normally fairly quiet and not much trouble, enjoying reading and "making things" she was very tolerant. My friends sat round her kitchen table and painted; we played cricket on her back lawn; Vanessa and I once made a den in the airing cupboard lying on the freshly-laundered sheets; when I wanted to change to a different bedroom that was agreed to. My hobbies took up space in the kitchen: budgerigars, fret-saw, plywood and poster paints occupying one end of the draining board; my bicycle lived in

A Precarious 'Normality': Roehampton 1

the hall; endless telephone conversations with Vanessa went on her phone bill; my puppy (acquired later) ran round the house making puddles and barking, I climbed everywhere, jumped off the terrace over her hydrangeas (but not into them); ate the bitter-sweet crab apples.

But Mother was continually planning on uprooting, yearning for somewhere of her own. Did she ever realise how lucky we were? Or was her glass forever half empty?

*

I remember Mother taking me on a red, London, double-decker tram, somewhere in central London, probably in the summer '52 before they were taken out of service. Running on fixed rails trams just weren't manoeuverable enough as road traffic increased. We also travelled by trolley bus; these lasted into the '60s, powered by long arms linked to overhead electric cables, able to swing out round parked cars. Parking restrictions existed but infrequently enforced in those far off halcyon days.

The earliest walks closest to Auntie Gladys's house were to Putney Park Lane a leafy, unmade-up, gravel road, bordered by the back gardens of wealthy houses. We nicknamed this the "Cuckoo Lane" where we heard the first cuckoo of spring singing somewhere amongst tall leafy branches. We never actually saw it, its secretiveness, like the clear call easily mimicked, adding to its charm. At the end of the Cuckoo Lane across the road from Putney Heath, was a derelict house, razed almost to the ground, a bombsite open for small feet to explore, stepping over walls only a couple of bricks high.

It was up the Cuckoo Lane that I'd push my doll's pram, taking my large doll family of Bertha, Baby Honey, Lamby, Teddy, Golly and several others for a picnic on the Common; arranging them on the grass under a tree; packing all closely back in the pram to go home. Later the Cuckoo Lane was a good place to walk Scamp where one could let him off the lead.

Dark Cupboards, Dusty Skeletons

Above: doll family taken on picnics on the Common; far left "Teddy", far right "Lamby"; one of the two dolls behind was "Bertha", one in front, "Baby Honey" both named by Auntie Kay, another looks like a golliwog. Below "Lamby" leaning against a galvanised metal tub used as a paddling pool. Auntie Gladys's garden, 1952.

A Precarious 'Normality': Roehampton 1

My search for family led to families of dolls, then pets, then dream world people to focus on in lieu of relatives, having something to love being as indispensible as needing to feel loved.

Going someway downhill towards Putney was the nearest recreation ground, with swings, slides and roundabouts but I more often drifted up towards the Common. Once, seeing the curving colours of a rainbow from Auntie Gladys's back garden I was sure the arch must come down in the Cuckoo Lane and ran round to have a look. A Disney film about banshees, leprechauns and little folk had revealed a crock of gold at the end of the rainbow. When I got there the end had moved on, seeming to come down further away. Where else but the Cuckoo Lane to test the elusiveness of the crock of gold? It always did have a magical feel.

The nearest pond for shorter legs was what we called the "Little Dirty Pond". (Scio Pond on maps of Putney Heath.) I paddled round every inch of its boggy circumference; threw stones to make silver spreading ripples; dredged up odd bugs from its muddy depths (probably larvae of some kind); cut my toe on something sharp,

"Promise you won't be cross," I said before showing Mother, (thus prepared, she wasn't!); tried to persuade Scamp to swim in it – in spite of supposed spaniel ancestry on his father's side, he hated water; watched in fascination firemen trying to free a boy who'd got his leg stuck in a grating where the pond overflow went into a culvert under the road. Mother and I spent many long summer afternoons by the Little Dirty Pond, before walking home across the Common and past the war memorial for tea.

*

Now aged seven, fairly soon after we moved permanently back to Roehampton, I began taking myself to the Common to play, a much-valued freedom not known before. It had its downsides – vulnerability.

"Have you found a nest?" A strange man, youngish, appeared at the only entrance to the impenetrable hideaway I'd just discovered in some bushes on the Common.

"Is it a good one?" he smiled with apparent enthusiasm before I'd had time to answer. He seemed so keen, so sure I'd found a nest. I hadn't, wasn't sure what to say.

He came right in, sitting down on the earthy bank next to me. Voices came faintly through the thick bushes surrounding us, an elderly couple walking by. He seemed suddenly tense, said we must be very quiet, not make a

Dark Cupboards, Dusty Skeletons

sound. I didn't see why. They moved on. I don't remember how he moved from one stage to the next. I remember him holding me closely on his lap kissing my mouth, which I didn't like – in spite of dreaming myself to sleep every night by wrapping my own arms round my body, imagining the cuddles I'd missed since going to boarding school.
I can't remember now how he went about partly undressing himself and me. I remember standing in front of where he sat; him explaining carefully he wanted to touch my tummy with part of himself, that this would make me wet, it would be all right because he would wipe my tummy with his handkerchief. I liked this even less, really didn't want him to; shook my head, drew back.
"No," I said in a small voice, "No, I don't want you to."
Eventually he masturbated in front of me while I stood staring at this part of the adult male body never before seen.
Then he insisted on leaving separately. He would go first; I must wait there a few minutes. He disappeared. I waited, hoping he'd really gone, then squeezed out through the small spiky entrance. There was no sign of him.
I ran straight home, said nothing to Mother. This wasn't unusual. Children talked to one another, everyone knew what went on. No one told their parents brought up as we were not to mention private parts or strong feelings. Which ironically led to a situation where it was parents who remained innocent and ignorant.
One wet afternoon at Andrew's house we played hide-and-seek indoors. It was Andrew's sister Susan's and my turn to hide. We hid under a bed squashed up against the wall together, not immediately obvious to someone taking a casual glance underneath. Andrew, after searching vaguely, gave up and wandered off. We sat in semi-darkness and waited. I began to tell her about my peculiar encounter. Interest aroused she asked questions, the game forgotten. Finally, when all details had been elicited, she said,
"Perhaps he was a doctor who wanted to see if you were all right."
This solution had also occurred to me: after all doctors did undress people, touch them, examine parts normally clothed. And Susan, older than me, went to St Paul's Girls' School.
Our upbringings taught us that grown ups were always right. Wherever they did must have a good reason. Their authority must be respected. It was just children who were naughty, bad. Good, obedient, children did as they were told. Every God-fearing parent tried to instill obedience into their child.

A Precarious 'Normality': Roehampton 1

"Where were you?" asked Andrew crossly. "I looked under that bed!"
From the Robilliard's I heard that some of the boys playing on the Common had met strange men who'd sternly ordered them to take their trousers down. In a climate where obedience was often enforced by corporal punishment they knew better than to argue with such an authority figure as a tall strong man towering over them.
My experience was unpleasant but a one-off thing in which violence didn't feature. Perhaps I was lucky in that voices close by alarmed the abuser. What he did was *against* the law but the incident less damaging than corporal punishment at Miss Gisborne's school which – although frightening, painful, secretive, humiliating, often unpredictable, leading to guilt and self-hate – was, nevertheless, completely *within* the law.

*

In my search for family I still had my inner world but outwardly pets replaced my doll family. Whenever I asked for a pet Mother would say: "I'll ask Auntie Gladys".
It was, after all, her house. But she always agreed (apart from mice).
Mother took me to a pet shop in Putney to buy goldfish, first an ordinary gold-coloured fish I named "Sixpence", then a more original choice, a grey fantail, "Flicker". They lived in an aquarium on top of the chest of drawers in my room. I'm afraid to say Mother ended up managing much of their feeding and cleaning. She tended to foster my interests, then looked after pets when I tired of them.
The large department store, Bentalls in Kingston, had a small pet department including a large wooden tray with sides low enough for small children to look over, in which a variety of tortoises of different sizes and shell markings crawled around on a thin layer of straw.
Auntie Gladys was initially enthusiastic:
"They'll eat garden pests."
I had to explain they were vegetarian.
Mother and I made more than one trip to Bentalls for a tortoise, once with Andrew and his younger brother, Nigel. We'd heard male tortoises had slight dents in the under part of their shells.
"I want one with a dent in its tummy," announced Nigel.
I managed to get two – a largish, light brown male and small female with darker, more pronounced markings. Olive and Oliver roamed Auntie Gladys's garden, munching happily throughout the summer. We knew they

Dark Cupboards, Dusty Skeletons

hibernated in winter so settled them in a cardboard box in the greenhouse. Unheated, the temperature must have dropped below zero, as they didn't survive.
My first budgerigar chosen from a pet shop aviary was bright green. I called him Dandy (after the children's comic). The second we bought from a breeder on the Dover House estate. She was blue. Beautiful birds, they later both won certificates when exhibited at a school summer fete. Dinky and Dandy would be let out to fly around my room where they'd choose to settle on the curtain rail above the window. Mother, with great sensitivity, discovered a way of getting them back into their cage by holding the tip of a tennis racquet next to the curtain rail for them to perch on, pushing their tummies very gently to get them to step on. Then one at a time they allowed themselves to be carried slowly and carefully to the open door of their cage where they would obligingly hop back inside.
I cut a hole with my fretsaw in a wooden side of their cage and attached a nesting box, hoping for eggs, but none materialised. Perhaps Dinky was too old. When alarmed Dandy would give her a difficult time, taking it out on her with a few angry pecks. Like with some married couples, she never retaliated. Women's rights hadn't reached the avian world.

*

Although in many ways I was still very dependent emotionally on my imaginary world and Mother needed to rest a lot, we did all sorts of things together during my four years of junior school and, thanks to Auntie Gladys's generosity, there was the stability of staying put.
Everything shut on Sundays; we never shopped. There was also an early closing day once a week when all shops shut at lunchtime for the afternoon, usually on Wednesdays or Thursdays, varying between different districts. I didn't know what a supermarket was. W. H. Smith in Putney had a system whereby one chose a book looking along shelves then took it to a cash desk. Mostly though, you had to wait for an assistant to serve you, take out goods asked for and lay them on the counter for inspection. If you didn't like it you had to ask for something else to be taken out; clothes came from glass cases behind the counter inaccessible to the customer.
We never had meals out, even fish 'n chips, rarely went to a café and then only for a cup of tea. The Joe Lyons chain provided cheap cups of tea. There were no Indian or Chinese restaurants, immigration of ethnic minority groups only just beginning in the 'fifties.

A Precarious 'Normality': Roehampton 1

At Hindhead Grannie very occasionally paid for a meal at The Huts Hotel. Mother took me to church fetes and garden parties in the Vicarage garden; religious festivals at the Church such as the autumn harvest festival. Occasionally we took the train to Worthing to visit "The Aunts" in Douglas Close. Auntie Janey and Auntie Bella were Mother's father's sisters, my great aunts. When older I took myself off to beach while mother chatted. We had an outing on a Greenline bus to Epping Forest and occasional day trips to the south coast.

*

I remember the 1952 "pea-souper". Shopping one afternoon in Putney the fog hadn't seemed too dense. Perhaps it thickened unexpectedly rapidly, as the red double-decker number 30 bus crawled, tortoise-fashion, along the Upper Richmond Road, the driver's lights hardly penetrating a few inches in front of the tires. The conductor got off; we were alone in an empty bus, yellow-grey fog closing us in.
"Where's he gone?" I asked.
"I think he's helping the driver."
I dosed on the seat as we inched forward.
Dusk was falling as Mother and I got off at Crestway, near the top of the hill, and began the short walk up towards Highdown Road.
Walking close together, hugging the low hedges and fences of front gardens, we could just see each other, dim grey ghosts drawn closer by the enveloping grey mass. This was fun: we knew the way like the backs of our hands so there was no fear of getting lost. We chatted and laughed, guessing how far we'd come. I experimented with holding a hand in front of my face. Six inches away I could see it; at arm's length it disappeared.
Then, quite suddenly, halfway up, our heads emerged from the soup layer. We stopped and looked at each other, feet still invisible below. I plunged my hand down, watched it vanish and reappear. Ahead a normal if murky world existed. Behind a flat yellow-grey sea, hiding who knew what.
In December 1952 most households still depended on coal and coke for heating, why this pea-souper occurred. Before, during wartime fuel shortages and rationing, the air had been cleaner. Later, after the Clean Air Acts, pea-soupers became a thing of the past. Many died from breathing difficulties and bronchial diseases, legacies of this fog. At the top of the hill in Auntie Gladys's house where the air was clearer, the sooty smog didn't

Dark Cupboards, Dusty Skeletons

bring a recurrence of Mother's chest problems. Which was fortunate for both of us.

Brand new, sky blue.
First bicycle, probably paid for by Grannie,
in Auntie Gladys's front garden with birdbath behind.
Summer 1952.

Almost immediately a puncture developed; I could only gaze longingly at it until Bill Chaloner had time to come round and patch the inner tube. He brought a bucket of water to submerge the tube and spot the telltale air bubbles showing where the patch was needed. I learnt about one-way valves and how to use the bicycle pump.

A Precarious 'Normality': Roehampton 1

On one of my first expeditions to the Village I decided, riskily, to try freewheeling all the way down Medfield Street without using the brakes. With the air rushing past my face I resisted the urge to pull up the levers. Gaining speed the bicycle flew faster and faster as I gripped the handlebars keeping it steady. On a shallow dip where a driveway crossed the pavement the front wheel bounced sideways and I came off. Picking myself up, shaken, I covered my face with my knitted gloves. An expensive black car pulled up; two well-dressed ladies put me inside, asked where I lived and drove me home. Mother took me to the doctor round the corner near Crestway. The nearest hospital was in Putney, a bus ride away; I'm not sure there were any casualty departments then; you only went to hospital if sent by a doctor. I was uninjured apart from grazes all over my face, on both cheeks, forehead, chin and nose, with the deepest cut, surprisingly, on the upper lip just under my nose.
Mother walked up to the Village later and collected the bicycle still in the driveway propped against a fence where it had been left by one of the ladies. Although people had fewer possessions then, there was less theft.
I was kept off school until the grazes had all healed – at least a fortnight. As soon as I felt better, before going back to school, I was allowed out again riding my bike up and down the Cuckoo Lane.

*

As Mother had approached Canon Campling to get me into Roehampton Church School I suppose she felt we ought to show an interest in church attendance. So each Sunday afternoon I was sent off to Sunday School at Holy Trinity Church to sit in a pew and listen to Canon Campling tell bible stories. It was from him I learned the parables and miracles: the *Prodigal Son, the Good Samaritan, Feeding the Five Thousand, Walking on Water, Healing the Sick,* Nativity stories, the Resurrection. I think we just sat on the hard wooden pews; don't remember having to kneel on hassocks for prayers. Once, to my delight, he took us up to the normally forbidden area behind the golden alter rail, to tell us about the white candles in gold candlesticks, exquisitely embroidered alter cloths, the model of the crucifixion (I've never understood why this is inspirational, reminding me only of man's inhumanity to man).
Oddly enough, although a church school, I don't remember the school ever taking us into the church. We did have hymn practice in the school hall each week with Mr Frazer. The boys called it "the torture chamber". I don't think

Dark Cupboards, Dusty Skeletons

we ever said prayers – Our Father's, Hail Mary's and rosaries becoming a thing of the past – but I enjoyed singing hymns, especially rousing ones like:

"Onward Christian soldiers, marching as to war,
With the cross of Jesus, going on before . . . "

Inevitably, playing with Ann Robilliard one Sunday who didn't have to go to Sunday School, I resisted. Mother seemed quite upset. So she took me more often to the Sunday morning service instead.
 Holy Trinity was a large church always fairly full. I remember sitting alone in a pew stretching my neck to watch as she went up to the alter and knelt down to receive Holy Communion, Canon Campling moving slowly along the row of his kneeling parishioners. First he offered each the silver chalice with the wine, the blood of Christ, holding it to their lips.
"Is it clean," I asked later, "everyone drinking from the same cup?"
"He turns it as he moves along," she said.
Then, slowly, raising a hand to bless each of the kneeling figures, he'd move back along the row with the small white discs representing the body of Christ, placing one between the lips of each.
When older I learnt which parts of the service to kneel for on the padded hassocks, when to stand for hymns constantly getting up and down; to find the right place in the hymn book from the number given on the board in front; when to sit on the hard wooden pew for the sermon. Religious worship wasn't meant to be comfortable.
Canon Campling's sermons from the pulpit weren't very comprehensible. To relieve the tedium Andrew's elder sister, Susan, suggested the game of listening for words beginning with each letter of the alphabet in turn, starting with "A" seeing if one could get through to "Z" before he finished.
I studied the choir boys (the choir took *only* boys) pink faces above white ruffs and black cassocks, mouths open wide singing lustily, picking out boys I knew at school.
The roof of Holy Trinity Church vaulted above us as I stood, aged eight, in a wooden pew with my mother at the Sunday morning service. We raised our voices to its heights, standing for the hymns, kneeling for prayers. A young West Indian man slipped quietly in further along the pew, immaculate in well-cut pale grey suit and dark tie, hands and face contrasting strongly with spotless white shirt. All God's children.

A Precarious 'Normality': Roehampton 1

The scent of flowers and incense wafted; softened wax rolled down flickering white candles; Canon Campling's deep voice intoned prayer. Grey haired and saintly in gently swaying white robes and black cassock, a hush fell while he climbed the pulpit steps to deliver his sermon. Mother and I, the West Indian and the rest of the congregation sat down expectantly.
Into this intense silence, burning with curiosity, I asked in a loud whisper, "Is he black all over?"
Mother's lack of response indicated this was not an appropriate moment.
When we were safely home I brought the matter up again, but she still hesitated giving only a lukewarm, unsatisfactory, answer:
"Well ... er ... yes ... ".
Perhaps it was rude to talk about what he was like under his clothes. I never mentioned it again.
Completely ignorant of racial prejudice, with no T.V. to broaden my outlook, no Geography lessons in a school geared only to English and Arithmetic for the eleven-plus exam, and until recently in an isolated boarding school in rural Berkshire, I'd only come across Little Black Sambo stories, my cuddly black golliwog and the fun-to-collect paper golliwogs hidden under Robertson's marmalade jars' labels. These images of black people were about as real as elves, fairies and Father Christmas. With no intention of rudeness or racism I was, quite simply, amazed and curious.

*

As with most children I had to get along with Mother's friends' children. Sheila was a friend of Mother's from their undergraduate days in Oxford. Another single mother whose marriage had also broken up, she had two children, Sarah, slightly younger than me, and Jonathon, older. She occasionally drove over from Wimbledon to take us out in her little black car. This had two seats in front for the grown ups and a boot that opened to the sky to reveal a 'dicky' with an upholstered leather seat where her children and I were sat. With no safety straps – cars never had them then – this sounds hair-raising but with so little traffic actually quite safe. The little hump-backed car would chug serenely along with Sarah and I chatting and giggling in the open dicky. We got on well, despite seeing each other only infrequently. Sheila usually took us for a walk or picnic in some beauty spot Mother and I couldn't get to.
There were no parking restrictions, yellow lines and parking meters hadn't been invented. Traffic lights, few and far between, were designed to change

Dark Cupboards, Dusty Skeletons

when a car crossed a rubbery strip on the road. Boys enjoyed jumping on these to make them change.
The mums sat inside the car and talked about things they didn't want us to know, plenty of taboo topics in in those gossipy days. Sheila worked as a hospital almoner, had her own house in Wimbledon and her husband, Basil, a doctor, had gone to America. Outings by car were a rare experience for me, as for most children.
We first met Mother's friend Daphne and her small daughter Ann in one of the small shops in the Village when I was very young, and stopped to chat. Ann, a year older, was then "Wendy", her father, Ivan. Their tall narrow terraced house in Roehampton on many floors (perhaps only three but seemed more when I was smaller!) had a basement with kitchen at the back opening onto a tiny back garden. I think the living room was on the first floor at the front where Ann's birthday party was held. Aged seven this was probably the first I'd been to; there weren't many parties in those post-war years. We all sat on a circle of chairs playing party games such as pass-the-parcel and musical chairs.
Halfway up the hill from the Village their house overlooked an open grassy part of The Common with the war memorial to the left and Roehampton Church School opposite to the right. Ivan's motorbike would often be parked outside with sidecar for Daphne and Ann. This looked exciting; I envied Ann the sidecar. Most families had no motorised transport, just rather basic black pushbikes. Soon after I started at the Church School Daphne, Ivan and Ann moved to Sanderstead in Surrey. Mother had really taken to Daphne saying she was such a nice person. So we visited occasionally, travelling by train. Expected to play happily with Mother's friends' children, although tagging along well with Ann I never really took to her.

*

My first proper beach holiday was somewhere on the south coast, I think Bexhill, probably '52 aged seven. Mother read the *Church Times* newspaper advertising Pathfinder Holidays where, she thought, one would meet "nice people". Later holidays at Shanklin on the Isle of Wight were definitely Pathfinder so Bexhill may have been as well.
We stayed in a holiday camp block only a few yards from a sandy beach with set meals provided in a separate dining room where we were allocated a table to ourselves. I remember the weather being sunny and spending a lot of

A Precarious 'Normality': Roehampton 1

time on the beach in my beloved grey shorts and T-shirt, or new, blue, stretchy, grow-with-the-child swimming costume.

I was bought my first kite, a small square light-weight wood frame covered in tissue paper, and learned how to fly it; built moated sandcastles with bucket and spade, watched the tide come in and fill the moat, paddled in rock pools. The camp organised a children's theatre trip by coach. I remember nothing of the performance, only that at the end children were invited onto the stage, wanting to go but when there not able to follow the movements in time with the others, which must have been a painful experience for Mother in the audience. A holiday friend, an older boy Terry, on the beach with his mother, whom I really took to, helped me fish in rock pools. Great fun. On this holiday for the first time I was given not only a bucket and spade but also a larger fishing net with longer wood handle than ever before, to happily spend afternoons dipping in the salt water rock pools, swishing around, peering in to see what I'd caught hidden amongst the inevitable scoop of seaweed. Mostly tiny crabs and shrimps and, most curious, a pipe fish (its name learned later from a picture) which disappointingly didn't look like a fish. The biggest thrill of all was clearly recognizable as a fish with fins and gills, about four inches long. I had caught a *real* fish! No one talked conservation in those days. My bucket got very full, its occupants very crowded. Even at age seven I could appreciate they might feel stifled. I carried the bucket with its precious cargo back to our small, twin-bedded room in the holiday camp block just beyond the beach. In the ensuite bathroom I ran a bath of cool fresh water and tipped in the occupants of my bucket, anticipating the lovely freedom they would have swimming around. To my surprise they all rapidly expired.

Mother, sometime later unbeknown to me, quietly emptied the bath of its corpses. Apparently, after I was in bed and asleep she ran a warm bath for herself, telling me next morning that the bath had felt "very fishy"!

Dark Cupboards, Dusty Skeletons

Above: building sandcastles in warm sunshine.

Below: fishing in a rock pool, left behind by the tide.

Summer holiday, Bexhill 1952 ? Mother never dated photos or added place names.

A Precarious 'Normality': Roehampton 1

Kite flying at a holiday camp, Bexhill 1952.

Mother eventually came up with an ingenious compromise to her unhappiness with my beloved grey shorts she felt to be so unladylike. (In the ethos of the time, they were!) One day she produced what looked like a short, navy blue skirt; not something I was keen to wear. But on further examination the 'skirt' turned out to be divided in the centre like shorts, having a separate space for each leg. I happily took to wearing this substitute all the time out of school, including when roller-skating with Andrew up and down Highdown Road. Worried they might be too short at the back to hide

Dark Cupboards, Dusty Skeletons

knicker-legs Andrew helpfully offered to skate behind, reassuring that nothing showed which shouldn't.

"Lamby" as King of the Castle,

Holiday camp buildings behind.

Bexhill, 1952.

It's not easy in retrospect to pin down precise dates of summer holidays but as I remember being eight when learning to swim, 1953 was probably the year we had a Church of England Pathfinder holiday on the Isle of Wight. Independent girls' boarding, Upper Chine School Shanklin, enjoyed beautiful buildings in extensive grounds, neatly cut sweeping lawns, well-stocked flowerbeds, leafy mature trees. The deep gorge of The Chine ran through the grounds down to the sea, crossed by a bridge from the main school building. The Pathfinder holiday organisation hired most of the school and grounds.

We shared a room for two in a pleasant cottagey house, perhaps a school boarding house in term time. A communal dining room in the main building offered three meals a day with families at separate tables. We were allocated

A Precarious 'Normality': Roehampton 1

a table for two conspicuously in the centre of the room, once again a noticeably fatherless situation.

One of my chief memories is of learning to swim in the school's open-air swimming pool. Mother had helped me practice breaststroke lying on my tummy on the stool in Auntie Gladys's bathroom. On holiday I went in the pool on my own while she rested, plenty of other adult holiday makers also being in the water. A kind lady, seeing me trying to swim, helpfully put a hand under my chin to keep it above water. Suddenly it happened – there I was moving arms and legs and staying afloat without support – once learned never forgotten as with riding a bicycle.

Singing with other children in groups round an upright piano I learnt popular modern gospel songs, such as:

> "Wide, wide as the ocean,
> High as the heavens above,
> Deep, deep as the deepest sea,
> Is my Saviour's love.
> I though so unworthy,
> Still am a child of his care,
> For his word teaches me,
> That his love reaches me,
> Everywhere".

The large school hall with stage was the venue for entertainment put together by holiday guests, mainly adult, watched by everyone.

I made friends with a little girl, Deborah, younger than me, daughter of a clergyman who wore a white dog collar, holidaying with his family.

The school was within walking distance of a sandy beach down a steep cliff path beside The Chine, where I fished and swam while Mother basked in the sun. We returned for a second holiday at Upper Chine School the following year, carrying small suitcases, crossing the Solent on the ferry.

*

Dark Cupboards, Dusty Skeletons

Second Pathfinder holiday at Upper Chine School, Shanklin, Isle of Wight, wearing grow-with-the-child blue, stretchy, costume.

*

At school I spent two years with blustery Mr Frazer. He took the first-year juniors, the seven to eight-year-olds, then moved with the class to take the second-year juniors.
"How unfortunate!" observed Mother – having to spend two years with him. But I have some positive memories; don't look back on this as so disastrous. Mr Frazer sat at his desk in front of the class with Angela Brown beside him, looking at the nib of her pen. She was something of a favourite. He would sometimes examine our pen nibs if he thought we might be dipping them too far into inkwells, likely to create blots. Had she dipped hers too deep?

A Precarious 'Normality': Roehampton 1

Smiling, joking, he pretended he was going to smack her hand. She stood next to him giggling. Then, having made his point about the nib, he smiled, "Oh no! It would be wrong to hit a girl!"
Wrong for a man to hit a girl? This was new to me.
Mr Frazer, short, stout and crusty-tempered, was in no way the epitomy of the gallant male, but it was from him (ignorant of men as I was) that I first became aware of the chivalrous attitudes and good manners towards women that British middle-class men regarded as decent.
It was usually the slower boys who got into trouble. If you were a girl and you were bright, as I was, there was never much trouble. I never had problems; was in any case already very frightened of adult authority, shy and unsettled to start with.
He told us that when he'd first started teaching boys came to school barefoot unable to afford shoes. He used to take them round after school knocking on doors asking if anyone had a pair of old shoes they could give a boy.
Barry in dark green corduroy suit with short trousers, stood beside Mr. Frazer at his desk at the front of the class. Barry was from the children's home at the top of Medfield Street. "Sir" was very serious, talking quietly. I listened. It was about stealing classroom supplies – paper, blotting paper, other stuff.
"Do you want me to tell Uncle Bill, ask him how much more stuff you've got there?"
Mr. Frazer wasn't shouting now, he was gentle, very grave. He told Barry,
"That's a nice suit you've got on," trying to raise the self-esteem of this orphaned boy from the children's home. Nice clothes weren't so easily come by in those post-war years. Barry didn't get "The Slap".
In those days Great Britain was still a colonial power and London had not yet been overtaken by Tokyo as the largest city. Our infant attitudes were shaped by this – attitudes to ourselves and the world.
"Which is the biggest city in the world?" Mr Frazer asked the class.
"London?" someone ventured tentatively.
"London," he repeated, looking pleased.
I had a sudden feeling of 'rightness'; somehow I'd known all along. Of course Great Britain – our country – would be the best and most powerful with the biggest city in the world.
Mr Frazer was teaching us to read double figure numbers. I think virtually everyone had got them, except Michael Beasley. He was called out to stand

Dark Cupboards, Dusty Skeletons

in front of the class by the blackboard on its easel. Mr. Frazer wrote "64" on the board in white chalk.

"What's that?" he asked.

Michael, clearly terrified, blurted out the first number that came into his head: "Twenty-nine."

"NO!" roared Sir, turning red. He tried another number – with the same result.

Sir covered his face with his hands. He staggered across the classroom to the mantlepiece, rested his arms along the top, laid his head in his arms. Michael Beasley stood paralyzed; the class watched nervously in total silence anticipating the biggest explosion yet. After an eternity Mr Frazer straightened, staggered back to his desk, told Michael to sit down. I never knew him give any boy "The Slap" for not understanding, although Michael probably thought he might.

Another time as some boys were organising the mid-morning milk that arrived each morning in a metal crate full of small third-pint glass bottles, some got spilt. He lost patience and bent four boys over a front row desk under the horrified gaze of our student teacher from the local Froebal College. Definitely not how she was being trained to manage a class of young children.

An important part of our position in the world and British society involved learning good B.B.C. English, the "Queen's English". I had always heard this at home and I don't suppose Mother would have contemplated a school where it wasn't spoken. All the teachers spoke well – the children adopted the same accent. Now, regional accent is regarded as a sign of identity and individuality; then it was a sign of that endlessly thorny question – which class you belonged to.

Four-letter words were not known or not repeated. I learnt them in secondary school. The word "blimey" became commonplace until Mr Whitaker told us in morning assembly it meant:

"God make me blind".

We gasped in horror at what we'd all been unwittingly saying.

Mr Frazer's second-year junior class was to have had a school outing to see the Queen as she toured the streets of London after the coronation. With only a few families having black and white television the only sight of the Queen we might otherwise have had was a newspaper picture. At the last moment we were told the trip was cancelled but if any parent wished to take their

A Precarious 'Normality': Roehampton 1

child out of school for the day to see the Queen that would be permitted. This was a verbal message transmitted by ourselves. I don't think the school had a duplicator. We were never given notes to take home. Surprisingly, Mother took to the idea with enthusiasm:
"Oh yes, we'll go, shall we! That would be rather nice, wouldn't it, to see the Queen!"
She wrote the obligatory absence note to take into school. Normally frugal, especially where knick-knacks were concerned, she bought me a souvenir blower for the occasion. Cone-shaped with spiraling red white and blue stripes, a tassel of white paper strips, the small end had a blower which made a noise like a particularly inconsiderate car horn and an angry elephant all rolled into one. She equipped herself with her old Box Brownie camera.

We took two red London double decker buses to Wandsworth, positioned ourselves on the edge of the pavement for a good view, and stood there waiting.

As the cavalcade came past I blew as loudly as I could. The Queen looked in our direction, frowning slightly, perhaps wondering where the charging elephants were coming from. Mother, gazing besottedly, without taking her eyes from this once-in-a-lifetime vision, pressed the tiny lever on the side of the Box Brownie. The shutter clicked mockingly. Everything was over in a fraction of a second: the black limousine moving past crowds further along, its royal rear bumper vanishing. We'd had our allotted glimpse.

Together we studied our own personal black and white photo of the Queen. "There. You can see her eyes!" said Mother, pleased with her achievement. I peered at the two grey smudges in the picture indicating a moving subject. Certainly there were two blurred dashes where eyes should be. As a record of our demonstration of loyalty, the main subject looked uninspiring. The surrounding crowds, stationary, were clear enough, total strangers sharing the experience.

I was the only child in my class taken to see the Queen that day. A unique occasion. Never another where parents were told they could take their children out of school. For any event.

*

Mr Frazer was keen we should do art and handicrafts. I was good at these. Teaching focused very much on the three R's for the eleven-plus exam so there wasn't much time for anything else. He told us all to make something at home to bring into school. I made a paper-maché cup and saucer moulded

Dark Cupboards, Dusty Skeletons

round those we used at home, painted pink with green spots, then finished with clear varnish to harden the surface.
"Can we have them back, Sir?" someone asked.
When I asked for mine he said,
"Oh no, I must have something to show the inspector if he comes round."
I didn't really mind. Was actually quite pleased.
Then on prize day I was awarded a magnificent paintbox – two rows of little jars of poster paints unlike any I'd seen before – for "Art and Handicraft". The only prize which wasn't a book. A special prize just for me.
The class play didn't go so well. Being so shy, I was given a small walk-on part, one of three fairies. The rehearsals went well and I was looking forward to the performance without much in the way of nerves.
Then the evening before, at home with Mother, I cleared my throat slightly. Almost on cue, as though she'd been waiting for this, she said,
"You've got a cold. You'll have to stay at home tomorrow."
"But what about the play?"
She didn't answer.
I felt I was letting them down, but supposed it wouldn't matter too much; there would still be two fairies. I spent a dull day at home, slightly disappointed. Did she feel humiliated by the small part? Did she think I was too nervous? Shy herself, as she always said, did she feel I was getting an opportunity she never had to develop confidence? Was it a protest at time being taken from academic pursuits? I'll never know.
The day after the play I asked for an absence note. She said I didn't need one. This was exceptional; I always took a letter when away from school. In class, as I stood next to his desk, Mr Frazer asked quietly,
"Why were you away yesterday?"
"I had a cold, Sir."
"Where's your note?"
"Please Sir, I haven't got one."
He looked thoughtful, grunted, said no more.
This was the only school play during four years of junior school, and as things fell out, the only play I had the opportunity to participate in throughout schooldays.
However the top quarter of each class usually won end-of-year prizes, with hindsight an iniquitous system immensely discouraging for those who didn't. I received prizes in both years in Mr Frazer's classes, the first just "For

A Precarious 'Normality': Roehampton 1

Progress", an Enid Blyton book *The Buttercup Farm Family;* the second year the lovely box of poster paints. I rather came to take an end-of-year prize for granted, that I'd be one of those whose name would be called on prize day to stand up and walk out to collect one.

*

An older girl, Margaret Lambert, stood near me in the playground announcing loudly to other girls that she knew something about my father, "But . . . Oh! . . . We mustn't tell her. It would break her heart if she knew."
I did tell Mother about this, asked what it was I didn't know. She didn't reply but was probably more upset by this bit of Village gossip than I was. Perhaps something to do with my supposed illegitimacy?

*

My best friend Andrew, eighteen months younger than me, had been accelerated a year. When I first knew him he was six, I was seven. In the second year juniors Mr Frazer sat us separately, although I was still next to a boy, Adrian Titcombe.

Andrew was supposed to play with the older boys in the upper playground but stayed with me in the lower playground with the girls and younger boys. At one time he was told he must go to the boys' playground. He did – for a few days – then nipped down the hill again and played with me. Sharp teachers' eyes always noticed everything but, understandingly, nothing was said. As the younger boys were with the girls at playtime it was less obvious for him to be with me. If I'd gone up to the boys' playground I'd have stuck out like a sore thumb, my navy pleated tunic amongst all those grey shorts and pullovers.

*

His surname was Horsey. In class Mr Frazer, short, stout and old-fashioned, came out with the obvious joke,
"Have you finished yet, Donkey?"
"Yes Sir."
Grin: "Oh, you know your name then!"
Small polite smile.

*

"Do you like your own face?" Andrew asked one day out of the blue.
"No!"
Quite a few children of my generation didn't like their own faces, why he'd asked. He never revealed how he felt about his own.

Dark Cupboards, Dusty Skeletons

Andrew, aged six, in Auntie Gladys's back garden, summer 1953.

We spent a lot of time playing together out of school, sometimes at my house, sometimes his. We played in the sandpit next to their chicken run with his elder sister, Susan, and younger brother, Nigel; we played hide-and-seek in his house, made endless white paper darts which, thrown out of an upstairs window for extra height, travelled further covering their lawn. We painted sitting round Auntie Gladys's kitchen table, roller-skated on paving stones for hours in Highdown Road (quieter than Dover House Road), listened spellbound to Auntie Janet's rendering of Greek myths when she visited, sat around on winter days chatting in front of our coal fire, sat in a circle on cushions on the floor in their lounge playing a card game "Cheating", where the object was to get rid of all your cards by any means

A Precarious 'Normality': Roehampton 1

without being seen – sitting on them was acceptable provided no one saw you do it. We tried to dig up their recently died and buried goldfish but couldn't find it, played cricket on their lawn. Neither household had television.

Mrs Horsey, watching from their kitchen window, called me "Elizabeth the Peacemaker." She said I calmed quarrels between her children, found solutions.

There were more rules in their house: they weren't allowed on the Common on their own or allowed to have fires. Consequently fires developed something of a fascination and they were always being sent to bed for experimenting.

Andrew was a gentler temperament than his younger brother Nigel, who got into fights at school.

"I wouldn't have sent him there if I'd known it was so rough." said their mother. On the other hand I don't think they were too keen on Andrew's best friend being a girl, boys should be boyish.

He loved playing boasting, would say,

"Let's play boasting," which he always won. "I've got . . . a bigger house/ chickens/more pocket money/a sandpit/a nanny . . ." (who fetched him and younger brother Nigel from school each day). The list went on and on. His father being a retired naval officer, the family was wealthier than my single parent situation. I think Mother, overhearing, was more upset by this boasting than I was; she couldn't give me what he had.

*

School summer playtimes were on the expanse of rough grass with a few small hawthorn bushes on Putney Heath behind Holy Trinity Church, sloping gently from the top of the hill down to the lower playground with a steep incline just before the hard asphalt surface. One of the few rules was that we weren't allowed to run down this steep slope and had to use the bare sandy gravel path at the end furthest from the buildings where the gradient was shallower. One side of this patch of Common we weren't allowed to play in had low bushes, a botanical boundary we were strictly forbidden to vanish into; on the other metal railings at the back of the church restricted limits. Mrs Herbert kept a watchful eye open for anyone straying into bushes.

At different times we practiced learning to whistle tunes ever more piercingly or to make owl hoots by blowing through our thumbs into cupped

Dark Cupboards, Dusty Skeletons

hands. This took many trials before the knack would be discovered almost accidentally. The trick was to leave a gap below one's lips so the air circled round and came out. By putting a thick blade of grass between one's thumb joints and blowing hard through the thin gap very satisfying screeches could be made suddenly behind someone. Rather like the reed in a flute I suppose but much less tuneful. As everyone was half expecting it and doing it themselves, nobody jumped. When grass was seeding we had 'battles' throwing 'dart' grass heads which stuck to clothing.

In school we scratched busily away, dip pens with split nibs shoved feverishly into porcelain inkwells as we struggled with compositions or sums, getting steadily covered in ink. Teaching was almost exclusively Arithmetic and English in preparation for the Eleven-Plus exam. We'd never heard of a group project. Nature study, in a form never taught in the classroom, came at playtime on the Common.

We would rush out on sunny summer days to spend hours minutely examining clover patches for the lucky four-leafed ones, some patches getting reputations for being luckier than others. We grovelled in the bare peaty-black earth between the roots of a cluster of small hawthorn trees looking hopefully for squirrels' hordes of acorns, burying our own treasure troves of sandy oval pebbles or scarlet berries and finding each others'. No one worried about getting dirty. The issue of dirty hands never even glimmered in anyone's mind.

Once I spotted a greeny-grey lizard sunning itself stretched along a twig among tiny oval leaves. Desperate to have it as a pet I inched feverishly forward – then grabbed. It was gone in a flash.

We sat in small clusters on the dry grass chatting, sharing jokes and riddles, updating each other on the current rude story going round, usually of a lavatory nature. We experimented with chewing the succulent stems of different grasses and discovered the juiciest stems to chew when pulled out of their grassy sheaths. Again, no one worried about hygiene – the possibility of getting worms never mentioned – I never heard of anyone who did.

In autumn we collected large red-orange leaves burnished by the sun and made leaf skeletons by carefully tearing away the fragile papery parts between the wiry veins. Autumn was also the time for conker fights, conkers collected having holes drilled and string tied through them at home, then brought into school in pockets. Winding the string tightly round his fist in

A Precarious 'Normality': Roehampton 1

preparation for the kill the owner would proclaim it a "two-er" or "three-er" depending on the number of past victories. Advice flew round as to whom to pick for an adversary:
"Don't play him, he's got a six-er!"
One stuck to the rules but could increase one's chances by refusing to play a sure winner. The ground became littered with the golden brown fragments of smashed heroes.

Autumn also brought berries. We discussed the horrific deadliness of poisonous deadly nightshade, red, green and purple berries twining secretively up the inside of hawthorn bushes. We gazed in awe at the finality of their potential. You definitely died if you swallowed one of those. This didn't stop me picking them and squashing the pulpy centres between finger and thumb to find the tiny seeds. Any ripe blackberries would be quickly eaten.

I hunted for bendy branches to pick from low hazel bushes and hide safely until after school to take home and make bows and arrows, hazel boughs being said to be more springy.

Andrew and I experimented with patiently rubbing two sticks together to make fire having heard it *could* be done, soon running out of patience, realising this was futile. So we hunted for fragments of broken glass among the tufts of dry grass; bright pin-points of concentrated sunlight flickered on the ground when we picked them up. Sunlight focused on our hands created sudden burning heat, the glass quickly dropped. Maybe we could create fire more easily by propping a broken shard against a pebble, leaving a hot bright spot on a tinder of wisps of dry grass for longer.

Inevitably while we waited, chatting about something else, the bell went. We ran down the hill to line up in the playground. Andrew suddenly remembered the tiny pyre and, daringly defying the summons, ran back up the now deserted Common to dismantle our fire-making construction. The teachers must have seen him but didn't react maybe thinking he'd left something up there, which said a lot for the understanding ethos of the school.

*

One afternoon at Roehampton Mother told me a lady psychologist friend of Mrs Chaloner's would be coming round to talk to us about the boarding school I'd been to. She added quickly, leaning down close:
"Oh, I don't expect you remember it."

Dark Cupboards, Dusty Skeletons

"Oh yes I do," I assured her eagerly.
At last someone wanted to talk about it.
A middle-aged lady knocked on the front door. She wore a dark cloak, beige-checked with matching fringe – slightly eccentric. Otherwise her black, below-the-knee skirt, brown stockings and sensible shoes looked normal.
She marched straight across the hall to me.
"And how old were you when you went to boarding school?" she demanded.
"I was four" I replied, truthfully.
Mother interrupted quickly,
"Oh no you weren't. You were five."
Startled by the suddenness of her attack I mumbled sheepishly,
"Oh, I thought I was four."
The lady seemed taken aback too.
Mother began to talk to her rapidly, the way grown-ups did. They talked for a few minutes, still standing in the hall. Then the lady left.
Later I asked,
"Why did you say I was five? I went to Miss Gisborne's when I was four."
Mother, no longer feeling threatened, was ready to concede.
"Well," she said, " I always thought of you as five."
But I wasn't.

*

I must have been early junior age, perhaps eight or nine, when an unheard of event occurred: for some reason I was left overnight at Grannie's house "Brambletye" with Auntie Janet. Why, I have no idea. Neither Mother nor Grannie were there, just the two of us. I have very few memories of Grannie the rare times we visited when she *was* there, just a vague shape in an armchair in her sitting room or sun lounge, not seeming too pleased to see us. Auntie Gladys is much clearer; I remember things she said, what she did, how she looked. But then I did spend much more time with her.
I called in the night when I woke – too good an opportunity to miss after night isolation at boarding school – and Auntie Janet came and stood by my bed in her ankle length nightie, reassuring, then saying she must get back to sleep, she had to go to the dentist's tomorrow.
Next morning Mother arrived, three of the family, amazingly, briefly together, and being in Grannie's house perhaps gave her some sort of presence. I recall only this one occasion when Auntie Janet was at Hindhead

A Precarious 'Normality': Roehampton 1

with us, although the house had three bedrooms. I loved Auntie Janet being there as well as ourselves. All together.
The morning passed all too soon.
When Auntie Janet began to talk about her taxi the realisation came that this unprecedented family gathering was to be very fleeting – had barely existed. I had to act. Rummaging in the garage I found some pieces of old rope.
The front garden at Brambletye had a high barrage of rhododendrons and azaleas between lawn and pavement. Planted by the grandfather who'd died when I was two months old, they were all in full bloom, an exquisite mass of scented orange, crimson, yellow, snow-white and magenta blossoms. A narrow gap permitted access for a path to the front door, a wider gap the driveway to the garage. Each had gates made of crossed wooden beams rather like five-barred gates.
Mother and Auntie Janet were absorbed chatting in the kitchen. I nipped out and spent some time winding ropes round and round the gates and posts tying plenty of tight knots. I was good at knots. Knots were the sort of thing we played with and practiced in the days before television.
Auntie Janet's taxi duly arrived and was spotted through a gap in the rhododendrons. She tripped quickly down the path in her neat beige suit, shiny leather handbag on one arm, grey hair tightly drawn back into a bun in the nape of her neck, not a hair out of place, running with her characteristic quick, nervous movements down the path.
Arriving at the narrower gate she tried to open it – then fiddled agitatedly with the rope trying to see how it might undo. The taxi sat and waited. I stood watching. Then she moved over to the garage gate and experimented there, peering short sightedly through her glasses, pulling bits of rope this way and that. Even more complicated twists held her in. The taxi still waited. She appealed for help; regrettably this wasn't what I had in mind. Back, to have another go at the smaller gate outside which the taxi hovered with its engine running. A taxi was a great luxury in those post-war years, not to be kept waiting, adding expense. Her gloved fingers began fumbling with the knots. I watched with bated breath, hoping she wouldn't be able to undo them, wouldn't be able to go . . .
It was enormously disappointing when she did eventually manage to dismantle my efforts. The gate opened, she dived into the taxi, the door shut. I stood watching it pull away, a hole opening up inside full of gnawing regret. She'd gone and that was that.

Dark Cupboards, Dusty Skeletons

Well, I had tried to keep the family together.

*

Auntie Janet, visiting Roehampton, sat on a chair in the bay window of the dining room (which had become our sitting room) by the telephone table. I danced up with Andrew in tow.
"Tell us a story," I demanded. "About the ancient Greeks."
I wanted to show her off to Andrew, how marvellous she was at stories. She paused, thinking for only a few seconds, before launching into *Theseus and the Minotaur*. Sitting, hunching forward slightly, in her neat beige suit, grey hair pulled back into a bun fastened with hair pins in the nape of her neck, she spoke slowly, mysteriously, holding us spellbound until the grand finalé with the beast being slaughtered by the young hero.
Afterwards, Andrew said suitably awestruck,
"She looks like a pixie."
This was one of the few times I scored over him. A favourite pastime of his was to initiate boasting sessions which, coming from a wealthier family, he always won hands down. I wasn't much bothered by him winning, Mother was.
"That awful boasting," she would say. But I had an aunt who could tell fascinating stories like he'd never heard before.
Persephone in the Underworld was another story she enchanted me with. I wasn't so sure about the snakes of Medusa's hair, still a phobia since nightmares at boarding school. Icarus's attempts to fly were another one. Interest thus stimulated, I got her to tell me the names of all the Greek gods, their equivalent Roman names and what they represented, all committed to memory.

*

On another visit to Roehampton Auntie Janet got ready to take me out. I put my coat on.
"Where are your gloves?" she demanded.
I didn't have any. She disapproved. An upper class lady *never* went out without gloves. Obviously I wasn't being brought up properly. Auntie Gladys, overhearing, with her unerring sense of humour later rocked with laughter at the idea of tomboy me, happiest in shorts, being expected to wear gloves like a lady.
The idea that little girls should be ladylike was a problem for someone growing up in a family of independent women – brought up to be highly

A Precarious 'Normality': Roehampton 1

independent, perhaps over-independent, from an early age – and who wanted to be a tomboy in shorts. I felt silly in a skirt. It changed my personality. I became demur, unable to be myself, felt closed in, artificial. To get home from school and change into shorts or slacks was a great relief. The first thing I did. Now I could roller skate, climb trees, or just be myself – unfettered by that *thing* flapping round my legs. Briefly physically freed, more confident, able to expand, I could begin to live.

Mother felt one should be intelligent, charming, beautiful, healthy – a healthy mind in a healthy body – otherwise one was NO GOOD. She managed all these except health: an Oxford graduate, dress-conscious, sometimes a little artificial.

"Oh My Dear! How dreadful for you!" she would say with all the right mannerisms, dressed in her slim-fitting, fashionably ladylike clothes.

One had to be all these things in order to be socially acceptable in the circles the Thomson family aspired to after great-grandfather made a fortune as a pawnbroker (out of others' hardships, although he must also have saved many from the dreaded workhouse).

These ideas constrained her; she could become 'heavy', moralising; creativity not considered important: in the sixth form she'd been expected to give up the violin, focus on Oxbridge entrance.

"I want people to remember me as I was," she said in old age, "not as I am now." Assuming others lived by the same rules and taboos, never seeing a person's lifelong essence as defining.

Mother often wasn't there, but when she was, wasn't tired or ill, she created moments to treasure. Trouble was, after being away at boarding school, her not being around, I found it difficult to really trust, feel safe deep down, the possibility ever present she might turn life upside down again.

"Ruth! You must eat your butter ration!" said grandmother. Butter was considered a luxury in post-war years, much nicer, more nutritious than margarine. No one worried about cholesterol in days when every scrap had to be eeked out to get enough calories. Mother had been giving her butter ration to me.

When I was quite small, before going to boarding school, I remember having "hugs" on her lap. Sitting there with her arms round me warm, comfortable, safe. After that she brought me up not to expect demonstrative hugs or kisses, although she once told a story about a little boy who'd got lost. At the police station they'd asked,

Dark Cupboards, Dusty Skeletons

"What does your mother look like?"
He answered,
"She's the most beautiful woman in the world."
Shortly after a tired, downtrodden looking woman rushed in. His mother.
"I always remembered that story," said Mother, "to their children mothers are beautiful."
I wondered – hadn't she known she was the most beautiful person in the world?
At boarding school I was the only one seeing a parent at weekends. Mother resisted pressure from Miss Gisborne not to. The others stayed the whole term; the two-day half term meant playing all day (without much to do) instead of lessons. Parents rarely visited; most I never saw. But Mother visited, chatted to Miss Gisborne; also, once, Auntie Kay, who took me for a walk across the golf course when Mother couldn't make it.
Waiting by the bus stop in Putney, the wind was icy.
"Stand behind me," Mother said, "I'll shelter you." Her thin body didn't give protection but the offer was warming.
When I was at Roehampton with her, if I couldn't sleep, I could go downstairs in the evening, say,
"I can't go to sleep". She would come back upstairs with me – perhaps chat a few minutes, settle me down again – then I would sleep.
She spent some of the little money she had on my interests, hobbies, things to do in the days before television. Coming from a teaching family she was good at providing absorbing, mind-stretching, activities.

*

At the end of term it was announced that three or four of the brightest pupils in Mr Frazer's second year junior class were to skip the third year juniors' and move straight to the top class, the fourth year juniors', where they would spend two years. Mr Whitaker probably had to juggle places. But Mother, having only a couple of years before got me moved down to Mr Frazer's first year junior class, now seemed outraged that those skipping a year didn't include me. Mr Whitaker can't have found her an easy parent. At home she finally announced,
"They'll get stale." (Sour grapes!)
I don't remember having any feelings one way or the other, just the awareness that Mother did. The following year with Mrs Clack, a lovely teacher, would be the best yet; looking back I'm glad I didn't miss out.

A Precarious 'Normality': Roehampton 1

At the end of the second year juniors' Andrew, my best friend, left Roehampton Church School, it still being accepted in the '50s that middle class boys aged seven or eight should be sent away to boarding school. His father had been in the Royal Navy. A couple of years later two preparatory boarding schools would be considered for Prince Charles: Cheam School and St Peter's Seaford. Prince Charles went to Cheam, Andrew to St Peter's. Pleased to be going, (another boasting point) he showed off the pile of new clothes bought, marked with name tapes. He was eight.

"It's much too young to go to boarding school," said Joan Chaloner, the psychologist next door.

"I went when I was four." I piped.

No reply.

When the time came for him to go home on the last afternoon of the summer holidays he wanted me to stand at the corner of Highdown Road, looking up Dover House Road while he walked backwards, very slowly, waving all the way. A long drawn-out goodbye. When he disappeared round the bend I waited awhile to be sure he wouldn't reappear and find me gone, knowing this was helping him cope.

Settled but Only Temporarily: Roehampton 2

Back at Roehampton Church School aged nine in September '54, I was again with Mrs Clack who now took the third-year juniors'. Having been placed in her second-year class when first at the school – before going down to Mr Frazer's class right for my age group – I already knew her. As a career woman Mrs Clack seemed sympathetic to Mother's situation: they were both educated working mothers. Mother and I got on well with her. An extremely dedicated teacher who obviously enjoyed her job her class invariably quiet and orderly, she explained things clearly on the blackboard. Her classroom had modern, light-coloured wood, level-topped, double desks with the ubiquitous white porcelain inkwells. The register was called first thing each morning using christian and surname,
"Elizabeth Wallace?"
"Yes, Mrs Clack." (*Never* just "Miss!")
After Assembly we'd have ten questions of mental arithmetic: random multiplication sums from tables learnt by heart, simple addition and subtraction, imperial (not metric) weights and measures. Then Mrs Clack gave out the answers for us to mark ourselves. She'd ask who'd got 10 right, 9, and so on; trusted to be honest we'd put hands up. Arithmetic on the blackboard followed by sums to work out came before break.
She sat me next to a new girl, Christine, probably Andrew's replacement. We soon became best friends until we left two years later to move on to separate secondary schools. Two bright, responsible girls who worked well together we were also stood next to each other in morning assembly, smiling to each other when our favourite hymn was announced, singing rousingly:
    Onward Christian soldiers,
    Going as to war
at the tops of our voices, or another favourite:

Settled but Only Temporarily: Roehampton 2

Oh hear us when we cry to thee,
For those in peril on the sea.

Always together in the playground, we'd wander round, chatting, playing with other girls, learning to do cartwheels and headstands, giggling explosively about anything and everything – even when harangued by the dinner lady, Mrs Herbert – having lots of fun. Rarely apart we had few quarrels, any occurring rapidly healed by the time-honoured schoolgirl ritual of linking little fingers and shaking gently.
"That's neater," Christine would tell me Mrs Clack had said when she'd taken her work up to be marked. Her middle name was Nita! She came each day on the number 30 bus from Putney as did several other children.
As Mr Frazer played the piano we still had him for recorder practice and singing lessons in the hall, traditional folk songs, the words read from paper booklets handed out. I came to know and enjoy many timeless ditties. We could choose. One song Mr Frazer objected to was *Little Brown Jug*, but he'd give way when passionately begged by several girls:
"Oh, please, *please*, Sir!"
With hindsight, might the little brown jug have been linked to alcohol? If so we were totally innocent. He banged out a variety of traditional folksongs on the upright piano, while we *Polly-Wolly-Doodled* at the tops of our voices.
I struggled to keep up with the recorder (other girls happily moved their fingers quickly and tunefully) and, for a very short time, the violin (too short to be relevant) on a school violin with a long crack down the wooden frame. In break times I taught myself to whistle, pursing my lips to practice until marginally tuneful sounds emerged instead of hissing air.
One enduring and endearing memory of Mr Frazer, short and squat, is of him with head thrown right back, face parallel to ceiling, speaking to tall, thin Cannon Campling who leant down over him. He had to adopt a similar stance struggling to light the hall gas-lamps, trying to get the hook on the end of a long pole to catch a metal loop hanging on a chain from the lamp. When pulled down the lamp lit. With head thrown back to see, Mr Frazer would wave the long pole struggling to get the hook through the loop. To turn the lamp off a similar loop the other side of the lamp needed pulling down.

Dark Cupboards, Dusty Skeletons

The headmaster, Mr Whitaker, would walk down the Common behind the church from his house, linked to the upper school, to his office in the lower school. At playtime Christine would run up to chat with me in tow.
"Hallo Puss!" he'd say.
"Puss" then meant something warm and furry which purred without the connotations it has today. Christine had short dark hair neatly cut, well-brushed, gleaming, a half-fringe and alert warm brown eyes. He'd taken a shine to her; it would usually be just her, with me, who ran up to chat.
Christine lived in an old converted Victorian house near East Putney station, a family of three in a small flat with just one bedroom where she slept with her parents, a tiny kitchen and equally tiny bathroom down curving steps from the living room. Her mother, the family breadwinner, worked in a small office up some narrow stairs near Putney Bridge. Christine once took me there to see her. Her father was very elderly, infirm and housebound; with so many men away in the war perhaps one of those who might not normally have married. He'd given Christine's mother the baby many women, unable to find husbands, longed for. Christine used to jokingly describe, not unkindly, him trying to get his socks on by holding them on the end of his crutch, adding a demonstration of how they'd fall off.
In school one day she said,
"My father's not my real father, he's my stepfather."
"What's your real father like?"
"Oh . . . he's young."
I told another girl Christine was friendly with and had invited to tea, who unfortunately repeated this story. On Open Day in Mrs Clack's classroom Christine's mother suddenly rounded on me.
"I've a bone to pick with you. What do you think you're doing telling people that Christine's father is her stepfather?"
"Christine told me."
"Christine would *never* say anything like that!"
Mother stood by silently, saying nothing.
Once home, away from the confrontation, she became indignant:
"It wasn't very polite of that girl to talk about Christine's father when she'd been invited to tea at their house."
"She really did tell me that."
"I knew it was true because you came straight home and told me."

Settled but Only Temporarily: Roehampton 2

Unusually Mother stood up for me. I hadn't expected to be believed, had so many difficulties putting things across. If the word of an adult conflicted with the word of a child it was usually assumed to be the child who was lying. I didn't quite see how coming home and telling her proved I hadn't made it up but she seemed satisfied it had.

In school a day or two later I tackled Christine.
"You *did* say your father was your stepfather."
She looked drawn, embarrassed.
"Yes . . . well . . . I didn't want her to say anything to you."
I left it at that. She obviously didn't want to talk about it. So Christine had fantasies about her 'real' father. I wasn't the only one to daydream about imaginary relatives although for some inexplicable reason never an imaginary father. Despite this hiccup we remained best friends although neither of our mothers seemed keen on the relationship.

*

In Mrs Clack's class we were all given a hearing test with what was probably 1950s state of the art technology: headphones through which numbers read out became fainter and fainter until one couldn't hear any more. I had to give up writing the numbers down well before the others. Used to doing well in class I felt a bit taken aback, looked round to see others still writing, even guiltily trying the unforgivable cheat of sneaking a peek at what the girl next to me was writing. This didn't work, I couldn't see. Mother had to take me to the clinic in Putney. A lady stood about a yard away and spoke to me – I had no trouble hearing – she dismissed the problem saying I must have had a cold on the day. But I hadn't.

As a young adult I often struggled when others seemed to be hearing. I'd be trying to catch odd words, piece them together to make sense, understand the conversation. Background noise made things worse. Slight deafness due to the side effects of measles perhaps? In the mid-1940s there was no immunisation.

This can't have helped with my trouble with talking although there were other reasons for this: was what I wanted to say 'right'? I felt blocked, anxious, self-conscious, had had little practice at a repressive Catholic boarding school where no one talked much. And Mother was anxious about what I might come out with, especially about the dubious family situation.

Dark Cupboards, Dusty Skeletons

In my teens I overheard another girl, criticised for something just said, reply triumphantly:
"How do I *know* what I'm going to say until I've said it?"
I always turned words over carefully before opening my mouth: would it be ok, could never chatter unselfconsciously as other girls did, tried to give answers that seemed permissible, expected.
But taking turns reading a children's novel aloud in class would be no problem: words in a book must be right. In Mrs Clack's class we read *Twice in a Blue Moon*. Keeping my finger in the page the class was reading so as to be ready if told to read, I'd read on ahead keen to discover what happened. I'm sure the book title is correct but can't now find any reference to it on the web.
I did least well in girls' P.T. (Physical Training), especially at netball the only team game played, probably not being assertive enough or too dreamy to be quick in the uptake. But most girls' PT lessons were more individually organised using balls, beanbags and skipping ropes. Occasionally we'd be put into Tug-of-War teams with a long thick rope. Boys had separate PT lessons. One warm fine day Mrs Clack told us girls to take off outer clothes and go into the upper playground in vests and knickers, probably a modern, liberated, progressive approach to PT. I wasn't keen, but had to. We weren't out very long. A man walked across the Common to lean against the railings, and watch. Years later I heard Putney Heath was notorious for paedophiles; we were soon taken indoors out of sight never again to have the idealised freedom of PT in underwear.
One day an old scholar, slightly older than us, appeared in our classroom on a visit. He wore black monk's robes belted at the waist with a white, tasselled cord, the uniform of Christ's Hospital School. Afterwards Mrs Clack talked to us, saying how marvellous it was that a small school like ours should get boys into such a prestigious school as Christ's Hospital. She was immensely proud.

*

Christine came up to me in the playground one day with Josephine Shead asking if anyone wanted white mice. Hers had multiplied – as mice do! Christine and I both jumped at the chance, I hardly daring to hope they'd actually materialize: some adult would find out and put a stop to it. But only the next day (perhaps worried we'd change our minds) two glass jam jars were surreptitiously produced at morning break covered by metal lids

Settled but Only Temporarily: Roehampton 2

punched with air holes. Inside each jar, tucked up in cotton wool, was an exquisitely captivating albino mouse. Magenta eyes peered back at us, pink whiskered noses woffled with interest, slim paler pink tails wrapped themselves seductively round tufts of cotton wool. Quickly changing hands before anyone saw, the jars were transferred to pockets of navy gabardine raincoats hanging in the cloakroom and left until "home time".

Auntie Gladys, normally the ideal landlady in allowing any pet asked for, had a phobia of mice. So at first, having transferred my charming little woffly-nosed companion to larger accommodation than the jam jar, I hid the cardboard box on the top shelf of the cupboard in my room. One night as I lay in bed in darkness an alarming, noisy scuffling issued forth. Afraid the mouse might be escaping I moved it next day to an old glass aquarium with higher sides.

Christine kept hers secretly on the steps down to their bathroom, difficult to conceal in such a small flat. Her mother eventually discovered it. The mouse had to go. I went with her to the vet where she hoped they might find a home for her pet, but the pleasant young woman at the desk said kindly all they could do was put it down. Did Christine want them to do that? She nodded dumbly. A large tear rolled down her cheek. I had to do something so said I'd look after her mouse and took it home with me.

I first hid the aquarium with both mice in a small cupboard in the garage. Whether the chauffeur, whose employer rented Auntie Gladys's garage for his large expensive black car, discovered them there, I don't know. A friendly middle-aged man in uniform who let me sit in the upmarket, beautifully upholstered car while he hosed it down, if he did find them he never let on to Auntie Gladys. But thinking he might I moved them to the tool shed at the end of the garden underneath a shelf, hiding the aquarium under some old fabric netting used to protect ripening black currants from greedy birds. Some days later, putting food scraps in, I discovered the netting hanging down inside the aquarium. The mice had presumably scrambled up to make their escape. Whether the gardener had discovered them or just moved the netting, I never knew. The mice vanished forever hopefully to live better lives elsewhere.

*

In winter a thin stream trickled down our sloping patch of Common. Mrs Herbert, the dinner lady, grey-haired, well-wrapped in warm hat and scarf, would stand nearby, gloved hand round the metal clanger of her hand bell,

Dark Cupboards, Dusty Skeletons

ready to knock it sharply against the brass dome to deter anyone who seemed likely to run through and get wet feet. Her crossness hid genuine concern:
"You'll be sorry when you're older and get rheumatism."
Some boys once covered an ankle-deep puddle with dead leaves. Thus booby-trapped I ran straight through getting a soaking wet foot, sat with it in Mr Frazer's class, not feeling uncomfortable or complaining to anyone. A wet cold foot was all worth the fun.
We had a great time on the Common in the snow, throwing snowballs, rolling snowmen, woollen knitted gloves already in holes quickly saturated, fingers red and numb. Less commendably we put snow down necks. Having done this to one boy, to my alarm I suddenly noticed Mrs Herbert only a few feet away. The boy complained but she only looked slightly amused telling him not to make a fuss.
Mrs Herbert's sharp eyes nipped most problems in the bud before they began, there was never much trouble. One clang of the hand bell meant, "Stop! Don't do that!"
I don't remember any fear of getting into trouble; did they think I was too shy? A vigorous shake of the bell would signal the end of dinner break, time to run down to the playground and line up in classes. We all knew what the different sounds meant.
In damp soggy winter weather we were less often allowed on the Common having to stay on the relatively dry asphalt playground well-wrapped in belted navy gabardine raincoats, shoelaces trailing from solid brown leather lace-ups, grey knee-length socks slipped in wrinkles round ankles – elastic garters declining to keep them up during active play. Garters were made from a strip of white elastic hand-stitched by mothers into circles, hopefully not too loose, not too tight for the calf they had to fit. Elastic was also used for attaching knitted woollen gloves to the ends of coat sleeves to prevent them getting dropped and lost. The worst was elastic in the legs of thick, navy blue knickers – very uncomfortable on sensitive inside thighs if slightly too tight. I'd be forever pushing knicker legs up and down through the pleats in my school tunic trying to find a less worrying place.
Playground games included a "craze" for 'French' knitting with home-made equipment: an empty wooden cotton reel with four small nails hammered into the top around which to wind scraps of brightly coloured wool forming a long 'tail' through the centre hole – all scrap materials.

Settled but Only Temporarily: Roehampton 2

Another was Cat's Cradle needing only a small piece of string or wool, also scrap, the ends tied together, looped round both hands held sideways palms facing in. Then you bent a longest finger to pick up a loop, continuing picking up loops to form a net: the Cat's Cradle.

Singing games absorbed a lot of break time. In one game two girls stood facing each other holding up arms, hands clasped tightly to each others', singing. Others would run round and round under the 'bridge':

"Oranges and Lemons say the bells of Saint Clemen's
You owe me five farthings say the bells of St Martin's . . ."
ending with:
"Here comes a candle to light you to bed
And here comes a chopper to chop off your head
Chip chop, chip chop, the last man's DEAD ! "

Raised arms would come down capturing someone . . . that person would be "out" . . . the rest played on until no one was left, beheading as capital punishment living on in children's folk rhymes.

And another singing game presumably from Great Britain's maritime past for which actions have slipped from memory:

"The big ship sails on the ally-ally-ooo,
The ally-ally-ooo, the ally-ally-ooo,
The big ship sails on the ally-ally-ooo,
On the last day of September.
The captain says it will never, never dooo,
Never, never dooo, never, never dooo,
The captain says it will never, never dooo,
On the last day of September."

We played hopscotch drawing ten squares on the asphalt playground surface with a piece of chalk if anyone had brought one in, or, if not, with a stone chosen for its graphic qualities from rough ground on the playground's edge. A small flat stone, which wouldn't roll, would be searched for, to throw down into the numbered squares in turn, starting with the first, the nearest, progressing up to ten at the far end. You had to get the stone in the right square: if it went over the edge of the line it was the next person's turn. After their turn you had another throw. If the stone

Dark Cupboards, Dusty Skeletons

went into the square aimed for, one hopped from one foot to two all the way up and back, balancing on one leg to lean down and pick up one's stone on the way back. The winner was the first person to go successfully through all the squares. A game for two or three girls. I don't remember what the boys did, just having a hazy impression of them rushing around in the background somewhere.

*

Mr Whitaker didn't believe in homework. He said if the teaching was done properly it shouldn't be necessary. We never had any. I don't think Mother really agreed but I coped much better with school when it didn't encroach on home. A relatively high percentage passed the eleven-plus exam getting those scarce, much coveted, grammar school places.

He lived on school premises, I think with his wife whom I wouldn't have recognised, and an office in the lower school. He seemed keen for eleven-year-olds to move on to the new comprehensive school in Putney taking all levels of ability; perhaps he'd seen how much disappointment the eleven-plus exam could cause. We saw Mr Whitaker mostly in morning assembly, where he once told us,

"I do care about all of you, even if I sometimes show it in rather odd ways. Don't I Christopher?"

"Yes Sir," muttered Christopher resignedly, a nice boy not usually in trouble. There was much less anxiety about accidents then than now, but Mt Whitaker had a bee in his bonnet about stone throwing. After he'd caned Christopher for this (privately in his office) he explained to us that when a boy himself he'd seen another boy lose an eye through being hit by a stone. I've no memory of accidents at school, apart from minor cuts and bruises, although we had so much freedom at break times.

Mr Whitaker did genuinely seem to like children. Although he occasionally used corporal punishment that was the way things were. He caned only boys and only on the hand without any sex or power motive.

The hall had three high gothic windows with different panes of glass: two reinforced, frosted, gloomy and grimy. One day Mr Whitaker explained to us in assembly that the only one with nice clear glass had been replaced by the local authority, which paid for repairs, and he much preferred it to the others. He then told us that this had been broken by a hapless culprit who'd thrown a ball through it and come to him in fear and trembling. How surprised the boy had been, he told us, to be given a pat on the head, a

Settled but Only Temporarily: Roehampton 2

three-penny bit and an apple. He emphasised which window had the clear pane of glass, how much nicer it looked, pointing out the ones he hoped would soon be replaced with clear glass paid for by the local authority – *after* being broken. He all but invited the naughtier boys to have a go but I don't remember any of them testing his sincerity on this one. Although a humane man, as he occasionally used the cane perhaps they thought it better not to risk it.

The cane was generally considered essential in the interests of that great god of 1950s child-rearing: *"Discipline"*. Many parents might have worried about laxity in boys' behaviour in a school without such disciplinary methods. Having a child that might be thought 'spoilt' or 'out of control' was a parents' nightmare, the worst scenario. Good self-esteem, confidence and the rights of the child were simply not part of the agenda. But nevertheless we had a great deal of freedom.

One of the naughtier boys, Kim, was eggshell bald from ringworm. One day in morning assembly Mr Whitaker sent him down the hill to the lower school with a message for Mrs Hill. In this contrived absence Mr Whitaker talked seriously to the school about Kim's problems. We were told about his illness and that we shouldn't tease him about his lack of hair. A similar situation arose before the fathers' cricket match. We were all told not to ask Duncan why his father wasn't playing. His father had died in the war.

*

Although wary of deadly nightshade I wasn't bothered about toadstools and spent one long exciting autumn dinner break ferreting in damp spots under bushes for the tiny forest which had magically sprung up overnight. Red caps with creamy spongy undersides, curving stems and pointed brown caps with fins underneath – a revelation to discover a dozen different shapes, colours and sizes. I picked them and stashed my finds away carefully under a bush to take home after school, only to find they'd turned into disappointing mushy brown sludge during afternoon lessons.

When spring came again we went up onto the Common to build dens under the hawthorn blossom and experiment with trying to weave mats from blades of grass. I remember Mr Whitaker saying how lucky we were to have the Common. Taken for granted, as children do take their worlds for granted, it didn't mean much until I passed an inner city school with its high brick walls surrounding a bleak monotonous playground and realised what we had.

Dark Cupboards, Dusty Skeletons

School portrait, aged 10,
Mrs Clack's 3rd year junior class,
summer term, 1955.

Break time activities went in fads or crazes. One summer it was handstands and cartwheels. Bare limbs went wheeling gracefully round the playground, red and white check dresses firmly tucked up into knicker-leg elastic, long plaits brushing the smooth grey asphalt or rough yellowing grass as we circled upside down. In the lower playground the outside of the lavatory's' brick wall came in useful for handstands: facing it one threw one's hands down flat continuing the momentum by kicking upwards and balancing upside down, feet against the wall behind. Softer grassy slopes on the Common were better for headstands. Carefully positioning head and hands on the ground in a triangle you could slowly raise your feet and straighten upwards. Thus balanced it was possible to stay upside down for some while until your head hurt or boredom set in. No one worried about glimpses of thick regulation navy blue knickers. The older boys were in a

Settled but Only Temporarily: Roehampton 2

separate playground or on the higher part of the Common, few passers-by went along the road. Thick navy blue knickers were totally, unattractively decent, anyway!

I remember the occasional quarrel when close friends would temporarily fall out but mostly there was little bullying, teasing or unpleasantness perhaps because we had plenty of space and other things to do. I never felt afraid of any child. Some friendly rough and tumble went on with the boys the aim being to get your opponent spread-eagled on his back on the ground, sit astride him and, leaning forward, pin his wrists to the ground. Usually these 'fights' took place on the grass, no one got hurt, it was all perfectly good-natured. Once a boy pulled me over in the playground. Feeling defeated I reached out as he ran off and grabbed an ankle. He came down on the hard asphalt with a terrific smack. Frightened by the impact, I was afraid he'd be angry. But he picked himself up and, subdued but still friendly, said,

"You certainly can hurt me!"

In cold weather the boys' red peaked caps with school badge, a black silhouette of the church spire, must have caused them some anguish. Us girls would run past raising an arm at the last moment to catch the cap under the peak and knock it off backwards. The first thought of the owner was to retrieve his cap, so retribution rarely followed as we'd be well away by the time it was back on his head.

The first priority on getting out of the classroom was often the lavatory. These were outside in both top and bottom playgrounds: smelly, dark, dank, usually with wet seats and no paper. No temptation to linger. In the lower school girls' separate cubicles had more privacy than boys; we passed the entrance to the out-of-sight boys' urinals to get to them. I'm not sure whether we washed our hands afterwards or whether it was ever suggested we should. The basins in the upper playground were, in any case, away from the girls' lavatories inside the main building containing the hall. Perhaps contact with a few germs helped build immunity?

I don't remember any children in the school from ethnic minority groups so racism had not yet become an issue. Surprise would have been felt if it were suggested that rhymes we all knew such as,

> "Eeny meeny miney mo,
> Catch a nigger by his toe,"   might be offensive.

Dark Cupboards, Dusty Skeletons

In Mrs Clack's class Christine and I went one evening a week to the women's teacher training Froebel College down Roehampton Lane, where we linked up with 'our' class student and other students, for sessions of art and craft, nature study, physical games and activities. The College had spacious, well-kept grounds, gym and art facilities. Students tried out teaching skills and techniques on a class-sized group; we benefited from opportunities and equipment the Church School couldn't offer.
*
Tall, saintly, white-haired, and stooping slightly, Canon Campling, passing Christine and myself outside the church in Ponsonby Road, smiled at me rather than her. Taken by surprise I didn't have the good manners to respond before he'd moved on. Mr Whitaker would always say "Hello" to Christine, a favourite of his he'd nicknamed "Puss" which, it needs to be emphasised, didn't have the connotations it does now! But I wasn't used to people prioritising *me*. Mentioning this to Mother she seemed to think I was something of a protégé of Canon Campling's.
Inevitably, one Sunday playing with Ann Robilliard who didn't have to go to Sunday School, I resisted. Mother seemed quite upset. So she took me more often to the Sunday morning service instead, arranging Confirmation classes out of school with a young lady living in one of the newly built blocks of flats. Twelve-year olds, once confirmed, might take Holy Communion. I learned to follow the order of service in my dark-red leather-bound *Book of Common Prayer*. Set responses had to be learned, intoned in the dim church interior:
Priest: "Praise ye the Lord."
Congregation: "The Lord's name be praised."
Also, psalms for that Sunday had to be found and followed. I'd been given a small navy-blue Bible with a few colour illustrations of life in the Holy Land. All rather joyless and soul-destroying. Suffering from severe depression in my early teens I finally abandoned Confirmation classes and the Church of England generally, including bedtime prayers.
*

In Mrs Clack's class I came top in end-of-year tests giving me the chance to have first choice of children's novels chosen as prizes by Mrs Clack and laid out on her desk. I first chose *Jennings At School* by Anthony

Settled but Only Temporarily: Roehampton 2

Buckeridge, but Mrs Clack said she hadn't many boys' books so could I choose another? I picked *White Boots* about ice-skating by Noel Streatfield, awarded for:
"Top of the Class and Art".
On prize-giving day, after the top year had received their prizes, my name was called first for Mrs Clack's class. I stood up from where I sat cross-legged on the floor with my class, and made my way to the table at the front. There is a photo of me, aged ten, receiving my prize for coming top of the class. Mrs Clack is standing on the right, smiling.

Mrs Clack is far right. I've no idea who the lady giving out the prizes could have been. Invited in for the occasion, she wasn't part of the school. Rochampton Church School prize giving, end of summer term 1954.

Dark Cupboards, Dusty Skeletons

LONDON COUNTY COUNCIL
ROEHAMPTON CHURCH SCHOOL

REPORT FOR YEAR ENDING July, 1955

Name: Elizabeth Wallace Number in Class: 42
Class: 2 Position in Class: 1

SUBJECT		ASSESSMENT	REMARKS
ENGLISH	Reading	20/20 A	Outstanding ability
	Composition	15/20 B-	Excellent progress
	Grammar	18/20 A-	
	Comprehension	17/20 A-	
ARITHMETIC		82/100 B+	Good, careful work
HISTORY		13/20 C	Satisfactory
GEOGRAPHY		C	"
SCIENCE	Nature Study	14/20 C	Shows interest
ART		A	Great ability
WRITING		19/20 A-	Always very neat
HANDWORK	Needlework	B	Good work
OTHER SUBJECTS	P.T.	C -	Rather poor

RELIGIOUS KNOWLEDGE: 19/20 Excellent   Attendance: Good

GENERAL REPORT: Elizabeth has great academic ability, and applies herself readily to all her work. I am very pleased with her year's progress, and she deserves to be top of the class.

Dr Clack — Class Master/Class Mistress   Head Master/Head Mistress

The lowest mark, a "C – Rather poor", was for PT (Physical Training). Teaching being geared to Arithmetic and English for the eleven plus exam we didn't really have any History, Geography or Science lessons – hence the low marks, probably the same for everyone. My only surviving school report: Mother threw out the rest.

*

Mother was sitting in the audience, always there at prize-givings, on open days, and summer school fetes, although she said she had to work on the only sports day we had when I won the obstacle race. She was delighted when she read on my end-of-year report written by Mrs Clack:

Settled but Only Temporarily: Roehampton 2

"Elizabeth has great academic ability . . . and deserves to be top of the class".

Label inside
White Boots, prize
for "Top of the Class"
(no room to add: "and Art"
as originally announced)
Roehampton Church
School, June
1955.

The year before Mother had been disappointed I wasn't one of four brighter children moved straight into the top juniors' skipping a year, my year being too full; for each year the school had only one class of about forty children. She thought I should have been pushed on as well. But I was definitely much happier with Mrs Clack, the only junior school woman teacher, and with best friend Christine. Mrs Clack was a lovely person and a good teacher. Did she realise Mother had been disappointed hence the top mark? So the delightful photo of me receiving my prize hides undertones: that Mother took friendships, relationships, integration, for granted, or didn't consider them important. Academic achievement was the thing. She wanted me to do well, be a feather in her cap but, as I grew older, didn't like me rivaling her own success. Anxious to please I was never good at coping with double bind situations: damned if you do, damned if you don't.
I never really settled into secondary school. After many early changes eleven was a bad time for yet another move and worse was ahead, long-crushed feelings forcing themselves to the fore swamping achievement.
Nevertheless it's a charming photo a reminder of one of the better moments of childhood, so perhaps I should hold it there before the rest gains a power it shouldn't have: myself looking delighted, a happy moment, the pearl in the oyster to take away.

Dark Cupboards, Dusty Skeletons

From the school summer fete:

"Awarded to Elizabeth Wallace whose blue budgerigar . . . was adjudged First Prize Winner at the Roehampton Church School Parent-Teacher Association's Exhibition held on 18th June 1955."

Well done, Dinky, for meticulous preening to look your best. Dandy also won a certificate, the only two awarded.

In the holidays Andrew came home from boarding school. Middle class parents weren't keen on sons playing with girls, it wasn't manly. At the beginning of the holidays Mother suggested we leave it to him to make contact: he was in a boys' world now. Seeing me his mother brought up the possibility of going round to theirs. I said,
"We thought we'd leave it to him."
She looked immensely relieved, replied quickly,
"I think that's a *very* good idea."
However, Andrew did appear fairly soon and showed me how to draw submarines being blown up. We settled happily at Auntie Gladys's kitchen table with pencils and paper to experiment with differing designs on this theme.
"I drew a really good one at school," he said indignantly "and showed it to the headmaster. But he said, 'What's that? A Christmas tree growing on a submarine?' "

Settled but Only Temporarily: Roehampton 2

He also talked about corporal punishment. The dormitory monitor had the power the administer a mild form of this to the other boys if they talked after lights out, as well as more serious punishment by teachers.
At the end of the holidays he said,
"Let's do that thing again. Where I walk backwards and you stand at the corner waving."
When ill in the school sanatorium he wrote to me, a penciled letter full of schoolboy jokes.
"Have Pip's maggots eggs hatched yet?"
Pip was their budgerigar; 'maggots' had a line through it.
I took the letter round to give his mother thinking she might miss him and like to see it.
Next holidays he said,
"You didn't answer."

*

Ann Robilliard appeared one day saying her grandfather was ill lying in his bedroom upstairs next door with an oxygen mask covering his face. She and Christopher had to take turns sitting with him. He wasn't to be left alone in case he briefly regained consciousness or his breathing changed. She said how frightened she was watching him lying there, listening to heavy breathing, knowing he might go at any minute, waiting for his breath to falter when she would have to rush and tell her mum, afraid he might die.
Two days later he did pass away, though not when Ann was with him. Neither of us had had much contact with death. She visited and we asked Mother a lot of questions which she answered patiently. I think Ann felt freer to ask at my house than in the inevitably tense atmosphere of her own.
A year older than me, Ann took the eleven-plus exam earlier. When the results came, seeing her in the playground, I asked where she was going. A three-tier secondary school system existed: grammar, central and secondary modern. She was playing two-balls against a wall, seemed uncommunicative, intent on her game.
"A central school," she said briefly.
"Not a grammar school then," I thought.

*

Mother was difficult to confide in about anything that really mattered, not demonstrative, affectionate, joking, often tired needing to rest. She wasn't happy with our family situation, wishing things were more 'normal' (whatever that is) and easily shocked. Most devastating: she'd often been not there. But she came from a family of teachers and was very good at providing activities, responding to endless demands from a bright child of, "I'm bored! What shall I do *now?*"

Even on a low income she provided a stimulating range of activities probably helped by Auntie Gladys not charging rent. And I think she also enjoyed many of the things we did together. Education, in a broader sense, went on all the time at home. Not having done much art or handicrafts herself, she made a big effort to provide for my interests, finding out about captivating activities. When I asked her for money for some trip or hobby she usually encouraged by providing it, if at all able to. The following is just a smattering of what she came up with.

Mixing things,
watched with interest – might it be good to eat?
"Claremont", Summer, 1955.

Settled but Only Temporarily: Roehampton 2

I always had wax crayons, coloured pencils and paper for drawing, tracing (greaseproof paper), black carbon paper for multiplying copies, a small flat metal paintbox with ten tiny rectangular water colour blocks to experiment with mixing colours, comb painting with cardboard 'combs', made patterns with letter stencils. Mother organised painting activities: sessions with friends, usually Andrew and Nigel round Auntie Gladys's kitchen table. Scissors and glue were always available to cut pictures from magazines and newspapers, make scrapbooks, fold paper and cut shapes to make circular paper doilies and dancing ladies when opened out, Christmas decorations: fringes, paper chains, lanterns from coloured paper, crinkly crêpe paper, soft tissue paper.

Mrs Chaloner gave me a book, *Things To Do* for a birthday present. I still have it. She also passed on children's magazines with activity ideas Mother sometimes helped with. I was always "making things", constructed a multitude of creations from paper maché, cardboard boxes, shoeboxes, bits of wood. Everything could be used. Freedom to experiment led to various unexpected results: in the greenhouse trying drops of left-over oil paint on water, dipping paper in, discovering quite by accident the marbling effect produced. Now expensive kits are sold.

Indoors I tried pouring oil into a jam jar of water: the oil floated, wouldn't mix; I put the stalk of a small white cut flower in a bottle of dark blue ink, discovered tiny blue veins appeared in the flower where the liquid had been sucked up; dripped ink on blotting paper, added drops of water, watched the ink spread in artistically concentric rings.

Mother had a box of old electrical plugs she let me experiment with. I worked out how to wire a light bulb to a plug. The question was, would it work? In case of danger she insisted on testing it herself, kneeling by the socket on a rubber mat for insulation. I felt elated when the bulb lit up (with no ill effects). If Mother wanted a plug changed she called the electrician, a plumber for a blocked sink. In the 1920s St Paul's Girls' School hadn't taught her practical skills.

Without regard for the sexual stereotyping common in the 'fifties, Mother provided boys' toys (as well as a doll family, dolls' tea set, dolls' pram and cot). She'd played cricket at St. Paul's; I had a cricket bat. Meccano was more of a struggle. We made a chair following instructions in the small paper manual, then I looked at a picture of an intriguing looking car with wheels, asked enthusiastically,

Dark Cupboards, Dusty Skeletons

"How do you make that?"
She shrugged helplessly:
"Well . . . I don't know!"
I packed the Meccano away in its cardboard box. Unfortunately it never came out much again.

We got on better with my fretsaw kit. I learnt to drill holes, thread the blade through a hole, screw it tight again in the saw. I managed a hole in the wooden budgerigar cage for a nesting box (Andrew's budgies bred, mine didn't). In thin, three- or five-ply wood, curves could be sawed, simple puzzles made.

Earlier on I'd had a metal clockwork, wind-up, train but only a small circular track; short of money she never bought more track or any points to vary what could be done with this rather limited set.

One Christmas Mother bought a toy film viewer with battery operated light and celluloid Mickey Mouse film wound manually round two wooden spools, able to project still pictures onto a plain wall in darkened room, a simplified mini-version of the bigger slide projectors at school. Vanessa had a better projector from Gamages' well-known London department store: quickly turning a handle created a *moving* image. (Her father had come back to live with them. "Things always did go right for her," Mother observed. Vanessa didn't agree.) Mother also produced a thin paper children's picture book explaining movie-making, with pictures of a tiny clown at the top right corner of each page. If you flicked the pages quickly the clown appeared to somersault.

On dark winter evenings we drew the kitchen curtains and turned the lights out to experiment with a children's photographic printing kit. The film negatives had been developed at the chemist's leaving printing on light sensitive photographic paper, to us. By carefully following the instructions clear black and white pictures magically emerged from the little trays of chemicals. Neither of us had done anything so scientific before, Mother having specialised in foreign languages at school did minimal science.

Settled but Only Temporarily: Roehampton 2

Addison's ironmonger's in the High Street, Roehampton Village.

An invaluable '50s source for "making things".

She'd give me money to go to Addison's Ironmonger's in the Village to buy oil paint, nails, glue. Orange boxes – presumably having been used to transport oranges – could be collected free from the greengrocer's, but were difficult to work with as they tended to splinter easily. I could use carpentry tools from the garden shed, even the big saw. With no adult male to supervise I had *carte blanche* to experiment.

Mother had never learnt to cook but she could sew. She taught me how to use the old Singer hand sewing machine Grannie had passed on and she herself had learnt on as a child: how to turn its handle with one hand while guiding the "material" under the needle with the other, the somewhat complicated technique for threading cotton around numerous hooks, and how to change the bobbin. I pinned bought paper patterns onto material then cut out simple skirts and blouses to stitch together and wear, also making dolls' clothes from scraps in Mother's "piece box" of different sizes, colours and patterns. From an army surplus shop we bought an old blue parachute to cut up and sew.

She helped me with different stitches for embroidery: blanket stitch, cross stitch, knots, chain stitch. I made tiny embroidered tablemats from scraps

Dark Cupboards, Dusty Skeletons

of coloured felt. Knitting advanced to learning purl, plain and cable stitches, casting on and off, rescuing a dropped stitch. I'd begun with thick wooden knitting needles, graduating through plastic (or were they bakelite?) through to four thin silver metal needles – without knobs on ends to stop stitches falling off – for knitting socks. I learned to crochet using a single needle with a tiny hook on its end.

Early on a large blunt bodkin seemed easier for starting to learn hand sewing, and discovering how to fasten thread securely so it wouldn't pull out. Next came threading ordinary sharp thin needles, licking the end of the cotton thread to make it slip more easily through the tiny eye; learning to sew on buttons – first stitching one loosely then winding round and round the loose threads; making buttonholes with blanket stitch; darning socks by sewing strands of wool one way across the hole, then weaving perpendicular threads through; stitching patches over tears; mending seams; threading new elastic with a safety pin through thick navy-blue knicker legs.

We didn't cook much, Mother had never learnt, hated it, having only mastered very basic cooking and there were few exciting ingredients in those post-war years. In any case Kitty (Auntie Gladys's live-in maid) before she left, reigned supreme in the kitchen with Polly, her green parrot, in his cage on one end of the long draining board. But I learnt to peel vegetables with a small hand potato-peeler, press oranges round and round a circular glass squeezer to make juice. We never had parties to prepare for, never baked cakes.

Nature came indoors. Mrs Chaloner suggested growing sliced off carrot tops on saucers containing a little water, watching them sprout; also buying mustard and cress seeds to grow as a sandwich filling by sprinkling on an old, damp flannel spread on a small china plate (I wasn't too keen on eating the result but the growing part was fun).

In autumn I found pointed things to bore holes in conkers, threading string through for conker fights. Oven baking made them even harder, less likely to break when hit by someone else's. Dry, papery-thin garden flowers or leaves, pressed for several days under heavy volumes of *The Children's Encyclopedia* by Arthur Mee, made good pictures glued on sheets of paper. We knew we shouldn't pick garden flowers but no one ever talked about conservation in those far-off days – at least, not to schoolchildren. There was some feeling it wasn't right to take birds' eggs, the fairly common

Settled but Only Temporarily: Roehampton 2

hobby of making a pinhole each end, blowing out the yolk and displaying egg collections in cabinets, beginning to die out. I tried this, blowing unsuccessfully.

Baby birds regularly fell out of nests and needed makeshift cages constructed as a home from home, but sadly they always perished. Goldfish Flicker and Sixpence needed cleaning and their tank furniture redesigned to give them a change. Ladybirds, ever attractive with their scarlet and black wings, could be collected and kept in jam jars with suitable leaves to feed on. School friends kept stick insects, silk worms, made ginger beer from ginger beer 'plants'.

Making books was always an ongoing major activity. I'd develop what Mother called a 'craze' on some topic: birds, dinosaurs, astronomy. (Never having heard the word "project".) One book was entitled *A True History of Birds*, not really a history rather information about different species; I just liked the sound of this title. Moving on to an astronomy craze I traced endless pictures of the moon and solar system, copied statistics – still remembering the order of planets in the solar system, how many million miles the first four are from the sun. Mother and I gazed out of the dining room window at the night sky through ancient field glasses captured from a German prisoner during the First World War by distant Australian cousin, Ted Mitchinson, he'd given to Grannie's family when spending army leave with them.

Auntie Janet looked through my homemade books with drawings of dinosaurs.

"What a lot one doesn't know," she commented wistfully. Apparently dinosaurs weren't mentioned in classical literature!

*

My greatest ten-year-old literary enterprise was *Peter, Paul and Capico City* inspired by Nicholas Stuart Gray's *How Many Miles To Fabylon?* borrowed from Putney Library. Rescued from Mother's flat after she passed away, my book had survived various moves and turnouts, 'Prelims' consisted of title page, 'Contents' giving chapter headings, a list of the fifteen main coloured illustrations, all with page numbers and fantasy map. Having no access to a typewriter these were followed by forty-four pages of hand-written, lower-case 'text', intended to mimic real text; I'd long since mastered joined-up handwriting. Dark rectangular marks in the centre show where small bits of Selotape had joined the pages. Mother wouldn't let me

Dark Cupboards, Dusty Skeletons

put a strip straight down the centre – too wasteful. Expensive Selotape must be used sparingly. Carefully bound, the outside cover was blue cloth stuck on cardboard; the title inked on the fabric in thick black letters, the dust jacket orange sugar paper decorated with spotted toadstools.

Twins Peter and Paul were king's sons and lived in a castle in Capico City, having lessons with a private tutor. They're not allowed to leave the city but, the theme of the book being getting up to mischief, they sneak out to have fun. Reread decades later the charm of the story seems to lie mainly in characterisation, narrative flow and, surprisingly, speech not being my forte, dialogue – dramatics being somewhat thin! The story continues with a toadstool turning out to be magic and granting wishes. They visit Fam's Farm, climb down an old well (*á la* Enid Blyton style adventure stories), meet a witch who turns them into snowstorms – they snow over Capico City so as to have snowball fights next day – climb magic trees which fight, get very dirty. The story ends with the twins' tenth birthday and permission granted to play outside the city walls.

Other 'great' works that survived are a *Pets Enrollment Scroll* another attempt at creating the longed for 'family', giving Name, Colour, Type of Pet, Date Bought, several editions of a *Pets Mag*, with animal stories, poems, drawings and newspaper cuttings. A newspaper, several homemade books of poems and rhymes, some copied some original.

I never wrote about my own inner dream world. That was too private. And perhaps too vulnerable.

Most books read came from Putney Library. Of course all children loved Enid Blyton's un-put-down-able adventure stories, especially difficult to abandon at bedtime when Mother came to turn out the light just when the Famous Five had been captured by the baddies and locked in a remote, inaccessible cave somewhere. Adults didn't consider Enid Blyton good literature. Mother was always trying to introduce me to children's classics or. "good" books: *Swallows and Amazons, Bambi, Heidi, The Ship That Flew*, the Narnia series, stories by Joan Aitkin, the William books. William and his mates weren't always good. A 'good' book meant something with deeper meaning, not shallow, didn't necessarily mean not subversive. Much of what went on in books none of us would have dared do and adults would have stamped on.

Other popular authors were Capt. W.E. Johns who wrote the Biggles books, Malcolm Saville, and Violet Needham some of whose children's

Settled but Only Temporarily: Roehampton 2

novels would now be politically incorrect, one containing a description of a young boy tortured on a medieval rack. Mother showed me how to find books in the library by looking along the shelves under authors' surnames in alphabetical order, told me of books I might like (and considered 'good') or, with my library tickets, took them out of the library for me herself.

Books offered plenty to feed my own inner fantasy world, providing new characters, which also came from Children's Hour plays on the wireless.

My non-fiction reading was mainly on keeping pets, books bought with Christmas or birthday present money. And in the Village, spotting one of those personal hand-written notices stuck in a shop window for *The Children's Encyclopaedia* by Arthur Mee, offered second-hand for £3, I took down the address of the council house on the Dover House Road estate. Mother willingly agreed to walk there with me and buy it from an elderly lady with grown up family. The ten thick, weighty, navy-blue volumes cost more than she earned in a week. How did we manage to carry them up the hill all the way home? Probably in more than one trip, each of us with two or three under arms. Well worth the effort and money though: I spent many happy hours browsing through the volumes learning interesting facts, studying the numerous black and white photos and colour illustrations.

Ordering and labelling my own few books, I played at setting up my own library, "Mother Moon's Library".

Comics became a weekly reading experience, collected from the newsagent in the Village on Saturday mornings or, for a short while, delivered with Auntie Gladys's daily newspaper. *Swift* and *Girl* were the junior and female equivalents of the boys' *Eagle. Dandy,* and *Beano* with naughty *Dennis the Menace,* were cheaper, less upmarket, contained pictures of corporal punishment. What was considered 'good' children's literature rarely had this.

I listened to BBC Children's Hour plays on our rather antiquated "wireless". In a particularly gripping play the hero nearly got strangled by a huge anaconda in the Maldives Islands. Of course this happened just at the end of an episode and you had to wait a week for the next to find out whether he died or escaped. I eventually realised one was usually left at some cliff-hanger, quickly resolved next time. The rain forest, then known as "the jungle", was a place where exciting adventures and exploration took place (remnants of an Empire mentality?) with no concept of conservation.

Dark Cupboards, Dusty Skeletons

Plays weren't always factually accurate: anacondas are a South American snake. Children's radio plays of John Masefield's *Box of Delights* and Charles Dickens' *Nicholas Nickleby* have also stayed in memory. Mother and I listened together to radio comedies *A Life of Bliss*, *Take It From Here* (Jimmy Edwards) amongst others. Mother always listened to the Oxford and Cambridge Boat Race but disappointingly, in the mid-fifties, Oxford, her university and the city I knew, never seemed to win.

I dressed up and invented charades, acting them out for Mother to guess the chosen word. (She pretended she couldn't.) Once went next door to perform charades with the Chaloner's grandchildren while Mrs Chaloner guessed. Arranging my dolls in rows I would provide each with a scrap of paper and crayon to play 'schools' where I was teacher. (Oh! The delicious power of it!) Then there were plays with home-made glove puppets showing above a screen rigged up from chairs draped with a rug or blanket, or setting out tiny metal farm or zoo animals with home-made scenery cut from scraps of card: animal pens, trees, fields, jungle.

Mother bought a second-hand upright piano which she sometimes played, while I improvised dances. She rarely opened her violin case.

She also acquired from somewhere an ancient second-hand portable gramophone, the case covered in black cloth peeling off corners to reveal bare wood beneath. We took the bus into Putney and I chose a large shiny black, 78 rpm record of *The Teddy Bears' Picnic*. The gramophone, powered by a stiff wind-up metal handle on the side, was only good for one 78 rpm record when fully wound. Winding was hard work. I didn't play it often. When the record began to revolve, one had to lift the arm with the needle, placing the point very gently on the edge of the record so as not to scratch it. Inevitably scratches appeared. You could hear the needle crackle over them every time the record revolved. The sound came from vents in the box and at the end of the arm. A tinny sounding, rather grinding version of *The Teddy Bears' Picnic* would emerge.

Desperate to show off the gramophone, I played it during a one-off visit from Canon Campling (looking after his flock), interrupting his conversation with Mother, unable to wait 'til they'd finished. His face, between saintly white hair and circular white dog collar, took on a fixed expression. He listened politely for a few moments before asking me to turn it off. The reverend gentleman must have felt really lost that day in deep dank woods with primeval bears.

Settled but Only Temporarily: Roehampton 2

We listened to music on the wireless: Mother especially liked *Music While You Work* each morning while she got chores done in the kitchen. I much enjoyed the theme tune for the Children's Hour play of *Nicholas Nickleby* and wrote to the BBC to ask what it was; they answered and I bought a 45rpm record of Katchaturian's *Mazurka*.

Music didn't play a big part in our lives. There was no continual background of piped music as now, music wasn't heard in cafés or shops. I never heard much pop music. If it was beginning, it hadn't become widespread; Mother would certainly have disapproved anyway – not sufficiently cultured.

In front of warm, cheerful flames of our coal fire in Auntie Gladys's dining room, she taught me card games: Clock Patience, Happy Families, Snap, Old Maid, and board games: Snakes and Ladders, Ludo, Halma, Draughts – she'd never learnt Chess.

Pencil and paper games in front of the fire included Hangman (improved spelling), Noughts and Crosses, Boxes, Battleships. As I became skilled at developing winning strategies perhaps she let me win, thinking of her cup of tea when the game finished, developing the art of losing as part of a winning strategy in her own end game. And why not?

A lot was picked up listening to Mother speak in her clear Oxford accent with wide vocabulary, explaining things, one to one conversations with no interruptions from other family members, unfamiliar words expertly pronounced, explanations by a teacher from a family of teachers. A disadvantage would be never learning to merge into group conversations: anticipate when a speaker was about to finish, able to continue seamlessly.

Mother needed to rest a lot. After lunch the chocolate peppermint creams would come out and she would settle, sometimes on her bed, sometimes sitting on the sofa by the fire, until teatime, dreaming perhaps of better days: the security of childhood with "Mother" and "Daddy", success at St Paul's, Oxford glory, Polish high society. When she felt lively, more energetic, there would be the occasional cushion fight, or brief rough and tumble on the lawn. I romped with Scamp as well, though being small he wasn't always too keen, grumbling loudly although never snapping.

Mother found an old mattress for me to practice somersaults and handstands. I had a pogo stick jumping on the front drive – a hard concrete surface – counting to improve on personal bests.

Dark Cupboards, Dusty Skeletons

We never did any decorating: the house wasn't ours. The old purple curtains in Mother's bedroom often caught on the handle of the open window, perished torn shreds spread out for all to see, or at any rate for the Chaloner's to see. How frequently they seemed accidently caught by the wind.

"Look," Mother would laugh, "The wind's blown the curtains again."

Mrs Chaloner eventually came to the rescue, offered a set of deep delphinium-blue curtains from a similar bay window in her own house, cast off but still in good condition, not torn. As my husband said, Mother always had a talent for getting people to do things for her.

*

Fire developed an almost fatal fascination. I'd play for hours with nightlights and candles, one winter's evening pouring paraffin out of a container onto a nightlight on a saucer on the linoleum floor in my bedroom. Holding a match to the wick hadn't seemed to work; it wouldn't light. For a moment nothing happened. Then a huge flame flared up, lighting the darkened room, singeing the fringe on my forehead. Backing away against the chest of drawers cut me off from the door. I thought I wasn't going to get out. Then, just as suddenly, the gigantic flame subsided, leaving the room in semi-darkness again. Mother, resting in another room, never knew.

Using the iron in the holidays upstairs in Mother's bedroom, I forgot to unplug it before leaving to meet Mother for dinner in the canteen at Queen Mary's Hospital.

"Did you turn the iron off?" she asked.

"No!" I said, suddenly gripped with fear, "I don't think I did."

She looked tired, cross.

"I'll phone Auntie Gladys when I've had my lunch."

Luckily Auntie had smelt scorching and climbed the stairs to switch the iron off. Having nearly burnt the house down I developed a neurosis about turning irons off.

In summer I built campfires on the disused vegetable patch at the end of the garden, boiling water in a small kettle to make tea. Early on in these experiments I spilt boiling water over my foot scalding it badly. Mother took me to the doctor (the nearest hospital was a bus ride away in Putney), who said the latest theory was *not* to cover scalds with greasy ointment and bandages as before, but expose them to the air. She prescribed a lotion,

Settled but Only Temporarily: Roehampton 2

Gentian Violet, to put on the scabs. Mother found an old gym shoe and cut away the top. So I went to school, to Mrs Clack's class, with a violently purple foot open for all to see. No one seemed too concerned – these things happened – children sometimes had minor accidents.

In winter I played with our open coal fire heating the poker until it was red hot, then white hot, pushing it through bits of paper to make neat round holes edged with burnt brown rings; made curves and patterns in paper; watched the poker slowly cool to orange, red, lastly black with a wisp of smoke. Experimenting with burning tissue paper, cardboard, wood chips, rubber bands (which stank when burnt), silver foil from sweet wrappings, paper clips, scraps of fabric, hair or Scamp's clipped fur which also burnt with a highly distinctive smell, I discovered what burnt easily, what didn't, watched things curl, blacken, change to charcoal, smoke and smoulder, burn with blue or green flames, flare up bright orange, or singe and turn brown, finally to disappear up the chimney as smoke. I rearranged pieces of glowing coal with the tongs, turning red sides up to give heat. Mother often didn't know what I was doing but I managed to look after myself, learning from mistakes without anyone to censor and, most importantly, to control fire.

*

Aged ten I asked for a dog and Auntie Gladys generously agreed. In an all-female family conscious of a lack of maleness in ourselves, this had to be a male dog. Scamp came from an upmarket private house nearby. His mother was a purebred, black, trimmed poodle named, "Arabesque", who'd 'got out' when "on heat". The lady who owned her thought she'd met the purebred cocker spaniel down the road, but he must have had a bit of something else as Scamp had terrier-type ears and high-pitched bark. Mother dubbed him a "Poo-Span Plus". She'd paid five pounds for him but said later she thought it too much as he had less pedigree than she'd been led to believe. Mostly black and curly, he had white toes and 'tie'. The last of Arabesque's litter to find a home, Mother persuaded his owner to keep him until the school holidays when I would be home all day to look after him. She was working part-time as a medical secretary at the artificial limb centre at Queen Mary's Hospital, Roehampton. Until then I was allowed to go round Saturday mornings to play with him in their garden.

Dark Cupboards, Dusty Skeletons

Scamp, Auntie Gladys's back garden, summer, 1955.

Mother tried at first to get him to sleep downstairs in his basket in the kitchen but he cried keeping people awake, so slept in her bedroom. She became very fond of Scamp; he became more her dog than mine. Canon Campling in one of his sermons told his congregation he was sure there were dogs in Heaven. Delighted, adoring Scamp, she wanted him with her in Heaven.

*

We made a special trip to Harrods' pet department to choose a beautiful pale grey rabbit I named "Sue". I designed and built her hutch, carefully measured with two opening doors, enclosed sleeping compartment and sloping roof. To buy wood Mother and I caught a number 30 bus to a timber merchant near Putney Bridge. Back home I totally independently measured and cut the boards to the right-sized pieces and nailed them together. They all fitted. Then I painted the hutch with green oil paint and

Settled but Only Temporarily: Roehampton 2

added a waterproof cover over the roof. Another advantage of not having a father: with that day and age's attitudes to women, girls simply didn't do things like making rabbit hutches. It would have been done for me.

Sue in her carefully designed and built hutch.
Auntie Gladys's back garden, summer 1956.

The hutch wasn't very big, Sue needed more space. Let out to roam the garden she nibbled where she chose, unfortunately developing a taste for pyrethrums eating all those in Auntie Gladys's lovely herbaceous borders right down to the roots. I'd watch Auntie Gladys walk down the garden and look. Good-natured as ever, she never said anything.

Sue used to escape through holes in the fence and go adventuring in neighbours' gardens, once even getting as far as Kitty and Nellie's, Auntie Gladys's spinster sisters-in-law, round the corner. When we were out one afternoon Auntie Gladys, spotting Sue come back through the fence, tottered stiffly down the garden, bent down awkwardly, picked her up and returned her to the safety of her hutch. I was surprised Sue let her, she could easily have made a dash for it, but perhaps she'd had enough excitement for one day!

*

Dark Cupboards, Dusty Skeletons

Sue in Scamp's basket.
"Let the dog see the rabbit," didn't apply.
Scamp took to her very well although he *would* follow
her around poking at her with his nose. When irritated
she'd turn, jump at him with her front
paws and shoo him off.

Although in many ways I still felt very emotionally dependent on my imaginary world and Mother needed to rest a lot, we did a lot together during my four years of junior school, an easier phase of childhood, and thanks to Auntie Gladys there was the never-before-experienced stability of staying put. A first ! Mother took me shopping in Putney and to the library on the number 30 bus from Crestway. We shopped all over London – buying my much-worn beige duffel coat with wooden toggles from Harrods in Knightsbridge – at Barkers in Kensington High Street, Gamages, the Army and Navy Stores, at Bentalls department store in Kingston travelling from Roehampton on the number 85 bus. As everything shut on Sundays – one was supposed to go to church – we couldn't shop Sundays.

You had to stand and wait to be served by an assistant who brought out goods asked for and laid them on the counter for inspection. I wanted a boys' snake belt: elastic stripes in duller colours with snake-like silver metal fastening, worn through loops in shorts' waists to hold them up

Settled but Only Temporarily: Roehampton 2

instead of braces. The male assistant laying out a selection of colours, far from seeming keen to make a sale, made no secret of thinking it odd one should be bought for a girl. I became too embarrassed to make a choice. Mother, indignantly supportive, picked up some different coloured belts, and turned her back to the assistant for me to choose with more privacy. Silently I pointed to a bright orange and blue one. She paid; we left; I wore it a lot.

In warm weather she introduced me to Roehampton Outdoor Swimming Pool travelling on the number 72 bus from Roehampton Lane.

At Richmond Ice Skating Rink; she showed me how to skate. After that I took myself learning to ice skate wearing her rather too-large, brown leather, adult-sized boots, toes stuffed with newspaper. They'd been brought back from her year in Lwów. New boots would have cost too much.

By tube we visited London Airport. I suppose we'd expected to see handsome air pilots striding purposefully around in smart uniforms; laughed together over a cup of tea at the unexpected touristy-ness of it: the roof garden café, pop music blearing out from loud speakers.

A couple of times Mother hired motorboats on the river at Richmond. In mid-river we (or was it me?) experimented with turning off the engine and drifting silently for a minute or two then turned the ignition key, doing what we'd been told by the boatman *should* start the engine again – but didn't. The two of us sat helplessly wondering what to do, gazing at gently sparkling water on all sides. A passing man on the bank seeing our plight helpfully managed somehow to get the engine running again. Did we throw him the mooring rope? Memory fades.

We visited Kew Gardens, the entrance fee much less costly than now. One attempt, with Vanessa and Scamp, ended disastrously when we were stopped at the gate. Mother hadn't known dogs weren't allowed in. Was there anywhere we could leave him? There was a man who might have him for a short while but I thought he wouldn't be happy left with a stranger. Vanessa seemed understandably upset the promised outing hadn't come off.

Mother took me to church fetes and garden parties in Canon Campling's large vicarage garden, church festivals such as the autumn harvest display in the church, taking an apple or orange to leave, and Palm Sunday celebrations when all children were given a dried white *real* palm leaf

Dark Cupboards, Dusty Skeletons

woven into the shape of a cross. At Christmas a crib appeared at the front of the church. Drawing Christmas cards I coloured a rather scrappy one for baby Jesus, which Mother thought ever so sweet taking it into the church where it somehow appeared in the crib beside the baby. If I'd known she was going to do that I'd have made more effort.

She took me to the cinema in Putney. We saw *Lassie* about a collie dog who nearly got shot by bad men, perhaps the first film we went to; *The Forbidden Planet* my first science fiction film; an early three-dimensional film for which special glasses were issued made from white card with coloured plastic lenses; *Oklahoma*, a Rogers and Hammerstein American musical which I loved; "*The Baby and the Battleship*" (1956) a comedy about ordinary sailors trying to secretly care for a baby they'd accidentally taken aboard a battleship; *The Admirable Crichton* where an upper class family with servants, wrecked on a desert island, comes to depend on the butler, the only practical man, to take command over his social superiors to ensure survival of all; *Snow White* a Disney cartoon; another Disney cartoon about Irish leprechauns, banshees, little folk and the crock of gold at the end of the rainbow; *Reach for the Sky* a second world war film about the legless pilot Douglas Bader, played by Kenneth More who became a favourite film star; *Pollyanna*, rather sentimental: looking round at Mother in the darkened auditorium I saw a few tears rolling down her cheeks – Pollyanna hadn't meant to be naughty – what did this remind her of from her own childhood; and an American epic historical romance *Gone With the Wind* later banned for depicting ethnic and racial prejudices which, of course, nobody considered then, Britain being full of a multitude of prejudices.

We visited "The Aunts" in their tiny flat at 14a Douglas Close Worthing two grey-haired old ladies sitting in armchairs. Auntie Janey and Auntie Bella were Mother's father's sisters, my great aunts. Neither ever married. They always sent a ten-shilling note for birthdays and Christmas and I'd write to thank them until they died in the late '50s. Auntie Belle, who also lived in Worthing, was the widow of Grannie's brother, Walter. Mother always spoke warmly of her but never took me to see her.

Fares were cheap. We had occasional outings on single decker Greenline country buses, one to Epping Forest, another to Frensham Ponds and day trips to the south coast. On one to Hindhead we looked down into The

Settled but Only Temporarily: Roehampton 2

Devil's Punchbowl – an intriguingly memorable name to a young child – looking much more bowl-shaped than it does today.

One winter was so cold even the larger ponds on Putney Heath froze solid and I skated on Kingsmere in Mother's brown leather ice-skating boots dug out of the old blue trunk in her bedroom, again managing well enough with screwed up paper pushed into the toes. We both had narrow feet: double-A fitting. Everyone, it seemed, gravitated towards the pond during that cold snap; I met classmates I didn't normally see out of school or speak to in school, discovered a new side to Michael Beasley as we stood on the ice enjoying a friendly chat – a totally different image to that of 'naughty boy' put across by teachers.

Another trip to Kingsmere was on a sunny summer's afternoon to sail the boat I'd made. A flat oblong piece of wood laboriously sawed into the shape of a prow at one end, with mast, and a white sail cut and sewn from an old sheet, tied fore and aft with string. Mother settled herself on the dry tufts of Kingsmere's grassy shore. Taking off shoes and socks I found a long stick to push the boat out and waded into the muddy water up to my thighs. Tired of manoeuvring it around the shallows I pushed it out to deeper waters with the end of the stick.

"Now it's gone," said Mother, "you can't get it back."

I wasn't so sure. Blown by a light breeze the boat drifted further out. Perhaps to stop me getting wet trying to retrieve it, Mother suggested we move round to the other side of the pond and sit there under the trees. I watched the white sail slowly move further and further out, a white speck in the centre of the glinting brown water; then – slowly, slowly – drift nearer to where we sat until I could again wade out to the tops of my thighs and just reach far enough to pull the boat in with the end of the stick. Delighted, I wallowed in achievement: I'd made a sailing boat which worked well enough to sail right across the pond.

Longer walks were to the windmill, near another larger pond Queensmere, always a thrill to gaze at this strange building with its sails standing out against blue sky, soft white clouds scudding behind. What was it for? I had no idea. But somehow it always held its charm as a focal point on Wimbledon Common.

One other visit to a pond in Richmond Park (Adams Pond on the map, although we never knew the name) was also one of those "red letter days" as Mother called them. Equipped with small toy shop fishing net on the end

Dark Cupboards, Dusty Skeletons

of a bamboo stick and glass jam jar with string handle tied tightly round its neck, I'd wade in dipping randomly among the clumps of pondweed, whilst Mother sat and rested after the longish walk. Once, getting a net full of weed I tipped it into the jam jar seeing nothing so exciting as a tadpole or water snail. Then, holding the jar up once the weed had settled, I was utterly thrilled to spot a tiny silver fish swimming round inside its glass circumference. I'd caught a *real* fish. Home again I showed it to Mrs Chaloner who said it was a stickleback – you could tell by the three spines along its back.

On one visit to the same pond in Richmond Park, at one end peering under a low wall crumbling from lapping water, I discovered rows of tiny brown froglets, hiding just above the ripples. Another first.

We'd enter the Park through Roehampton Gate after a lengthy walk along Crestway, through the alleyway behind the artificial limb hospital where Mother worked, across Roehampton Lane and down Clarence Lane beside the Froebal Collage: over a mile. From a map I worked out that straight, unbending, Clarence Lane was about half-a-mile in length: could be used as a measure to estimate distance. Inside the Gate we would walk on, spot deer antlers among the bracken, rams with curling horns on the rough open grass, carrying our picnic looking for a good place to sit.

An even longer walk would be to the Pen Ponds in the centre of the Park where one sunny spring day I found, amongst the rushes, hundreds of shiny black tadpoles wriggling in a couple of inches of water above the sandy grit. Catching them in my hands I put as many as possible in my glass jam jar and carried them all home, conscious that it was a warm day and they were somewhat overcrowded. At home I immediately drew some cool fresh water in the metal watering can from the tank in the greenhouse (knowing they wouldn't like tap water), poured it into an old aquarium and tipped the tadpoles in, sure this would bring them great relief after their hot journey. To my utter disappointment they all promptly stopped wriggling and expired. I worked out this must have been due to the abrupt change in temperature.

The idea of conservation was never mentioned to children in the 'fifties. No one suggested it might be wrong to take tadpoles from their natural habitat. What I did hear, either at school, or in church, or both, was that plants and animals had been put on this Earth by God for man to use, and how wonderful that He had provided for us in this way.

Settled but Only Temporarily: Roehampton 2

*

It was quite normal in the 1950s for children to be turned out of the house on their own after breakfast until high tea late afternoon, with wrapped sandwiches for lunch, older children often having younger ones in their care. Many of my generation remember this freedom as the best part of childhood. With no television there was little to do indoors, mothers tended to be house proud, upset by messy play, children's lives generally more disciplined and restricted. Coming back to Roehampton after boarding school there'd been my new sky-blue bicycle to roam off on; then street play with friends bringing new freedoms – skipping, hopscotch chalked on paving stones, jumping on a pogo stick, walking tall on wooden stilts homemade by Joan Chaloner next door, skating along pavements on adjustable grow-with-the-feet, bare metal roller skates.

Playing by myself on the Common, I jumped dark stagnant steams oozing with rotten leaves, leaped lumpy grass hillocks, discovered new dells and copses to hide in, got to recognise every mound and hollow, collected acorns pulled out of fairy hat cups and that eternal must-have autumn treasure of shiny golden brown conkers; in winter picked dangling catkins and furry pussy willow, studied minutely every frost-covered blade and leaf.

Surrounded by snow I'm alone, revelling in being alone. This Common where I come to play transformed from a green world – sometimes lush green, sometimes brilliant yellowing orange – into pure white desert. A pretty desert for all that it's frozen, uncompromising. Here I come each day out of school; here is freedom, a shaking off of restraint, a dialogue with myself, unchannelled. Usually a smattering of others but today, no one. Just precious freedom in a frozen white world, alone in vast whiteness, transformed, each thin hard black twig contrasting a delicate white layer above, softly decorated. Catkins dangle, hang still in hazel bushes, no birds sing, no traffic rumbles on unseen roads, an immobilised silence, no smell of wet leaves, damp grass. The stream, pale opal, hard, bearing my weight, stays silent, unflowing, white ice shining, crystallised.

In my top two years of junior school Mother worked during school holidays as a medical secretary at St Mary's Artificial Limb Centre, typing letters for doctors. Aged ten and eleven I wasn't bothered about being left. Auntie Gladys was around, the twins Kenneth and Alec, who'd moved into

Dark Cupboards, Dusty Skeletons

the Chaloner's house next door, wanted to play. We scrambled back and forth over the fence and their garage roof, garden space effectively doubled. Meeting Mother for dinner in the hospital canteen was a ten-minute walk. We'd queue at the buffet for a hot meal out of huge metal containers as at school, sit on benches at long bare wood tables. Cheap canteen food was for the workers manufacturing artificial limbs. Many patients, minus an arm or leg, would be trying them out in the hospital grounds. I became used to seeing amputated limbs, metal replacements strapped on, seriously disabled people managing amazingly well.

*

Although smitten with debilitating shyness I was also highly independent, would go anywhere, which confused those who assumed a shy child would also be clingy. Mother would put me on a train with a small suitcase to be met at the other end by total strangers; people neither of us had ever met. We both took it for granted that this was what was 'done' with children: I would be all right. Mother got adverts from the newspaper, the *Church Times*. "Nice People" could be met in this way she thought, these of course always being middle class. Having been to boarding school so young, integrating with other children, being familiar with public transport (cheap and frequent), being used to roaming off on my own while Mother rested, going on holiday alone seemed a natural development. And I had my private dream world to take with me, inseparable, my own inner, if precarious, security.

When did I first start travelling alone on main line trains? Aged nine, ten? Mother would take me to Paddington on the tube, settle me into a carriage on a train to Oxford; after an hour's journey clear station signs announced where to get off. First unaccompanied holidays were to my two maiden aunts as stepping stones to greater adventures. Auntie Janet had me to stay in the school holidays when she wasn't teaching, to give Mother a rest.

The Boving family, who owned 5 Rawlinson Road in North Oxford, lived downstairs. First Auntie Janet rented their flat above, then Auntie Kay retired from the Bank moved in with her, until Janet in the autumn of '55 bought 63 Sandfield Road Headington with their mother's money and moved there with bedridden Grannie and resident home help portly Mabel Violet Alexandra Higgins in her 'fifties, whose wonderfully long name aroused some comment and still remembered in toto!

Settled but Only Temporarily: Roehampton 2

Auntie Kay remained in the Rawlinson Road flat, now with a spare room. Scamp was still a puppy when he came too, travelling with me by train to Oxford. Arriving on the bus from the station Auntie Kay showed me my room over the porch, then said Scamp should stay with her other guest, adult friend Mary, while she took me to the bathroom to wash. Unsure how Scamp would react to being left, I protested. Always forceful, she insisted. Coming back from the bathroom we met Mary rushing downstairs in a panic. Scamp, convinced he'd been abandoned, had jumped through the open upstairs window, slithered down the sloping porch roof and leapt off the end into space. Wherever I went, he was going too. Mary found him below on the gravel drive looking bemused, but unhurt.

Auntie Kay took me swimming in the river – she didn't swim herself – and punting, walking to the boat yard off the Banbury Road. My letters home have survived.

5, Rawlinson Rd. 1st August [1955 ?]
My Dearest Mum,
I have arrived safely and Scamp was very good in the train. His blanket is on the end of my bed, and he is going to sleep there. Tonight he is going to have some scraps of meat (not grissily [sic]).
When I first got to Auntie Kays, she showed me my room. Kays friend looked after Scamp for a minute and he ran away and jumped out of my bedroom window and slid down the roof (which is over the front door) and jumped onto the ground. Kays friend hurried down stairs and opened the door and found Scamp waiting for her. He was perfectly all right.
This afternoon we went down to the river and I swam in the river. It is just a place in the river where lots of children bathe. It is very deep in the middle and it is deeper than me. I tried diving. Auntie Kay said I was getting on very well and tomorrow after-noon we are going to a swimming pool in the river where I can dive with my feet out of the water. I don't think Christine [my best friend] has ever swum in a river.
I carried Scamp out to the middle of the river out of his depth and put him in. He swam to shore. He kept his head well above water by paddling madly with his front paws and splashing a good deal.
Tomorrow we may go punting if I do not go swimming. We will go punting up the Cherwell which is a different river.
Before tea Kay and I went down to the Bovings and they saw Scamp.

Dark Cupboards, Dusty Skeletons

Auntie Kay says that if it is rainy she will take me to a film called "A Kid for Two Farthings". But I do not know what will happen to Scamp. Anyhow it does not look like rain.
I hope I can stay with Auntie Kay until Saturday and then come on to Hindhead with Janet and Scamp.
With lots of love from Elizabeth.
P.S. When Scamp came out of the water I thought he wasn't my dog. [With curly fur slicked down.]

Auntie Janet had discovered Miss Gisborne had moved to a large detached house at the junction of Rawlinson and Banbury roads. She took me to see her, knocking on the door without prior arrangement.

5 Rawlinson Rd. Oxford   2nd August [1955?]
Dear Mum
This Morning I went to see Miss Gisborne. She wasn't to [sic] bad. At first Nurse bought Barry [her black labrador] in because she did not know that I had Scamp. Then she took Barry out and left him in the garden.
When we left Nurse gave me a sixpence to buy ice-cream with. I am going to bring the sixpence home and treashure [sic] it. [This was such an unusual act of kindness from those two, but within a day or two I'd spent the sixpence.]
Then I said "Goodbye" to Janet [who was going into Oxford] and went home.
This afternoon we went down to the river again and I bathed. I practiced my diving and I learned to float on my back. When I float on my back I do the breast-stroke with my legs and do the crawl with my arms. I am not quite sure of the proper stroke.
When we were down by the river I let Scamp off the lead. There is a big meadow which runs right down to the rivers edge and is called Port Meadow. There are no cattle in it because they have been taken out so that the owner of the meadow can get some kind of a weed out of the grass, because the weed is not good for cattle.
This evening at seven Kay's friend [Mary] is going. You will be surprised to know where she is going. She is going to stay with a friend in ROEHAMPTON. The friends name is Gabrielle Cross. You would not know her because she is staying in a house which I think that she is looking after their house while they are away.
Last night Scamp slept in my room on the floor. He did not want to sleep on the bed because it was to [sic] hot. In the night he kept on giving little

Settled but Only Temporarily: Roehampton 2

woofs as Mary or Kay went by. I kept having to scold him because otherwise his woofs would grow louder and turn into loud barks. Because of having to scold him all the time I did not get to sleep till after Kay and Mary had gone to bed and they went to bed at midnight. After that I got to sleep all right.

I got up at seven and took Scamp outside the house on the lead. When I went upstairs again I found Kay and her friend were just getting up. They gave me a cup of tea and then they went to early morning mass. [Auntie Kay had converted to Catholicism] I took Scamp down to the place where the swings are by the canal, and then I came back. Kay and her friend were not back, so I read a little bit of "Worsol Gummige" [about a scarecrow who comes alive] till Kay and Mary came back. Then we had breakfast.

This morning Kay gave Scamp a bone which he chewed for about five minutes and then he went and buried it. He had to have it out of doors because Kay does not like him to have bones in the house.

With love and best wishes from Elizabeth.

P.S. Scamp has a surprise <u>for you.</u> (it is something to show you).

5 Rawlinson Rd.
[No date; drawing of Scamp top left corner]
Dear Mum

I hope that you are well. Yesterday when we went to Port Meadow I saw two goldfinches. I knew they were goldfinches because I have seen lots of pictures of goldfinches. The goldfinches were sitting on two thistles and they had gold tips on the tips of there [sic] wings.

Last night when Kay called Scamp out of my room, to take him outside I did not wake up. Even when Kay brought him back to my room and switched on the light and even after he had climbed over me, I still did not wake up. I must have been very tired.

Today we went on the river in a punt. I sat on the front of the boat and dangled my feet in the water. It was nice and cool.

Auntie Kay says that she will ring you friday night about me coming home.

Scamp seems all right. He ate his breakfast this morning and at lunch he had some scraps of liver.

This night we have had a high tea because Kay is going to choir practice. [at St Aloysius in central Oxford.] Upstairs in Auntie Kays sitting room there are lots of book-shelves with Mr. Bovings books in. He has two copies of the Observers book of Wild Flowers. I have been looking at them.

Dark Cupboards, Dusty Skeletons

With love and best wishes from ELIZABETH. xxxxxx [Three rows of kisses.]

Auntie Kay put me back on the train – in a carriage with a young man she said she thought looked reliable – to be met at Paddington.

Staying with Auntie Janet after she'd moved back to Headington, I took Christmas and birthday gifts of book tokens and cash down to the Children's Bookshop in Broad Street, by bus, spending many happy hours browsing and choosing.

Auntie Janet produced an old black adult-sized sit-up-and-beg woman's bicycle, wartime utility style, for me to explore the countryside and surrounding villages. Cycling through Islip came a first glimpse of genuine Romany gypsies, swarthy, black-haired, with colourfully painted horse-drawn caravan, shiny pots and pans dangling from hooks. Making it as far as Kidlington this also became newly discovered territory a memorable, first-time, round trip of about twenty miles.

Once, taken in to see Grannie, a thin querulous invalid lying in a high bed in her own downstairs room, Auntie Janet monologued for a couple of minutes while I looked on not knowing what to say. Leaving the room a feeling of disappointment lingered.

Janet bought the first car I remember a family member owning: a beige Morris Minor registration 288 AFC, later passed on to Mother to be dubbed by my children, "Granny's Little Tortoise Car." I must have been ten or eleven. She'd take me out in it, quite a novelty to a child who rarely went in a car, then leave it parked with me in it for quite a while, getting bored. On a hill I experimented with releasing the hand brake, the car began to roll backwards, suddenly scared I quickly pulled it on again.

*

At some stage during the last two years of junior school the thorny question of "class" (now an unmentionable) reared its ugly head. Possibly from playground talk about cockneys being moved from East End slums into the new Roehampton tower block council estates. Accent was incredibly and totally unjustifiably important in those far-off days: a working class or Irish accent instantly betrayed the speaker. But my memory is of all Church school children speaking well, including some visited who lived on the new estates. Nevertheless, despite this mixed social milieu I became horribly class-conscious.

Settled but Only Temporarily: Roehampton 2

The milkman and newspaper boy came every day to Auntie Gladys's detached, upmarket house, coal was delivered by a horse with nosebag pulling a cart, a baker's van brought bread, the laundry was collected and returned. They all came to the back door via the tradesmen's entrance, except the newspaper boy who put Auntie Gladys's daily paper through the front letterbox. Heard came one day each week to do the garden, a chauffeur kept his employer's car in the garage Auntie Gladys rented out.

"We're not really *upper* middle class", Mother said, "we don't have enough money. But we're not *lower* middle class either." I suppose she meant with our life style, interests, good speech and her Oxford education. She invented a new class for us: "middle middle-class". I became aware that class was an explosive issue. It mattered. But although mixing with friends from all surrounding neighbourhood types, I was totally unaware of ethnic minority, non-Christian groups: West Indian, Chinese, Jews, Moslems, Sikhs, Hindus. Immigration, beginning mainly in the 'fifties, hadn't yet reached Roehampton Village.

Even my middle class relatives seemed afraid I might become unbearably snobbish. To broaden my outlook Auntie Janet gave me a children's novel, *The Family from One End Street*, about a large working class family. I never took to it, couldn't identify with this huge, close-knit, poor family in a tiny terraced house, with cockney accents, patched clothes, and father's cloth cap. The children's literature I read tended to be about middle class children sent away to boarding school, coping brilliantly on their own with scary adventures (Enid Blyton). Highdown Road's large detached houses were home to the Wingate family whom Mrs Chaloner introduced me to: Caroline Wingate, my age, one of four children with elder sister Alison at St Paul's Girls' School and two younger brothers; and the twins, Kenneth and Alec who'd moved into the Chaloner's house and boarded at a boys' prep school. Andrew lived in an equally large detached house in Dover House Road. The film star, Jack Hawkins, lived a couple of turnings away although I only ever saw him on celluloid. In Barnes cousin Vanessa also enjoyed a middle class neighbourhood opposite the reservoir.

Nearby in less upper class housing, friend Ann Robilliard lived a short walk away on the older, settled, council estate in Crestway in a small terraced house. A temporary early 'boyfriend', Raymond, lived on the new estate of recently built high-rise flats. Both were friends from the Church School and well spoken; perhaps Mr Whitaker was able to interview and select children with 'good' accents, the school being popular, oversubscribed, and not a regular state school.

Auntie Gladys talked about newspaper reports of the disruption of close communities caused by the building of the new Roehampton council estate, people being compulsorily moved by slum clearance from East End neighbourhoods they'd lived in for generations in close-knit communities. Much loved dogs and cats, forbidden in high-rise flats, had to be got rid of, often put down. A girl in my class, whose father was a policeman, lived in a small cottage in the centre of the Village. Other friends I visited, Janet Tomlinson and Susan Ford, lived in Putney.

*

Through Vanessa's mother, Audrey, more family-minded than Mother or Auntie Janet, I met distant cousins visiting 91 Lonsdale Road. Little boys Norman and Duncan from Rhodesia – where their father, Audrey's brother Peter, farmed tobacco – were two lively boys who kept dropping on the floor to good-naturedly rough and tumble with one another. Instantly they'd be sharply told to stop. It seemed odd this was forbidden – I did the same with school friends, nobody minded – but when we got home Mother said it was different out in Rhodesia because of the black servants. It sounds as though apartheid wasn't much fun for white children either. They had to behave with a dignity considered appropriate for a ruling elite and not scuffle on the floor like puppies or, presumably, the local native children.

I also met, just once at Vanessa's eleventh birthday party in Richmond Park, three brothers, David, Roger and Michael Thomson, also second-cousins, grandsons of Mother's Uncle Lewis, penultimate of my grandmother, Bertha's, eight siblings. David, the eldest, was much the same age as Vanessa and myself, his brothers a couple of years younger. At one point as we all milled around Vanessa came and gathered me up under a small tree with the Thomson brothers, apart from other party guests.

"Mummy says we have to talk to each other," she explained.

All I can remember is David telling us they called Roger "Podge" which I thought must be as it rhymed with "Rodge", but apparently he had been quite podgy. A photo of the five of us, with some of Vanessa's school friends also party guests, shows everyone standing in a Park pond ankle deep in murky brown water.

Settled but Only Temporarily: Roehampton 2

Cousin Vanessa's 11th birthday party, Adam's Pond, Richmond Park. Vanessa is third from left with pigtails. I'm far right. The three second-cousin Thomson brothers are dark-haired David, behind, sixth from left, and the two little boys front centre, Michael and Roger. August 1955.

A friend suggested we walk our dogs by a narrow river and let them off the lead. They both immediately dived in, emerging soaking wet.
"Oh," she said, "they shouldn't have done that, should they?"
I meekly agreed.
"We must punish them, mustn't we?"
She began hitting her large Alsatian with its leather lead, while I smacked Scamp. She got so carried away a woman on the other side of the river called across telling her to stop. Back at her house she surprised me by immediately telling her mother (I never told mine) who, instead of being quick to blame and condemn just tried to find out who the woman might have been. Neither of us knew. This story may elicit gasps of horror but corporal punishment was endemic in our 1950s lives. Many children suffered from it, saw adults as all-powerful. When we had the opportunity to control and do likewise, we took it. Dogs could be controlled by us.

Dark Cupboards, Dusty Skeletons

Children's literature frequently contained incidents of children being smacked, spanked, whipped or caned; radio plays even had sound effects!

*

As a young child I always looked forward to seeing my aunts although visits only happened briefly in school holidays. When a teenager things changed: not having their own families they both wanted to possess, mould, make me exclusively their own. By then I'd become too emotionally detached.

Auntie Janet always wore glasses with her grey hair tightly drawn back into a bun at the nape of her neck. Dressed in immaculate well-cut grey or beige suits, the seams of her stockings would always be dead straight. The eldest of the three sisters she was academically brilliant, prone to nervous breakdowns, painfully shy and found beginning teaching traumatic never having had any teacher training, fearful of losing control of a class even of nice, well-behaved girls in upmarket schools. She never wore make-up and unlike Kathleen had never been expected to marry. Nevertheless she could be sensitive and kind-hearted with younger children, less harsh, more tolerant than Auntie Kay. In the autumn of '55 when their mother had been ill living off milk from the doorstep, Janet organised the purchase of 63 Sandfield Road Headington (funded by her mother), a round comfortable residential care-er with the magnificent name of Mabel Violet Alexandra Higgins, and moved her mother to Oxford from Hindhead. Janet's headmistress at Headington School tried to persuade her to give up teaching, thought she couldn't manage both, but Janet soldiered determinedly on. Mother and I went to Hindhead and sold the house (I had time off school during the eleven plus exam year). When her mother died Auntie Janet had a bungalow purpose-built to her own requirements in Franklin Road Headington. She'd spent her life in all-female environments, when teaching going home for school holidays to be looked after by her mother until her parents moved to Hindhead, never really seeming to grow out of school. As a young child I saw more of Auntie Janet than Auntie Kay: when we'd lived in Headington, and at weekends from boarding school, then staying with her in junior school holidays. Gentler with younger children, when reaching the age of the girls she taught her attitude changed, became controlling, severe. I couldn't cope.

Auntie Kay was sociable, outgoing, attractive, said the idea of going to university had been anathema to her. Everyone had expected her to marry.

Settled but Only Temporarily: Roehampton 2

Since leaving school she'd worked as a clerk in the Bank of England and hated it, but was unlikely to get another job in the 'thirties depression. Perhaps because of this she threw herself into high life with a variety of boyfriends, much to the consternation of her parents. She fell out with her mother and moved away from home. Then, at some stage, she underwent a religious conversion to Catholicism going on pilgrimages to Lourdes and Rome, actively trying to convert others which – now suffering from religious mania – she saw as a God-given duty. Mother had been closer to Kathleen than to Janet until I was born. She felt Kathleen was resentful that she'd married and had a child undermining their relationship. Nevertheless Kathleen was said (in a letter from Auntie Belle) to be very fond of me. We visited, sporadically, her rented rooms in London. She always seemed pleased to see us and I enjoyed seeing her. Bank clerks normally retired at forty-five; she moved in with Janet at Rawlinson Road, sharing the rent until '58 when she bought her semi-detached in Wolvercote with the bequest from their mother's will. Kathleen tended to make friends easily, then have rows, fall out with people. Janet and Kathleen didn't get on.

"Elizabeth must never know about this," Janet apparently told Mother. But what's the big deal about sisters not getting on? Why shouldn't I know? Forceful aunts came in quantity; uncles were mythical creatures, existing only in fantasy.

We never saw Auntie Janet, Auntie Kay or Grannie at Christmas. I should remember what I had and what happened on my birthdays and at Christmas. But on the whole, I don't. I do remember one Easter getting a wind-up analogue watch (digital battery watches being not yet generally available) wrapped in white cotton wool inside a large, patterned, cardboard egg. In those days a watch was a special high-tech present some children didn't have. Waking on Christmas morning my large, specially designed stocking, Christmassy white net with red trimmings, would be by my bed, opening about eight little packages all individually wrapped made a good start to the day. Less interestingly the toe invariably contained an orange tangerine. I don't remember much about what else was in the stocking, or what my separate larger, main Christmas presents were. Auntie Gladys would get me something for Christmas and birthdays, usually a book, as did Mrs Chaloner next door, and Vanessa's mother, Audrey. I still have children's books written inside on fly-leaves saying who they're from and the date given. Christmas Days were very quiet, we never went

Dark Cupboards, Dusty Skeletons

anywhere, had guests, saw relatives. The three of us would sit round the kitchen table for lunch: Mother, myself and, before we moved to Letchworth, Auntie Gladys. Mother would roast a chicken, a rare treat in those days affordable only on special occasions. Otherwise nothing much happened, even less on Boxing Day. Mother had to rest a lot having been ill with TB, feeling perennially tired.

I must have been about fifteen when Mother announced, "You don't want a Christmas stocking anymore, do you?" She'd enjoyed doing the stocking, she said, but had perhaps grown tired of it by then. I agreed I didn't.

The week after Christmas would usually be more exhilarating: if Christmas and Boxing Day were as silent as the grave a trip to a pantomime or circus livened things up. Lingering among early memories is singing rousingly along with a pantomime audience:

> "There's a worm at the bottom of the garden
> And his name is Wiggely Woo.
> There's a worm at the bottom of the garden,
> And he likes to say "How do you doooo . . ."

With, of course, a lovely, lively pink worm on stage.

Mother took me to Bertram Mill's circus where, to my huge delight, a clown's trousers fell down. I pestered Mother to arrange a second trip; we sat in cheaper seats "up in the gods", looking down inside the Big Top from a great height. Auntie Gladys teased:

"You just wanted to see if the clown's trousers fell down again."

She was absolutely right, overwhelmed with curiosity as I was as to whether or not it was a genuine accident. And, yes, they did fall down again.

Afterwards we went round the funfair stalls with a flea circus, saw the owner's bare arm bitten with bites where he fed his performers and 'fished' with magnets on poles. Another time of firsts.

One year we saw the utterly magical performance of *Where the Rainbow Ends*, an unrivalled classic amongst children's Christmas plays. Auntie Kay, bless her, bought tickets for the centre of the front row of the dress circle for Vanessa, me, Audrey, Mother, and herself, an all-female party (of course). For our family, an unusually large party of five, a rare family get-

Settled but Only Temporarily: Roehampton 2

together, and my only experience from this hallowed viewpoint. I remember the sense of pure magical mystery and enchantment created by colourful lighting, costumes and music, but not much of the story line. The web says this was a fantasy story about the journey of four children, two girls and two boys with a lion cub, in search of their parents (very relevant to fatherless girls). Much of the story is in Rainbow Land with talking animals, mythical creatures and a white witch. Travelling on a magic carpet they're guarded and helped by St George in shining armour ready as ever to fight and conquer the dragon of evil.

Unfortunately another of my clearest memories is of the interval. Vanessa and I weren't bought any snacks but she had with her a small tube of silver balls used to decorate iced cakes. While the three adults chatted enthusiastically to one another ignoring us, we leant over the balcony sucking these. One dropped out of Vanessa's mouth onto the audience in the stalls below. Giggling, we sent several more down until a mother with a son turned to look up as we quickly dodged back out of sight. We weren't always very well-behaved little girls despite our middle class backgrounds.

Birthdays were similarly unmemorable, Mother could never manage a party. In fact she discouraged me from going to Vanessa's parties – perhaps she thought I'd notice the lack. She made some excuse one year about it going on too late – I'd get tired – so the following year Vanessa's party included an overnight stay so I could go. Mother still desisted – giving the same reason – until Audrey explained Vanessa was very keen for me to go, hence the special overnight arrangement. So a small canvas camp bed was set up especially for me in the attic room at Lonsdale Road next to the large double bed all the others were to sleep in. In the end several of us, including myself, slept in the large bed, two in the camp bed and – needless to say – we were up past midnight. I didn't feel tired but the following year Mother again insisted I would.

For birthdays envelopes would arrive in the post from my two maiden aunts and two great aunts in Worthing, with ten-shilling notes or a book token, also a ten-shilling note from Vanessa's grandmother, Auntie Daisy. I enjoyed spending these, staying with Auntie Janet after Christmas, taking myself on the bus down into Oxford to browse in The Children's Bookshop in Broad Street, selling only children's books with a wide selection. But what money could be spent on was carefully regulated, nothing too frivolous would be approved.

Dark Cupboards, Dusty Skeletons

Bill, holding a pipe, and Ruth. Discovered clearing Mother's flat, she never showed me this photo when I asked about my father. Could it have been a wedding photo taken the day they married? There's no photo of the three of us together. Below: a first photo of me – with Mother – having not yet learnt to smile! Early 1945, probably the flat at 45 Gower Street.

Settled but Only Temporarily: Roehampton 2

Aged about ten I felt safe enough to ask again about that mysterious absent father I tried unsuccessfully to picture in my mind. Mother opened her blue trunk and produced a couple of letters. As he'd been moving about since leaving Gower Street he'd registered with a Royal Mail forwarding organisation. All one had to put on the envelope was the code below; not even a name, which seemed to further depersonalise him. When he moved he had only to notify this organisation; they would forward letters addressed with the code below. I remember some letters postmarked "Bow", otherwise giving no clue as to exactly where he might be.

BM/DTAT,
London W.C.1.　　[handwritten]
16th June 1955.
Dear Ruth,
It is a very long time since I have written to you. I am so sorry. Things have been somewhat precarious, and there have been times when I have not been too well – nothing really serious – probably mental tiredness more than anything.
I hope things are well with you. I hope, too, to be able to raise some surplus cash to send you in about a month's time or so – it will help with a holiday at least.
All good wishes,
Sincerely, Bill.

I never saw this letter but remember another note, written on an odd scrap of yellow paper, saying he'd had trouble with his eyes.

*

Back at school for the autumn term Mr Ayling, tall, young, dark-haired and single, took the top eleven-plus exam year in a classroom across the upper playground in the building also containing Mr Whitaker's house. On the first day of term Christine and I were delighted to discover we'd been sat together again In a double desk right at the back of a row in a corner, two responsible girls who worked well together All the brighter children had been paired at desks in two rows the same side of the classroom with the all-important blackboard at the front on the same side: John Faulkner and Rodney Wilson, Josephine Shead and Christine Garfield, Christine and myself, Duncan and three other bright boys.

Dark Cupboards, Dusty Skeletons

But, despite having come top of the class the year before, my marks at the beginning of the top year weren't good. Unaware of working any differently I'd no idea why, After two or three weeks they inexplicably improved. Mother said later,
"I really began to think you couldn't do it."
In Arithmetic we learnt the BODMAS memory aid for the right order of calculations in problems: Brackets first, then Division and Multiplication, lastly Addition and Subtraction, explained on the blackboard over and over. One parents' evening Mr Ayling told Mother he knew I was daydreaming when he went through sums on the blackboard but could never catch me out. I'd developed the knack of watching the first time a sum was explained, then drifting off into my own vivid fantasy world and, if a question was suddenly fired at me, switching on rapidly, looking at the blackboard, seeing what stage he'd got to, and coming up with the right answer. Daydreaming relieved boredom. In a mixed ability class with formal class teaching, things would be gone through again and again until the slowest had grasped it.

That autumn term Mother had to spend a week at Hindhead helping with the sale of Grannie's house. Grannie, too weak and ill to live independently, had been moved elsewhere. Andrew's mother took in "paying guests". To avoid missing school could I stay with them as a "paying guest"? But Andrew's mother said she hadn't a spare room so Mother took me with her and I enjoyed being at Grannie's for the last time while prospective purchasers viewed and Mother sorted possessions for removal. Mr Ayling wasn't pleased. Back at school he remarked pointedly in class about people ". . . gadding about all over the country".

The eleven-plus exam had basically two parts: English and Arithmetic, for which we were thoroughly grilled, Geography, History and Science being almost non-existent aspects of the curriculum. As light relief we did PT and Singing, no Art or Craft that year and, of course, had plenty of freedom to let off steam playing on the Common.

Religious education I remember as just Mr Frazer's weekly hymn practices when we had to sing lines over and over to get them absolutely right. The 'torture chamber' Rodney Wilson called it – but I enjoyed singing. Looking back it seems odd there wasn't more religious instruction in a church school.

Settled but Only Temporarily: Roehampton 2

During my last year the school got its first library. A wooden cupboard in the school hall (still lit by gas lighting) full of children's fiction.
The eleven-plus exam finally loomed.
"Supposing I don't pass?" I asked Mother, apprehensively. She was reassuring:
"It'll be all right. The school will say you should have passed. You'll get a grammar school place."
So that seemed all right. The exam passed uneventfully. I don't remember feeling particularly stressed or even much about taking it. Where did we sit the papers, in the hall or our classroom?
The day after the exams Mr Ayling got us all doing Arithmetic first thing, saying we couldn't just slack off because the exam was over. But, having made his point, classroom learning changed to something more progressive, more of which later.
When the results came through Mr Whitaker read them out in morning assembly, having carefully explained the categories: grammar, central, and secondary modern schools. We weren't given letters to take home. Possibly letters had already been sent, timed to arrive the same day, but we seemed to be left to relay the results ourselves, which may have been difficult for those without the coveted grammar school place. Anyway, I did have a grammar school pass so no problem there.
Mother decided to apply to Putney High School for Girls, I suppose with hindsight as it had an academic standard good enough for Oxbridge entry. I had to take the school's separate selective exam in January '56 on a freezing cold day – not that I minded the cold – travelling there by bus on my own, in snow. Mother seemed a bit horrified I never managed to finish the English composition in the time allocated, having chosen from titles offered a topic about a dog with a family of puppies and got too deeply involved to notice time passing.
At the interview, another separate occasion, I was asked to recite a poem. We'd been prepared for this at school, told one day to choose a poem to learn from a selection of about ten. Mine, about Robin Hood, ended:
". . . and winds his shadowy horn."
I pronounced "winds" as in winds that blow (short i); the young lady interviewer thought it was meant to be "winds" (long i) to emphasise air winding around inside the horn.

Dark Cupboards, Dusty Skeletons

"So you learnt the poem at home?" she asked, looking impressed, apparently thinking I'd been reading poetry on my own uncorrected, and this explained the mispronunciation. It didn't seem a good idea to admit I never read poetry at home.
"Yes," I said hesitantly.
"What poetry books do you have?"
This almost stumped me. I remembered seeing a dark blue volume with gold lettering among my mother's books.
"*The Oxford Book of English Verse*," I said even more hesitantly.
She moved on to a different question.
Mother was disappointed I hadn't won a scholarship to either Putney High School, or Oxford High School for Girls, where she'd also put me in for the entrance exam. Presumably I would have boarded.
"It would have been nice to be able to tell people," she said.
In Oxford Auntie Kay took me along. The interview didn't go well, a typical girls' schoolteacher, elderly, dull, grey-haired, didn't seem to think much of me.
Places were offered at both High Schools.
Auntie Janet phoned from Headington some while later, sounding depressed, Mother told me. Eventually, after talking about other matters, she'd asked:
"Didn't Elizabeth get a place then?"
"Oh yes!" said Mother brightly, "Of course!"
What she'd really wanted was to be able to say I'd won a scholarship. An ordinary place even at a highly academic, over-subscribed school hadn't been worth mentioning.

*

We didn't have TV. I read a lot, borrowing books from Putney Library, taking the number 30 bus from Crestway to Putney High Street. The children's library issued three library tickets: for one fiction book and two non-fiction. I didn't use my non-fiction tickets much but made a bee-line for adventure stories, such as *The Famous Five,* so popular often already borrowed thus unlikely to be found on the shelves unless unexpectedly lucky. Mother, up-to-date with current children's literature, helped me find good books, classics she'd probably read herself as a child. Janet gave me books or book tokens for Christmas and birthdays, Mother and Auntie

Settled but Only Temporarily: Roehampton 2

Janet valued education for girls. It was emotional life that went to pieces – confidence, trust, empathy.

Enid Blyton's gripping adventure stories, considered not 'good' literature, did get children speed reading to find out what happened. I was also given hand-me-down copies from their own childhoods of 'improving', moralising Victorian classics like *What Katy Did*, (injured and confined to bed through her own disobedience) and *The Water Babies* (with Mrs Be-Done-By-As-You-Did and Mrs Do-As-You-Would-Be-Done-By) the moral aspects going over my head.

I loved Elizabeth Goudge's *The Little White Horse, Henrietta's House*, and *Sister of the Angels*, only realising browsing through them again as an adult how Catholic orientated they were. As a child this also went over my head. Mother directed me to classics such as George McDonald's *At The Back of the North Wind,* Arthur Ransome's *Swallows and Amazons,* John Masefield's *The Box of Delights*. Someone gave me a beautiful hardcover edition of Kenneth Grahame's *Wind in the Willows* charmingly illustrated by Arthur Rackham. Auntie Janet gave me Janet Aiken's short stories, *All You've Ever Wanted,* among many other titles. Many children's novels were subversive – children got up to all sorts of naughty things coping amazingly well without adults around.

Some children's novels rivaled the video nasties worried about by modern parents. In one Biggles novel a central character is tied to pegs in the desert by the baddies and left to die eaten alive by colonies of particularly ferocious marauding ants. Although, of course, one always knew they would be bound to be rescued in the nick of time. Violet Needham, mentioned earlier, wouldn't now be acceptable. Some children's authors helpfully wrote entire series to while away winter hours, their characters becoming well-known. As well as several Enid Blyton series chronicling different groups of children, I read through most *Rupert Bear* stories in picture form, *Bunkle*, books, and *Billy Bunter* the Fat Owl of the Remove at Greyfriars' School.

The first term of that top junior year had been geared up purely to Arithmetic and English for the all-important eleven-plus exam. In the New Year we moved on to the more absorbing, and to us totally new, modern teaching method of "Projects". We could pair up with friends and choose our own topic. My idea was: *Ye Olde Roehampton*. No one else thought of

Dark Cupboards, Dusty Skeletons

that. Christine went along with this although she lived in Putney. I did most of the research for the Village and we had fun putting together a large wall poster with drawings and writings of the historical bits such as the drinking fountain with horse trough and war memorial.

Cherubs on the drinking fountain and horse trough in the centre of Roehampton Village.

With wide road space number 30 buses turned here for the return journey to Putney and beyond, as did number 72 buses to return along Roehampton Lane.

The building behind was a pub.

Date uncertain: may be from a visit decades later, but the fountain is unchanged since the 1950s.

Settled but Only Temporarily: Roehampton 2

Great War Memorial on Putney Heath at the top of Medfield St. passed every day on the way to school,

As it looked in the 1950s.

Steps and path by Addison's ironmonger's (on right) from Roehampton High Street to the fountain lower down the hill. As remembered from the 1950s.

Dark Cupboards, Dusty Skeletons

In school that winter during a cold snap (when the ponds froze) we all huddled on our chairs, in coats and scarves, round the antiquated solid fuel boiler at the front of the classroom. Mr Ayling organised spelling games it being too cold to do any serious work. I had to spell "balloon" normally no problem if written, but got muddled trying to spell it verbally.

Christine got quite keen on Mr Ayling who *was* young unlike her father. She wrote him a letter inviting him to tea but he told her rather abruptly in the classroom (but not in front of the class) he couldn't come.

In spring a family of starlings built a nest in the roof space above the double desk Christine and I shared. Every time the parent birds arrived with food for their young the kerfuffle sent down a shower of twigs, dry grass and thick grey dust onto Christine and myself. We told Mr Ayling who pointed out others sitting nearby weren't complaining. Unusually assertive I announced:

"We get the main shower!"

"Sir" moved us temporarily.

For a while we had a young lady student with us from the Froebel Teacher Training College. An interesting long slithery snake which appeared one day in a vivarium at the front of the classroom and stayed awhile, was probably hers. We stood watching as it curled round her hands when held.

Mr Ayling didn't have discipline problems his classes always being quiet and attentive. Only once did I see him administer corporal punishment during one playtime when he came into the classroom with one of the tougher boys, told him to bend over and whacked him once with a gym shoe. I don't know what the boy had done. We must have been in the classroom at playtime, not permitted in the younger classes unless raining.

In this top year a class photo was taken in the lower playground, as well as individual photos which had been placed on Mr Ayling's desk ready to be given out. We spotted him take out of its envelope the photo of his favourite, Rodney Wilson, look, and smile.

During summer dinner breaks Mr Ayling regularly took half-a-dozen of his favourite boys pond dipping or organised games of cricket with a hard ball (not allowed in unsupervised informal games) on the level part of the Common at the top of the slope. Christine once asked if we could go pond dipping too but he said slightly irritably:

"Oh no! I can't take everyone!"

Settled but Only Temporarily: Roehampton 2

She didn't make much headway; at break times he only did boys things with boys.

Out of school Christine and I went swimming together in the indoor pool in Putney; she took me to see where her mother worked; we went after school to the weekly activity sessions at the Froebal Teacher Training College with 'our' class student; we planned a trip to London airport but her parents wouldn't let her go (I went on my own) we shopped in Putney together.

She joined the Girl Guides and had a smart blue uniform. I thought about joining too until she said,

"I don't think you'd like Guides. There's too much lining up."

Mother, not unreasonably, wasn't keen to fork out for the uniform if I might decide not to go.

*

Once, in class, without thinking, I sat on the corner of a desk on an inkwell. A circular dark navy stain appeared on the seat of my red check gingham dress. Embarrassing. Mother commented that Mr Ayling, being a man, probably hadn't realised it needed washing out immediately. But she managed to make the stain disappear and I wore the dress to school again without feeling uncomfortable.

More embarrassing was starting periods at the then unusually early age of eleven and three months, having only found out about them a short while before. In those days parents often found it difficult to talk to their children about *anything* related to sex. With hindsight I think Mother must have engineered the situation so I would ask. I danced cheerfully from the separate lavatory into the bathroom next to it, where Mum was washing clothes.

"Somebody's had a nosebleed," I told her, bringing the reply:

"Oh yes . . . I'd been meaning to tell you about that . . ."

With hindsight I think she'd left the lavatory unflushed to encourage me to ask. She dealt with things that way. Lucky she did as not long after it happened. She showed me how to use a pink elastic sanitary belt and specially purchased white 'towels' with loops to hook onto the belt back and front under my thick regulation navy-blue knickers. The towel felt bulky and uncomfortable, at times hard with caked blood, or wet and apt to leak.

More negatively she also taught me the term "The Curse": in an educated, career women's world that's what it was. Much later I discovered other families saw the start of periods as something to be celebrated, meaning you were a women and could have babies. An attitude to fertility contrasting strikingly to that of my public school educated, 'liberated', female relatives.

'Periods' caused anxiety at school in case other children found out. None of the girls talked about them and I didn't want my secret known. The school was totally ungeared up to slim girls of my age having periods in that post-war era. With only basic unappetising foods available girls' physical development took place at a later age. I needed a change of sanitary towel during the day and had to take one to school carefully wrapped in paper (no plastic bags available) pushed deep into the pocket of my navy gabardine raincoat left hanging in the small cloakroom with other identical raincoats all crushed together, praying no one would accidentally put their hand in the wrong pocket.

Changing meant crossing the playground to the messy outside girls' lavatories with no loo paper, no locks on doors or bins for used towels. The used one then had to be smuggled back across the playground and hidden in the pocket to put in the dustbin at home. As far as I know no one ever did find out. Not even Christine. At that stage of my life menstruation didn't sit easily with my still tomboyish self: I was happier climbing around with the twins next-door, Kenneth and Alec.

Periods would later become heavier and more frequent – every three to three-and-a-half weeks. But I was a long way from thinking about marriage and family. Adjustment had to be made to the present family situation, that it wasn't going to change, that my institutionalised child dreams of family life would never happen.

Why did I menstruate so early? I wasn't anything like overweight; very few of our post-war austerity generation were. Apparently recent research has shown that girls without fathers often do menstruate earlier. No one seems to know why.

*

Various minor health problems many children suffered reared their ugly heads. Having no tonsils I tended to catch colds easily which annoyed Mother.

"You've caught *another* cold!" she would say, crossly.

Earlier on I was once off school for several weeks with a lingering cough. Vanessa told me the school attendance officer had come when she wasn't in

Settled but Only Temporarily: Roehampton 2

school for a while. "Bilious attacks" only occasionally bothered me unlike Ann Robilliard who often had them.

I developed warts on my fingers managing to bite off the smaller ones. The largest, on the back of my right index finger, had to be 'frozen' off at the clinic in Putney. A painful process although of course they said it wouldn't hurt. I preferred to deal with them myself. That also hurt, but at least I was in control; pain couldn't go beyond the bounds of what could be reasonably coped with.

I think you normally only went to hospital if referred by your doctor. I had a persistent verruca, possibly caught at the swimming pool, treated at Putney Hospital by a young doctor who wanted to try a new technique to vanish verrucas. This involved cutting away all the dead flesh around to the depth of the verruca, to 'starve' it. He said it wouldn't hurt: the flesh was dead. It wasn't. No anesthetic, of course. Mother took me the first time. For the second appointment she sent me on my own. Having had the remains of the verruca cut out in a minor op. I had to walk all the way back to the bus to travel back to Roehampton. Stoical (or unemotional) as ever, I never complained.

Mother felt the most important bits to take care of were "teeth and feet". Emotional stability never worried her. She took that for granted. I was always sent in alone to the dentist feeling deserted in my hour of need! The waiting room tried to evoke a deceptive serenity, but goldfish drifting lazily did nothing for exploding nerves within. Mother always maintained an ultra calm exterior so as not to panic me, wasn't sympathetic with fear, sometimes gave the impression of not caring unlike her own mother who'd apparently dissolved into floods of tears taking Kay to the dentist as she didn't want her daughter's overcrowded teeth pulled.

Called in I was expected to sit in the dreaded black chair. Full of foreboding while teeth were checked for fillings needed, I'd watch the dentist out of corner of my eye, fiddling with forbidding instruments in his unnaturally white coat, metal tools gleaming. Having started drilling he might pause, turn again to these mysterious instruments, while I watched, wondering if he'd finished yet, hoping . . . Through open french windows a sunny green lawn stretched beyond, doing nothing to reassure. Fillings were carried out with a slow drill without anesthetics,

"Our little buzzing bee," I was told encouragingly. Only for an extraction would you have 'gas' – a total anesthetic. Christine said she loved having

Dark Cupboards, Dusty Skeletons

gas, it made her feel marvellous. It did nothing for me, inducing only a horrible grogginess and fuzzy, muddled head.

"I've put four fillings in her back molars," a new young dentist told Mother. "There weren't any cavities but the enamel was weak and they definitely would have gone."

"Oooh!" Mother looked taken aback.

"The teeth definitely would have decayed," he assured her again. With the fillings already in there wasn't much she could do about it. I was just relieved the appointment was over and we were about to walk away up the path and out of the gate.

I never came away from the dentist without at least one filling (charged to the newly-nascent National Health Service). Mother felt it her duty to arrange regular visits: the *right* parental thing to do.

The older dentist who ran the practice had a large garden in front of his surgery with a beautifully trimmed lawn sporting a dovecote around which pure white doves cooed and fluttered. Whiter than the teeth about to be contaminated with grey metal fillings. Below, cropping the short grass, wandered several contented tortoises. They didn't have teeth, just hard gums which didn't give any trouble – a much more humane evolutionary design. I had pet tortoises too. Seeing he liked tortoises I took mine on a visit encouraged by Mother who, no doubt, saw a means of getting me to the dentist with fewer nerves and aggro. In a grubby green carpetbag, unzipped to let in air, they sat on the floor next the dentist's chair, rustling around in their straw while he drilled my teeth. Probably thanking God they didn't have teeth. When my head wasn't tipped back, I glanced down for reassurance. Surprisingly the dentist seemed a little cold towards them; I'd thought he'd be more interested.

One day Mother announced we were going to visit Auntie Kay. We took the bus into Putney, got off in the Upper Richmond Road and walked back a little way.

"This isn't the way to Auntie Kay's," I said. We stopped outside the dentist's gate. Fear rose in suffocating black waves, rushing upwards, a paralyzing, immobilising dread. It usually took at least two days to psyche myself up for a visit to the dentist, to cope with the pain and stress of fillings. Mother had thought it kinder not to tell me, to save me this agony. We would just pop in on the way to Auntie Kay's and it would all be over in no time. Unprepared, I was shocked into total paralysis, unable to move inside the gate. In the end, after lengthy argument, persuasion and bribes, Mother went in herself to avoid the fee for a broken appointment.

After the age of twelve I refused to go at all. My teeth responded by suddenly becoming amazingly cavity free. They gave no trouble throughout my teens; I never experienced the agonies of toothache and the newly-born National Health Service never got charged for treatment. In the '50s corporal punishment, with or without parental consent or even knowledge, wasn't the only legitimate physical abuse.

Mother eventually took my aching feet seriously, although admitting she had at first thought I was "putting it on, making it up", grumbling about having to walk. Finding it difficult to talk about myself I rarely complained about ailments, real or imagined. At boarding school there was no one to complain to – you just had to put up with it. Grannie seems to have been very anxious about her daughters so perhaps they'd played up to this. But Mother did take a mysterious stomachache seriously, possibly a precursor to periods, consulting the doctor, without assuming I was making it up. After an internal examination by our lady GP in rubber gloves, it eventually seemed to clear up of its own accord without treatment.

"You need a *balanced* diet, don't you," Mother would say. Wartime rationing had brought increased awareness of a healthy diet. My main meal of the day in term time was school dinner: gristly meat and two boiled veg. followed by cake and custard. In the evening at home, Mother would cook a snack, sit watching while I ate, often a one egg omelette or bowl of canned Heinz tomato soup, followed by a piece of apple at bedtime, in bed, "to clean your teeth", also cleaned by brushing with toothpaste. All bread was white. A feeling prevailed that easily digestible foods were better so children often suffered from constipation probably through not having enough roughage. Mother used to ask each day whether I'd "been". If not she'd produce senna tablets.

What we had for breakfast has now vanished from memory. Probably Puffed Wheat with full-fat milk and white sugar. Mother usually made afternoon tea, carried on a tray into the dining room to drink in front of the coal fire. Occasionally we had oranges, beginning to be available again after the war, slicing off the tops, pulping the inside with a knife, then tipping a spoonful or two of white sugar inside, sucking out the sweetened juice.

Dark Cupboards, Dusty Skeletons

At weekends after lunch I was allowed my favourite: two chocolate peppermint creams. Circular, these had delicious white peppermint cream inside a dark chocolate covering. The treat needed to last as long as possible: first I nibbled away the thin chocolate all round the edge leaving a chocolate sandwich, then used front teeth to detach the bottom chocolate layer from the cream, then licked the cream off the top chocolate layer with my tongue, lastly munching the top piece of thicker dark chocolate. Then all was gone.

Mother needed to rest a lot. She'd been lucky. Shortly before she developed tuberculosis a new drug cure had been introduced available free on the new National Health Service. Before this T.B. had been much feared: treatment had been an operation to cut out affected parts of the lung. People died. Being feared the disease became a taboo subject (as cancer did later) not talked about. Mother never said much about her illness this being something else not spoken of. But I remember her having to rest a lot while I roamed off on my own.

Unlike Auntie Janet, her father, my father, or myself, she didn't find her lack of energy frustrating. Resting, doing little, didn't leave her irritated, or wanting to be up and at it. Her ideal was always *not* having to do anything. Perhaps this had caused friction with my father, her mother and Janet successively, during the brief times she lived with them. She liked "the wealthy life" she said later, as portrayed in the '60s film *Dr Zhivago*.

*

Sex was shrouded in secrecy in a 'fifties upbringing, at any rate as far as the adults were concerned. They had to be protected. We found out what we needed to know from each other. Children talked to each other, rarely to adults. To adults it was an unmentionable and we were the innocents to be kept that way. Hence things that the adults should perhaps have known of: paedophiles in bushes, dirty stories in school, never reached their ears. They thought us safely cocooned in a world of innocence.

A cousin came to stay the night. We were both ten. After Mother had turned out the light and shut the bedroom door, in the safety and privacy of darkness, she suggested we take turns to tell each other all the rude stories we'd heard at school. Quite a repertoire. We entertained each other for some time until she told one which seemed to be going well, then fizzled out. I didn't see the point. It went something like this: the baker came to the door and the lady of the house said,

Settled but Only Temporarily: Roehampton 2

"Give me a bun."
He replied "I will if you take me upstairs."
This accomplished he laid down further conditions for the bun until the lady was lying on a bed without clothes on.
"And," said my cousin "you *know* what happened next!"
"No," I said blankly, "What?"
Whereupon she proceeded to tell me, very simply, perfectly accurately, and without a trace of embarrassment, the deep dark secret of the continuation of the human race. I have much to be grateful to her for. No one else within the family ever mentioned it. In fact her mother was upset because she thought I'd told *her* things she "didn't want her to know yet". Ill-feeling between our mothers over this persisted for years, I later discovered, without any of the adults really knowing who'd told what to whom. Now young children are properly informed in ways they can understand. There is no deep, dark secret.

*

A winter's Sunday lunch: this isn't the ideal family life of daydreams and if Mother decides to move again it will be "all change" anyway; nevertheless this moment in time crystallises like the ice particles outside the window.
The three of us sit down at the kitchen table for winter Sunday lunch: Auntie Gladys our landlady but more surrogate grandmother, my mother and my ten-year-old self. A grey, scrubbed wooden table – an incongruous foil for the sparkling silver cutlery and delicately floral plates – holds dishes of hot food. Opposite through steamy glass the back garden is deep in frost, thin-coned icicles hang from the upper window ledge. The grandfather clock in the hall, a black and white china pug proudly gracing its top, sings out midday with Westminster chimes. The black coke boiler in the kitchen corner, our main heat source, crackles softly drying clothes above. Auntie Gladys carves the joint as she always does, first drawing the knife across the long sword-like sharpener. She serves me some of the leaner slices. Passing the dishes we help ourselves to boiled cabbage mashed potatoes and gravy. Always a reluctant eater I partition my plate into sections and start on the meat. Mother looks worried, cross. Downward lines appear between her eyes. "Cross Lines", I call them. She explains for the umpteenth time that one should put a little of each food on the fork and eat it all together. That is what is *right*. But this is not

Dark Cupboards, Dusty Skeletons

school with its rigid coercions, so I continue with my strict divisions keeping the flavours separate. As I keep the sections of my life: home, school and imaginary family. Different people not encroaching on one another, those in my head more real than the others.

Mother is largely silent. Perhaps she is dreaming of having her own home, of the new council flat she applied for. An inspector came here, saw the four-bedroomed house with the name "Claremont" and no number, the polished furniture, the stained-glass window, didn't seem to think we were a priority.

She looks tired, doesn't eat much. She hates cold weather, fearful of what it might bring, suffering from a weak chest which gave way to tuberculosis not so long ago. Looking graceful in her delicate well-fitting clothes, softly-powdered face, dark hair permed in curls above her shoulders, when she speaks in her silver Oxford voice she doesn't reveal much.

After she left my father nearly ten years ago we spent a few weeks with my grandmother in Hindhead, lived with a friend in Potters Bar, then my aunt in Oxford. Now we are here in Roehampton with Auntie Gladys, whom Mother has managed to live with on and off since I was a baby. We have always come back between interludes elsewhere and boarding school. This house with Auntie Gladys, always here for us, is my home more than anywhere else.

Auntie's face is round, smile wrinkles lighten her eyes, her silvery hair is permed in frolicking waves, a pearl necklace bulges warmly beneath two chins. She jokes about the freeze-up, really hating having to carry buckets of cold water to flush the lavatory since the cistern froze. Cackling with laughter she says it is not "take up thy bed and walk" but "take up thy pail and walk". Well-versed as we are in the parable of Jesus healing the cripple, her joke brings relief both from the intense cold and a usually moribund depiction of Christianity.

Behind her I can see the dresser with rows of delicately patterned plates winking elegantly behind glass panels, part of the home she set up with her husband Jack. She often talks about Jack, how they'd married late and no children came along. Now Jack is dead and she has us, her 'family' sitting round the table. A surrogate grandmother. She knows she is too old to carry on here alone; if we move she will have to leave this house she

Settled but Only Temporarily: Roehampton 2

loves so much. Mother, desperate for her own home, talks about moving. Daringly assertive, I say:
"Why don't we just stay here? This is a nice house." Tailing off to finish lamely, "I think it's a nice house."
Mother falls silent. Auntie Gladys says "Ooh!" lets out a loud cackle of laughter, knows this isn't what Mother expected.

A tomboy in navy slacks and scarlet woollen polo neck, I'm not cold. On the corner of the draining board stand my poster paints, the only school prize ever which wasn't a book, presented for art and handicrafts. Little glass jars with screw lids and names I'd never heard of: vermilion, verdant green, ultramarine, yellow ochre, burnt sienna. I daydream about what I will paint, after lunch when the table is cleared and my friend arrives.

Our second course is bread-and-butter pudding – a good use of stale bread – polka-dotted with juicy black currants. Auntie picks up the glittering silver sugar dish with its dark blue glass bowl holding the fine white crystals. They fall through tiny holes in a special spoon to sprinkle across baked golden crusts. A layer of white, matching the frost outside. She passes the dish on to Mother; then it's my turn with the spoon. Trained from infancy that hard work comes before gratification and being extremely fond of currants, I carefully extract them one by one to pile at the side of my plate for a grand finalé. Then stoically tackle the character-building bit, pushing it down. Auntie Gladys cackles again with laughter; she finds this vastly amusing. Suddenly she makes a teasing dive with her spoon at my precious pile. Quickly I cover it protectively with my fork making a suitably indignant face. We carry on eating watching each other out of the corners of our eyes. She makes another dive – but I'm ready. It's a game we play whenever there's bread-and-butter pudding, until finally I scoop up all the glossy black currants into one delicious mouthful.

So here we sit finishing our Sunday meal, come together to pursue our different dreams of missed family life with varying degrees of satisfaction. Mother may be unhappy, decide to move when opportunity knocks – I will have to accept it as I have always done – but for the moment Auntie Gladys replaces the grandmother we rarely see and her house is the most permanent home I've known.

Dark Cupboards, Dusty Skeletons

Mother clears the dishes; Auntie Gladys leaves the table up to wash up. The grandfather clock chimes the half-hour, singing through our lives as it has always done, marking the passing of this moment of eternity; the china Pug smiles with oriental inscrutability; the solid black coke boiler crackles teasingly; its black cylindrical chimney vanishing into the wall takes the smoke I know not where. Neither do I care.

*

Auntie
Gladys had a terrific
sense of humour; the only adult
I regularly heard laugh
she always saw the
funny side.

He
looks
a little ugly
but I grew up with
this inscrutable oriental
pug sitting atop the
grandfather clock
in Auntie Gladys's hall.
If he should ever get broken
he might be one of a few
precious objects
taken to The
Repair
Shop !

Settled but Only Temporarily: Roehampton 2

Nothing was ever wasted.
"I hate waste," Mother would say. It was rare for anything to be turned out. I learned early:
"Save the pennies and the pounds will look after themselves,"
"Waste not, want not!"
She earned two pounds ten shillings a week as part-time medical secretary at Queen Mary's Hospital, the artificial limb centre in Roehampton. Auntie Gladys bought coke for the boiler, our weekend meat joint for three, paid the phone bill. Wartime domestic economies continued throughout the 'fifties. I would be given a quarter of an apple, peeled, to eat in bed; Mother would eat the peelings. When older I took pride in eating whole apples including the cores. Apples were usually the only fruit: we hardly ever had salad items, stringy outside leaves of cabbage were boiled, not taken off and thrown out, runner beans grown in the garden might be old and stringy. Pea pods, potato and carrot peelings *were* thrown out. Mrs Chaloner next door saved tealeaves and any organic waste to put on the compost heap for growing vegetables. Auntie Gladys was afraid this might encourage rats. I never saw any.
Socks would be darned, holes dubbed 'spuds' at school: a pink-white heel seen through an oval hole looked like a potato. Knitted woollen gloves would also get holes in winter leaving some fingers comfortably warm while others froze.
Mother had a small zipped navy-blue bag with *Muddles and Mendables* written on, for an odd button collection to replace those which fell off and got lost, hooks and eyes, poppers (press studs), scraps of wool for darning or mending holes in jersey elbows, knicker elastic and safety pins, spare suspenders for her suspender belt. Too much cotton cut off a reel would be saved and wound back on again, but I was always being nagged to cut off only exactly what I needed. A large brown cardboard "piece box" had scraps of fabric saved for repairs and patching. I was taught sayings designed to encourage thrift:
"A stitch in time, Saves nine."
Better to mend holes and tears quickly before they got bigger.
"See a pin and pick it up, And all the day you'll have good luck."
Pick up small dropped objects and stow them safely away for future use.
I don't remember any patches on children's clothes in school. Children's knees would put wear on garments so ours went bare all year round. Boys

Dark Cupboards, Dusty Skeletons

wore short grey trousers with buttoned flies. (When zipped flies arrived jokes multiplied about how zips might more easily slip down revealing all.) When my feet grew, Mother cut the toes out of one pair of brown leather sandals to give them an extra lease of life. Shoes cost.

Toothpaste had to be eeked out by squeezing from the bottom of the soft metal tube, then rolling up the tube tightly to extract every last smear. Mother bought the smallest tubes – she said she felt one used less when squeezing from a smaller one. A large tube or packet presumably might give a too-carefree feeling of abundance.

My husband's family didn't have either lavatory paper (they used old newspapers) or toothpaste. I was never taught to use lavatory paper and didn't regularly until my teens after we'd moved to Letchworth when Mother commented – disapprovingly – that lavatory paper was disappearing rather rapidly.

Scraps of ordinary white paper would be carefully stored, I used them for drawing or painting; crackly tissue paper was smoothed, folded and kept for wrapping; brown paper would be reused for parcels tied with recycled odd lengths of string knotted together. Mother watched me closely using Selotape, telling me not to cut off a fraction more than I needed; rolls of Selotape had to last. Glue was bought to mend a brown china teapot lid, broken when dropped. But post-war glue not being very effective the repair didn't stand up to steam and heat. Broken things were often hoarded because of a reluctance to throw them out, a hope they might one day somehow come in useful.

I was shown how to take photos with great care, never to waste a frame, not to open the back of the camera and let light in which would destroy the pictures on light-sensitive paper. Films for her Box Brownie camera didn't come cheap in our household.

A sofa and chair Mother owned she'd bought second-hand through hand-written notices in shop windows placed by people who had something they wanted to sell.

"We managed, didn't we?" Mother would say later. "I didn't want to worry you about money."

Even when she had money – after her mother had died leaving plenty and I'd left home – she couldn't buy anything not absolutely necessary. She'd developed a phobia of spending money, a lasting fear of being penniless, having nothing.

Settled but Only Temporarily: Roehampton 2

*

Clothes bought for me produced conflicts between tomboyish feminism and ladylike femininity. One winter I had a pair of dark navy slacks, ordinary ankle-length trousers. They were fine, not "pretty pretty", or over-feminine. My first pair of navy denim jeans was bought when I was ten or eleven. No one wore them much before. My chief memory of these is that when first washed they had so much starch in that when dry again they stood up on their own when leaned against Auntie Gladys's polished walnut wardrobe in Mother's bedroom.

One summer she produced a turquoise, leaf green and white floral sunsuit chosen and bought for me without consultation: a dress with thin, ribbon-width, shoulder straps and a little matching jacket of the same material, collarless with short sleeves, the lower edge finishing just below the bust (if I'd had one). This, she said, was called a bolero. The outfit was probably very pretty but I hated it. It made me feel silly, too limply feminine. They must have been fashionable that summer, Vanessa also had one and my chief memory is of her recently returned father draping our two boleros over his largely bald head and dancing up and down on their lawn to make us laugh. Briefly they seemed an advantage.

I'd developed a hammer toe twisting it at boarding school during endless hours lying awake in bed. Mother was very concerned that I should have shoes that fitted my growing feet properly. She took me to a shoe shop in Putney with an x-ray machine. No one worried about radiation. Wearing brand new, as yet unpurchased, shoes I stood on a tall pedestal, put my feet into the slot below, and looked down through the viewer. Mother and the assistant stood each side looking through side viewers. There were my feet, illuminated, vivid green, transparent. I could see the outline of the Clark's shoe, the outline of my toes inside and, most fascinating, the bones inside my feet. Mother and the shop assistant peering into the viewers, discussed whether my growing feet would have enough room.

Then I would be told to walk up and down, asked whether the heels slipped, whether the shoes were comfortable. Difficult to say as new, hard leather shoes often rubbed causing sores until worked in, but important to get right as shoes were a major financial outlay. Different half-sizes might be tried, viewed under the x-ray machine. Finally a decision would be reached, the shoes chosen packed carefully into a shoebox by the assistant. We would get the bus back to Roehampton carrying a bag of brand new

Dark Cupboards, Dusty Skeletons

shoes not allowed to be worn home, to be kept looking new for the time being. I'd be dying to try them on again once we got indoors.

*

The first time I ever cut my own hair, aged about ten, was the first time I ever felt happy with the way it looked. Until then Mother had taken me to the Village hairdresser, next to the fishmonger's, where I'd sit watching the mirror while Mother gave instructions: straight all round just below the ears, a parting on the left, a Kirby grip holding the longer side swept back across the forehead in a hard line. The grip, always falling out and getting lost, had caused much anguish at boarding school, getting me into trouble.
I wanted my hair short like a boy's.
"Well," said the young lady hairdresser to my mother, "why not let her have it short if that's what she wants."
An easy-going type with children of her own she clearly didn't see a problem with this.
"Oh NO!" came the shocked reply with the inevitable style repeated.
Towards the end of junior school, on a day when Mother wasn't around, I found a large pair of scissors and managed the job myself: a shaped bob that didn't need a Kirby grip to stop hair flopping over my face. Surprisingly Mother took it in her stride and didn't react. Perhaps when presented with the *fait accompli* she thought it looked OK after all. I kept that style though teenage years.

*

The Chaloner's lived next door at Dover Cottage: Mr and Mrs Chaloner and their two younger adult children Joan and Bill. The eldest, John, was married and living in Dulwich with two children, Jane and Stephen. It was a lucky chance for me they were neighbours; they tried to help with problems they saw and understood, provided activities to broaden horizons. Having them so close raised our quality of life. I loved going round to their house, being with them, although this didn't happen often. Mrs Chaloner was round and comfortable, with short grey wavy hair, wearing long loose-fitting skirts and cardigans; her grown up children called her "Mother Beadle". She wrote books on bringing up children under the name Len Chaloner (short for Leonora). Mother told me it was easier to get published if they thought you were a man (Leonard). Some of her work was based on that of the child psychoanalyst Melanie Klein's *Love*, Guilt and Reparation. The main memory I have of Mr Chaloner is that he liked to sunbathe

Settled but Only Temporarily: Roehampton 2

without clothes in a secluded spot between a bush and the fence at the bottom of their garden. If I drifted near, I would be called away in uncharacteristically stern tones. An unconventional rather bohemian family, I believe he was also a writer.

Two tall poplar trees graced their front garden with its small neatly cut lawn hidden from the pavement by thick hedges. We had more contact with them than any other neighbours, although all were pleasant with no unkind gossip or enmity I was aware of. The Chaloner's did things differently to us: calling their main room the "living room" rather than the "sitting room", a room going right through from front to back where door and steps led down to the garden. They ate their main meal in the evening instead of midday as we did.

Mrs Chaloner grew large marrows, cooked her own garden produce for her family. She told Mother the only time she could spend alone was in the bath, perhaps opening Mother's eyes to the realities of family life, Mother never being quick to spot her own advantages. She also told Mother how difficult it was explaining it to Joan when Joan's twin sister had died aged three. She surprised me one day by mentioning that her own mother produced any of her uneaten plates of food at the next meal, to be finished cold. "I hated it," she smiled. I couldn't imagine her treating her own children like that. She must have come a long way from her own childhood experiences.

She suggested activities: help with my home museum, I still have the Chaloner's contributions for this – real fossils, a small animal skull; she came up with the idea of dressing up and taking photos; always remembered my birthday usually giving books – *Things To Do*, and *George Cansdale's Zoo Book*; passed on magazines with ideas for things to do; introduced me to the Wingate family of four children on the corner of Highdown Road.

Mrs Chaloner also gave me a children's novel: *Mimff in Charge*, about a brother and sister who'd done something wrong (took a small rowing boat out to sea without asking) and as a punishment their parents went away for a long time. Looking back it's difficult not to wonder if this gift had a deeper significance, an attempt to bring into the open painful feelings she understood existed about my own early separations, to trigger discussion as to why I'd been sent to boarding school? My feeling that I must be innately bad? But I never liked the book much. Neither Mother nor I did talk.

Dark Cupboards, Dusty Skeletons

Mrs Chaloner often went to Dulwich to see her elder son John, and help with grandchildren, Jane and Stephen. John Chaloner wrote and illustrated children's books under the pen name Jon Chalon: *The Green Bus* had protagonists Jane and Stephen. Once, when they visited, I was invited round. We played charades. A black and white photo of the three of us in their front garden showed Jane and Stephen, comfortably dressed in old clothes, one posing in a handstand, the other about to bat a ball. I'm standing stiffly self-conscious in the blue-and-white flowery bolero dress Mother insisted on for the invitation. She later threw out a copy of the photo she'd been given, the difference all too obvious between their robust confidence and my painful shyness. When she drove Jane and Stephen home Mrs Chaloner took me along with them for the ride. They taught me the game of waving to other drivers to see if they would wave back. Some did. It was great fun.

Mrs Chaloner's daughter, Joan, studied, or worked, as a child psychologist and had a boyfriend, also John, who, Mother told me, didn't want children; a problem if they married. I think it was Joan who gave me the fossil ammonites and animal skull to add to my home 'museum'. She told me how to make papier-maché, soaking shreds of torn newspaper in water mixed with a little flour to make a sticky paste, shaping the sodden paper carefully round a bowl, leaving it for several days to dry out thoroughly, then decorating with water paints and finishing with a clear waterproof varnish bought from Addison's ironmonger's in the Village. She showed me a comical glove puppet she'd made herself with paper-maché head, "Simon the Cook", lively face beautifully shaped and painted, body of blue and white striped cloth. I launched into modelling an array of rather less expert heads for glove puppets.

Joan once took me into Putney to buy wood, metal brackets and screws for stilts, which she and John made. I spent many happy hours learning to balance, tottering about on Auntie Gladys's concrete driveway. She produced an old mattress, taught me backwards and forwards somersaults. I'd hang around chatting while she worked on her tiny black car. When the 'Big End' went the family seemed very depressed about what this might cost to repair. (The bottom end of a connecting rod that engages with the crankshaft).

I think it was Joan who made me my doll's house from an orange box (you got these free from greengrocers' in the Village; people used them for

Settled but Only Temporarily: Roehampton 2

firewood). Sandpapered and painted with green oil paint outside so no longer rough and splintery, it had real wallpaper inside, a tiny green door that opened and shut, scraps of genuine carpet on the floor (the luxury of it; my bedroom had linoleum!) and tiny sofa and chairs made from blocks of wood. I lost no time in sitting some of my tiniest dolls in them. I lent her the 'books' I'd written. To my delight, one day she turned out her room, gave me "Simon" the cook puppet with his enormous nose.

Mrs Chaloner's younger son, Bill, had worked at the Natural History museum, been on fossil-hunting expeditions. I found packages of fossils wrapped in newspaper in the cupboard under their stairs. One evening Bill, Joan and two visiting adult friends of theirs said we were going to play "Sardines". They explained this was a variation of hide-and-seek where, when you'd discovered someone hiding, instead of announcing this, you squeezed in and hid with them. Joan and I discovered Bill under their parent's big double bed. To a child unused to fun play with grown ups, lying squashed together in darkness, talking in whispers, seemed great fun.

Bill, in his early twenties, having been to Kingston Grammar School and university, now received call up papers for compulsory National Service. A noticeable atmosphere of dejection pervaded the family, obvious even to my ten-year-old self. Before joining up he had to learn to communicate via Morse code, each letter of the alphabet being sounded out by its own group of short dots and long dashes. Using two small buzzer machines connected by long wires Joan helped him practice sitting on opposite sides of their front garden lawn, buzzing rapid messages along the wires. I lay on my tummy on the grass beside her listening to the mysterious series of long and short beeps, intrigued.

I remember the day Bill left for the army, looking out of my bedroom window above the porch watching him get into the black car sent to fetch him, in smarter clothes than he usually wore: brown jacket and felt trilby. I'd never seen him in a hat before. Taking it off he threw it irritably onto the back seat before getting in behind the driver, looking thoroughly fed up. I hoped he'd look up and see me so I could wave goodbye, but he didn't.

Enthused by the sessions of Morse code, I set about learning the dots and dashes for each letter of the alphabet. Then wrote to "Gunner Chaloner" in Morse, underlining complete words so he'd know where they started and ended. He replied, also in Morse, but said he'd found my letter hard to

Dark Cupboards, Dusty Skeletons

understand! I must have got muddled. Some years later Bill met his fiancée getting engaged during a three-day trip by ship coming back from America. "Very quick," observed Mother.

*

At some point, maybe during my last year in junior school, the Chaloner's moved to a flat in Sheen, vanishing from my life – not such an unmitigated disaster as non-identical twins, Kenneth and Alec, about my age, moved in next door with their mother, stepfather, baby half-brother Christopher and "Nanny", a lovely young girl ever so fond of the twins, the focus of her life. She told me how much she missed them when they were away at prep boarding school in term time. During school holidays they sometimes stayed on her parents' farm. It was Nanny who mostly looked after them, reigning in the kitchen. I never saw much of their parents who worked, I believe, in a pub or nightclub somewhere in central London. Unlike Andrew's parents, they never seemed worried that being with a girl might impair masculinity: when the twins were home we spent a lot of time playing. This expanded to include things previously not allowed. We climbed the huge tree in the centre of their back garden, climbed over the garden fence into one another's gardens, then from fence top to their garage roof, from garage roof to brick parapet under an upstairs bedroom window, then into the house through the window. No one seemed to mind. We swatted flies with our hands, not easy, you had to be quick. Kenneth proudly said staying on Nanny's farm he'd once swatted sixty in a single day. They didn't have television either; the more middle class families I knew still seemed to be shunning it. Occasionally we'd be helped organise an indoor activity: I remember the three of us sitting round their dining room table with our stamp collections, swopping duplicates, sticking them into appropriate album pages for different countries. And they had a brown and white guinea-pig named Oscar to play with.

We could all swim; one warm sunny day their stepfather took us all to Roehampton Open-Air Swimming Pool. Alec carried several bags, ran a longer ways round, trying to build up his muscles to cope with a school bully.

One Easter holidays I couldn't play with the twins as they had chicken pox and were being kept in isolation in their bedroom. With else nothing to do I wandered into their front garden. An upstairs window opened, they leaned out to show off their spots.

Settled but Only Temporarily: Roehampton 2

"I want to catch chicken pox," I confided. (I can't now, for the life of me, think why!)
They munched happily huge chocolate Easter eggs wrapped in shiny paper. Generously, Kenneth threw a small piece down. More followed. Then a larger piece. Picking these up I also munched happily.
"You'll definitely catch chicken pox now," Kenneth said encouragingly.
I never did.
I remember seeing Andrew during my last year in junior school so our friendship must have lasted at least eighteen months after he left the Church school. Then faded. Perhaps he didn't want to play with girls anymore, or I spent all my time playing with Kenneth and Alec, or a mixture of both. Mother said Andrew once called. She'd told him I was with the boys next door. He didn't call again. We lost touch.

*

Adults I hardly knew sometimes asked,
"Do you like school?"
During that last year at the Church School, for the first time I could genuinely say,
"Yes!"
I was beginning to feel really settled, put down roots, grow in confidence. After all those early changes and disruptions the end of the fourth year juniors' would turn out to be a disastrous time for another change of school.

*

Over page:
Roehampton Church School:
top fourth year junior class, in the lower school
playground with part of the Common behind we were allowed
to play on. I'm in the third row up, third from right, not ready for the camera, not
smiling! Christine is in the same row sixth from right, between Susan Ford
with pigtails and Josephine Shead with glasses.
Mr Ayling is top left.
Summer 1956.

Dark Cupboards, Dusty Skeletons

Settled but Only Temporarily: Roehampton 2

Individual school portrait, fourth year junior class, Summer 1956.

I don't remember my place in class in the top year – nothing spectacular – but somewhere within the top ten or half-dozen. For my prize, "For English", I chose a children's novel *Under Black Banner* by Geoffrey Trease, an author I already knew and liked. Christine was also one of the lucky ones who won a prize, as in Mrs Clack's class.

Rodney Wilson and Ann Coysh won the two prizes for best all-round performance. No one knew before prize giving who these would be awarded to. (I knew it wouldn't be me!) As John Faulkner and Josephine Shead were academically top everyone assumed it would be them. But it wasn't. Mr Whitaker explained to parents gathered to watch the ceremony: "That accounts for Ann's look of surprise and Rodney's white face."

Both favourites of Mr Ayling's I felt he must have had a say in this allocation.

*

During the last few days of term Christine and I knocked on the door of Mr Whitaker's office with our autograph books. He wrote in her book first, then took mine thinking for a minute before drawing a caricature portrait of

Dark Cupboards, Dusty Skeletons

himself with a block of ice on his head and straws sticking out of his hair. Underneath he wrote:
"End of term always makes me feel as old as Methuselah with straws in my hair."
Comparing with Christine afterwards I discovered he'd put something different in her book – a different picture with different caption, each autograph personalised. I wish I'd kept the autograph book but Mother tended to announce,
"You don't want this, do you?"
At some stage it disappeared.
During those last few days Christine also asked Mr Whitaker and Mr Ayling to pose for a photo. (I wouldn't have dared!) She gave me a copy.

Mr Ayling and Mr Whitaker, headmaster, (right) outside the door to the fourth year top juniors' classroom, across the playground in the upper part of Roehampton Church School at the top of the hill in Ponsonby Road.

Taken by my best friend Christine, Summer, 1956.

On the last day of term at the end of school Christine and I hung around in the playground, just the two of us alone, everyone else had gone. Finally she said tensely,

Settled but Only Temporarily: Roehampton 2

"Well, I'm going home then," and left quickly to catch the number 30 bus into Putney. I hovered for a few minutes on my own in the now totally deserted playground, then went through the gate in the iron railings for the last time to start the half-mile walk home. Somehow I sensed things would never be the same again. They weren't. I never really settled into secondary school.

Christine and I didn't see much of each other after that, separated by different schools. Although Christine passed the eleven-plus she went to one of the new comprehensive schools in Putney that took children of all abilities, an attempt to do away with the negative feelings of failure of those who didn't win grammar school places.

*

When you're a child who actually owns a house isn't important – Auntie Gladys and I both thought of her house as home. We had to ask Auntie Gladys if I wanted a pet; she always agreed (except over mice). But mother wasn't happy and I was always aware I might be uprooted at any time. New tower blocks of flats were going up in Roehampton. Mother applied for one. A housing officer visited but clearly felt we weren't in an underprivileged situation with rooms in a four-bedroom detached house. Others had greater need of rehousing from East End slums.

Social life in Roehampton, built up over four years, fell apart. Auntie Gladys became ill, spending some weeks in hospital with skin cancer; she'd been a fairly heavy smoker.

The Chaloner's down-sized to a small flat in Sheen, Mrs Chaloner having first introduced me to the Wingate family with four children on the corner of Highdown Road. Mother and I visited her once or twice, by bus.

My godfather, The Reverend Christopher Hamel Cooke, had long since been transferred to Lichfield Cathedral.

Ann Robilliard had moved on to a central school the year before; our lives diverged.

Andrew had been at boarding school for two years. Mother tried to alleviate this break by once asking his younger brother, Nigel, to tea.

The twins next-door, Kenneth and Alec, were away at boarding school during term time, often staying on their Nanny's parents' farm in the holidays.

The Bradley's, Daphne, Ann and Ivan, had moved to Sanderstead soon after we'd moved permanently back to Roehampton. We made occasional visits

Dark Cupboards, Dusty Skeletons

by train but I'd never really got on well with Ann – it was our mothers who were friends.

Christine went to a new comprehensive school in Putney. The others in my year at the Church School dispersed to a multitude of secondary schools.

Vanessa was sent to a convent boarding school when she was ten, after her father returned to live with them. I remember him sitting in their kitchen marking her teddy bear by inking her school number on its leather-soled foot.

Auntie Kay, at forty-five, had retired from her job as a clerk in the Bank of England and moved from London to a flat in Oxford with Auntie Janet.

I drifted away from Holy Trinity Church after just a couple confirmation classes.

Grandmother, having become chronically ill and bedridden, was moved to Oxford, her lovely little house at Hindhead sold.

Mother, disappointed I hadn't won a scholarship, seemed to be suffering from burnout. As I was now twelve she thought of me as grown up – off her hands.

I still knew virtually nothing about my father, and apart from Vanessa and my two maiden aunts, had had little contact with other relatives: Grannie, the Aunts at Worthing, Thomson cousins in London.

But I was used to separations, had always accepted them, wasn't consciously aware of missing anyone. At this stage I still had my dream world to retreat into for emotional sustenance.

*

My generation tended to be thrown into new, strange situations: schools, holiday homes, clubs, where we knew no one but were expected to fit in. If you didn't it was your fault, there was something wrong with you – you were "spoilt", "shy", "proud", "wet" – and so on. But I did settle on unaccompanied holidays to Hatchgate Farm ("The Farm") at Cuckfield near Haywards Heath.

Staying on a *real* farm sounded romantic when Mother suggested it. She made arrangements for me to stay by post and telephone without visiting herself. I'd always liked animals, being outside, nature study, was keen to go. Mr and Mrs Seagrove usually took about half-a-dozen children, aged five to sixteen, so no shortage of company. Looking back this was probably the first time Mother put me on a train on my own to be met by strangers. Had she seen The Farm advertised in *The Church Times* as with Pathfinder

Settled but Only Temporarily: Roehampton 2

Holidays? The owners, an elderly couple, ran a small traditional dairy and livestock farm with poultry, dairy cows, apple orchards, soft fruit and some arable, I think largely hayfields, to feed the animals.

Hatchgate Farm, Cuckfield. 27th Aug. 1956
Dear Mum,
I arrived safely at the station and met Mr and Mrs [Seagrove] in the car.
The farm is very nice. There are several cows and chickens, turkeys, geese, ducks and guinea-fowl. Guinea-fowl are grey and shaped rather like grouse, only bigger. Also there are young turkeys.
Indoors we have six cats Peter, Winkle, Tinker and a kitten which are all black, and a tabby called John as well & Mick, who is a mixture I think of pershion [sic] and something else.
I have just got to go and feed the turkeys now with Leslie [another girl, a paying guest my age], but I will tell you more later.
Back again.
Then last but not least there is Sally who is a brown and white spaniel. She is about sixteen years old. Joyce, the land girl told me she was fifteen and Leslie says she is sixteen and Mrs Seagrove says she is seventeen.
Also there are two bulls called Hammond and Stegoras or some name like that. One cow is called Tin Hut because it used to live in one.
They all have names which are written in a book (Joyce the land girl know which is which) and the gallons of milk that a cow has given is put beside its name.
I think I forgot to tell you about the two livelyest [sic] occupants of the house. They are Susie and Jackie [Josie], two little cairn pups, which are five months old. They are very frisky and I had to take them for a short walk before breakfast.
I sleep in a very nice bed in a room with Brenda. She is a little girl from Trinidad, and she is black.
Give my love to Scamp. Love Elizabeth.

At some point sleeping arrangements changed, Lesley and I put together. Did Mother ask for this after my letter home? Brenda, easy going, less assertive than Lesley, must have been my first ethnic minority close friend. We ate meals sitting round a big wooden table in the farm kitchen with the Seagrove's and Joyce the land girl. Breakfast was the usual ubiquitous cornflakes but with a dollop of thick solid cream instead of milk. Rather dry, but the cream could be eeked out to moisten each spoonful of

Dark Cupboards, Dusty Skeletons

cornflake. Toast followed. As far as memory goes the main meal of the day was the standard meat and two veg. followed by pudding. If I wanted more water I could get up and fill my glass from the tap. Mrs Seagrove seemed slightly worried but said she thought water wouldn't do any harm. Upstairs, two to a bedroom, we whispered together about rumours of ghosts in the ancient farmhouse – had an earlier farmer hanged himself as Joyce told us? Downstairs in a small sitting room ensconced in armchairs we watched the tiny black and white television. The Farm became a special place: the timeless, mature old farmhouse, redbrick walls wrapped in creeper, insinuated itself into my dream world inhabited by storybook characters. Even the reality was almost a dream: soft eyes of contented milky cows; calves in the barn fed with babies bottles; brown and white feathery chickens which escaped and wandered necessitating hunts at dusk to save them from the fox, grabbing in fading light at a white blur under a hedge, hands closing on silky indignant feathers; grey speckled guinea fowl, black gobbling turkeys with scarlet combs; comfortable round brown ducks who quacked loudly; feral kittens living in the huge hay barn – we tamed a couple, capturing, cuddling, getting them used to being handled; Sally, the old brown and white spaniel sleeping in the sun outside the farmhouse door; the huge bull with a ring through his nose kept apart; the farmhouse door in two halves, lower shut, top open, in traditional, picturesque country style.

No horses: Mr Seagrove drove a grey van to deliver on his milk round. We stood in a cluster in the milking shed chatting to Joyce as she fitted milking tubes over cows' udders, while telling delicious ghost stories of the old farmhouse.

We picked gooseberries and redcurrants for the kitchen; mowed the front lawn with a push mower – Mrs Seagrove wanted all the daisies gone to create a smooth, totally green surface; collected dead branches for firewood from the small "plantation"; fed poultry and scraped floors of small wooden chicken houses caked with hard, dried dung; hunted for new-laid eggs; fetched the herd of cows from the fields for milking, learnt their names, gave them handfuls of cow 'cake' while being milked, took them back to the fields after milking and shut the gate; plucked newly-dead pink, fleshy chickens for dinner; brushed old Sally ("I knew she'd let you," Mrs Seagrove said to me); took the younger dogs for rambles; watched men build a haystack; minded younger children taking them to services in the

Settled but Only Temporarily: Roehampton 2

local parish church or playgrounds; when asked I regularly heard a younger boy read and wrote to his mother about his progress; the Seagrove's once took us to an auction of household antiques in Haywards Heath, Mrs Seagrove bought shining, golden horse brasses to hang among many other intriguing knick-knacks; in the evenings we sat in the farmhouse kitchen watching Joyce churn milk to make cream, churning on and on, trying ourselves, discovering how much strength it took to work the handle; heard stories about a small wooden hut which had housed three prisoners-of-war who'd worked on the farm; squelched in wellies through thick mud churned by tractor tyres and cows' hooves, squelching, squelching, all day long.

Joyce had been 'adopted' by the Seagrove's aged about fourteen – school leaving age – from a children's home to help with the farm work. She worked long hours doing much of the hard grind, the Seagrove's being elderly. We were told Mrs Seagrove had bought her some lovely dresses but only ever saw her in her rough, stained, hard-wearing working outfit of matching mid-brown top and trousers, and the inevitable wellies. Her reddish golden hair was cut fairly short. She gave the impression of being slightly ESN which may have been due to her children's home upbringing as she coped amazingly competently with farm work.

Milking took place twice a day, mechanically unless the machine broke down in which case the cows had to be hand milked by squeezing their udders, taking forever. Joyce showed us how, when fetching cows to be milked, to move a cow on if it strayed to munch a tasty patch by the side of the track, grabbing hold of its tail and hauling. The cows didn't seem to mind, sometimes got the message and obliged. Mostly they just contentedly followed one another. Joyce had a favourite cow she'd made a pet of as a calf, also named "Joyce" after her. Joyce the cow could be more temperamental than the other cows, knew she was onto a good thing being more assertive, less docile, might have been termed 'spoilt'. If there was one cow who decided she didn't want to come through the gate to be milked it was likely to be Joyce, needing to be coaxed, cajoled, pulled. Farm girl Joyce knew all the herd's individual quirks.

Among her many other chores Joyce also fed the feral cats putting down a single, large, round plate of food outside the farmhouse door in the sunshine, calling,

"Woooss! Woooss! Woooss!"

Dark Cupboards, Dusty Skeletons

A moment before not a cat would be in sight; then they'd suddenly materialise from every direction forming a circle round the plate, heads down in munching concentration, tails twitching happily.

We spent a lot of time around the farm with cheerful good-natured Joyce, helping, watching, chatting – feeling they worked her too hard. She didn't have the know-how to get herself out of the situation, find another job. She told us the postman had said he'd help. With hindsight the elderly Seagrove's seemed struggling to cope. Joyce, being young, strong, fit and very healthy, did much of the work to keep the farm going.

Mrs Seagrove took a shine to me, staying was fun and I returned at least three summers through to early teens. The old mellowed farmhouse with its ivy-wrapped walls became the venue for a revitalised version of my dream world albeit with different characters, essences of personalities captured from storybooks and radio plays. An emotionally sustaining world inside my own head, inseparable.

Left to right:
Brenda holding Susie,
Lesley holding Josie, myself with Old Sally below,
and Joyce the land girl holding a duck, or perhaps two?
Behind: The back of Hatchgate farmhouse
covered in creeper.
Summer, 1956.

Settled but Only Temporarily: Roehampton 2

Mother sat on a park bench in the sunshine chatting to her cousin Audrey while I ran around with Vanessa, both about eleven. All seemed to be going well: we were playing some game, running across the grass, laughing. I noticed the mums watching us closely as we played – looking serious, not in the same light-hearted mood as we were. Later, back at their house after I'd said something trivial – long forgotten – Audrey said suddenly,

"Oh! She *is* like you, Ruth!"

Mother, simpering slightly, with a touch of false modesty, replied,

"Oh! Poor *thing!*"

That was all, the conversation not taken further, not in front of us at any rate. Of course, with my light-coloured brown hair and slightly more sturdy physique, I wasn't like the delicate-boned, dark-haired Thomson's rumoured by Auntie Kay, probably incorrectly, to be Jewish in origin. I was like the father Mother had left – the father I wouldn't have recognised if we'd passed in the street. In the Thomson family view of the cosmos one had to be brilliant, charming, beautiful – and healthy – to be acceptable, even to one's own family.

Strong belief in the influence of genetics rather than environment – nature versus nurture – had existed since the early 19th century and used by the Nazis as justification for their actions during the war trying create a master race. In 1953 Watson, Crick and others published several landmark papers on DNA. The British weren't prepared to go to the same lengths as the Nazis but likewise maintained a strong belief in the influence of genetics. Perhaps mine, inherited from father, might not be up to scratch, to Thomson standards?

*

Despite a good year at school I still felt frightened of adults and authority, being shy, unassertive, somewhat blindly obedient, but lacking conscience: control had been based on fear.

"Something should have been done about my shyness," I told Mother: still in some ways 'stuck' as a four-year-old waiting to go home, untrusting, closed up when upset, unable to cry, or confide. Crying was shameful. Used to Mother not being there, not talking much, having feelings denied, angrily told,

Dark Cupboards, Dusty Skeletons

"You've *forgotten* that!" leaving me unable recognise intensely controlled feelings. She 'imagined' how I felt and told *me*. Assertively. Her own way of dealing with feelings.

Although we spent a lot of time together, at a deeper level I think settling back with Mother after boarding school never really happened. I stayed detached, dependent on fantasy, an inseparable world taken everywhere, with disastrous consequences when it broke down as it inevitably did.

I still had hammer toes from twisting them during long hours of lying awake in bed at boarding school, still bit tiny pieces of skin off the inside of my lips. Trained to go to church, I briefly became piously artificial. Men still seemed remote, idealised, terrifying, although lack of knowledge also meant lack of disillusionment.

But the relative stability of four years at Roehampton had brought benefits: academic achievement led to being wanted by secondary schools; friendships with other children although temporary, helped; mind-stretching activities at home developed knowledge; there'd been no sibling rivalry to create stress. Being able to go anywhere, superficially fit in and adapt, broadened experience.

Mother, discontented, wasn't disposed to count her blessings. Never energetic, hating domesticity yet longing for 'normal' family life, she wanted this without the inevitable chores, continually planning changes: convinced life would be better if she owned her own home – the glass forever half empty.

Universal education has stretched people's minds enormously but many of my generation felt emotionally damaged by school, either by teachers, or other children, or both. I was unlucky to have spent three years with Miss Gisborne, much luckier to have four years at the Church School.

Disaster and Collapse: Putney High School

The summer after leaving Roehampton Church School I holidayed at Hatchgate Farm, Cuckfield, in limbo again between two worlds. Family disruption had made school too important, gravitated towards to meet needs it had never been designed to fill.

The country bus from Haywards Heath stopped by the Wheatsheaf Inn. On the opposite side of the road an unmade up lane led down to Hatchgate Farm tucked away out of sight, a lovely old mellow-looking house covered in creeper surrounded by coppices, fields, vegetable patch, turkey and chicken runs, neatly cut lawns, old barns, haystacks and milking shed. The elderly owners Mr and Mrs Seagrove depended on Joyce, a live-in farmhand. Always happy to be there I got on well with other girls staying, but of course, when the holiday ended never saw or heard of any them again. Being used to friendships dissolving, taking for granted that that was the way things were, I didn't expect to see them again.

*

The first day of the autumn term, aged eleven, I put on my new Putney High School deep purple uniform (hating the colour) and walked up Dover Park Drive to wait for a number 85 red double decker bus along the road bordering the Common, which would turn down Putney Hill past my new school. An older girl from the Church School stopped to tell me this was a waste of time as the bus would be full, but that first day I persevered and waited, don't recall being late.

Brought up on new situations I don't remember feeling nervous. Putney High, run by the Girls' Public Day School Trust had a high academic standard, was the sort of school that prepared girls for Oxbridge where Mother expected me to go as she had done, the type of school she'd grown up in – highly academic and all-female – felt familiar and comfortable with, a world she knew. I hadn't had any input here, just gone along with

her decision. Putney High being probably the nearest school of high academic standard within easy travelling distance meant a short bus ride or longish walk – further than the Church School.
I've no memory of that first day at Putney High School. Each day a cooked dinner was provided in the school hall at long rectangular tables each seating about nine girls with a teacher at the head. Like home life this was yet another totally female environment of mostly unmarried women teachers, spinsters, my form teacher, Miss Lawson, being young – with hindsight obviously inexperienced – and somewhat plump with 'grand piano' legs. Different subjects were taught by specialist teachers who moved from class to class while pupils stayed put, except for lessons needing special facilities: physical education, art, music and science. I didn't relate to any of the teachers. They hardly knew us.
I couldn't cope with the soulless, humourless, female atmosphere, seeming so lacking in life and individuality, in some ways tending to mimic home atmosphere. Routine and formality were everything; the building seemed impersonal, barrack-like. A harsh electric bell would go off suddenly at intervals to mark the beginning and end of each lesson, jangling nerves. My classroom had four rigid rows of individual wooden desks with sloping tops, places were allocated, classes silent – no talking unless putting up one's hand to answer a question and permitted to speak. My hand never went up. With three forms for the first year (the Upper Thirds) the school was much bigger than the Church School, much more impersonal.
Homework became a major problem: I'd never had any before, hated school life intruding on home life, seemed unable to memorise anything; used to being near the top of the class felt demoralized by not doing so well in this highly selected group.
The playground was an asphalt square fenced in by high wire-netting and tall trees – I missed the Common – so break times were duller. I did get one fun game going with three or four other girls, trying to catch the falling autumn leaves as they twisted and turned unpredictably on their way to the ground, suddenly changing direction without warning. You had to be quick.
The girls all seemed bright, nice, kind, but I made no real friends although one girl, dark, curly-haired Jenny, did come to tea. I taught her Andrew's card game, "Cheating" which made her laugh. One other girl from my class at the Church School, Barbara Hardinge, was in my form but I'd never

really known her. We were the only two who moved on to highly selective Putney High. Despite being used to being sent off to strange places I didn't settle, became one of those children who never really do settle at secondary school; there's now more awareness this might happen, more help given.

To a family with high academic standards, independent women who'd done the virtually unheard of in getting to Oxbridge in the late 1920s and early 1930s, anything less was humiliating, it becoming difficult to have good self-esteem *without* academic qualifications as a prop. They may not have realised the extent to which competition was increasing. Earlier, fewer girls had had access to the type of education for sought-after places, or had parents who could afford to pay for an expensive education at a top public school followed by an Oxbridge college. My mother and aunt found it hard to value themselves (or me) as personalities without this type of 'success'. Paradoxically achievement seemed to undermine their self-esteem, many ordinary families leading fulfilling lives able to believe in themselves and each other without hardly a G.C.S.E. between them.

Fees at Putney High being graded according to income, Mother didn't have to pay anything her pay as medical secretary being too low. She said she thought they preferred to give scholarships to tempt parents who could afford to pay and might otherwise have gone elsewhere privately. Looking back Mother seemed to feel a bit demoralized, burnt out, felt that now I was turning twelve, growing up, I'd be off her hands. What a relief! She was losing interest. A crisis developed. I became depressed going for long walks at night. Mother, tired, unable to cope, went to bed. Looking back I could have been at risk of being considered in need of "Care and Protection", taken into some state institution.

*

Mr Whitaker had apparently told Mother when she'd seen him to discuss the next stage of my education that he wouldn't send his daughter to Putney High. He was keen on the new all inclusive comprehensive system which didn't segregate children by ability or, as in practice, social class, resulting in so much disappointment and demoralisation. Perhaps he knew Putney High would be rigid, formal, soul destroying. Auntie Gladys, loyally supportive as always, said she'd heard in the Village that girls weren't happy there. However, Mother once again rallied taking me for a medical examination with a white-coated male doctor at Queen Mary's Hospital where she worked. All went well until, with no warning, looking down I saw a small glass cylinder filling up with my blood; briefly feeling faint the whole world turned bright yellow. Mother was pleased as when the question of diet came up, one portion a week of liver and another of fish, amongst other things, was thought to be suitably nutritious. The doctor didn't find any medical problems. No solution there.

Alec from next door came round asking for me. Lying in bed upstairs I didn't want to play.

"She's outgrown her strength," Mother told him.

"You mean she's grown but her strength hasn't grown with her," he interpreted perceptively.

She changed G.P. to Dr Glyn whose house and surgery were on the corner of Highdown Road, the family with young children having recently moved there. To wait, you sat in their immaculate dining room next to his small surgery, on padded chairs round a polished dining table. I never saw any other patients, perhaps he was building up his practice. G.P.s then, although considered experts in all matters of heath, had little training in dealing with mental illness: he clumsily and inexpertly attempted hypnosis to help me talk about my problems, swinging a watch on a chain in front of my eyes like a pendulum, finally becoming visibly exasperated and annoyed,

Mother took me to visit a teenage children's home in Roehampton Lane for advice.

"Just adolescence!" they said.

We visited Mrs Chaloner in her flat in Sheen,

"You try and keep it to yourself," she advised, "don't worry Mother."

With hindsight I suppose she could see Mother was worried stiff.

*

During the spring term I drifted away from Putney High increasingly absent because of tiredness and depression. Past traumas catching up. Looking back it seems teaching staff may have realised rather belatedly serious problems were building up. Miss Barber, older and more experienced than my young form teacher Miss Lawson, took one of the other two upper third forms. On one of the last days spent in school I was unexpectedly told to sit at Miss Barber's table at dinnertime with other girls from her form, remember her joking with the girls, then trying to draw me in,

"Now, tell Elizabeth the joke!"

Disaster and Collapse: Putney High School

Unfortunately I was too far-gone to respond to this well meant attempt to help. After I'd left Miss Barber kindly finished the purple gingham, cotton summer knickers begun in her sewing lessons and sent them with a nice letter saying she didn't think I'd want an unfinished garment. Mother opened the package. I'm afraid I never wore the hated things; Mother must have eventually thrown them out. I can't now remember which day actually was the last spent at Putney High. At some undefined point during the spring term, it meant nothing.

The following was written for a Birkbeck creative writing course from the viewpoint of my twelve-year-old self. Although we were encouraged to 'fictionalise' to create interest, this story is basically true as remembered – the hated violently purple school hat, the disastrous art lesson, the purple gingham knickers, retreating to bed to escape . . .

I'm in bed again today. Can't remember when I last went to school. Mum came in earlier to get me up.
"Don't feel well," I mumbled from under the eiderdown. So she went out again and shut the door. When I started junior school she used to pull me out of bed. Now I've started secondary school at Putney High she says, "You've outgrown your strength," and leaves me to sleep, or better still daydream. But the postman interrupted by dropping something heavy through the letterbox.
Going into that school building feels like going into prison – trapped without fresh air the smell of Putney Heath calling – to the purple gloom of a dark fortress: the smell of carbolic soap, fading books, boiled white shirts, hydrochloric acid from the labs, until dinner when boiled purple cabbage stink gets into every corner.
Inbetween grey-haired, spinster schoolmistresses with grand piano legs write on blackboards in fogs of chalk. Row upon row of girls identity-less in black-purple uniforms, sit silently at wooden desks, shuffling paper, scribbling frantically, terrified of getting detentions. Just girls and women, no boys or men.
It's a school rule you have to wear their hat, a stupid purple bowl with brim, upside down on my head, making my face look fat and silly while thin elastic cuts under my chin. I used to walk into school just holding it. One day a voice beside me said testily:
"Shouldn't you be wearing your hat?"
I looked round and there was the headmistress, so I put the hideous thing on. I hate it; dark purple rage wells up at the thought of it. And the bright

301

Dark Cupboards, Dusty Skeletons

violet tunic is too large, floppy, uncomfortable. I feel silly in that too, hanging bulkily over too-tight knicker elastic and slipping, itchy grey wool socks held up by garters. The purple and grey striped tie throttles and chokes. They have purple for funerals in a foreign country somewhere, a symbol for the dead.

"I liked everything about it," I said when Mum asked after my first day. Best to give the right answer. Soon it turned sourer than bitter purple damsons stewed without sugar.

At my last school half-a-dozen of us were the top group in the class. Now I'm at the bottom. The top seems too distant to be reached – ever. Our headmaster at junior school said if teaching was done properly there shouldn't be any need for homework. We never had any. School was bearable if it didn't encroach on home, infringe freedom. Learning poetry and pages of French vocab all evening is a nightmare there's no escape from. My marks aren't good.

A new times-table we learnt the first week was: *three* order marks equal *one* detention. There's been this big thing in my form about who'd be first to get a det. If you get one there's a form for parents to sign. I can cope with being labeled bad at school, but what if Mum finds out? She already thinks I'm like my father who she left and I've never seen. Apparently I look more like him than her. The cross-looking science mistress with frown lines between her eyes put C – – on my last homework. Then crossed it out and put D. Does that mean I've got a detention? The first in the class? I'm not going back to find out.

Mum hoped I'd get a scholarship there.

"It would have been nice to be able to tell people," she said. Perhaps she felt that would have made it all worthwhile – all the struggle of being a single mother coping with gossip that I might be illegitimate.

"I can't go around waving a marriage certificate," she would say.

She went to see the headmistress who told her she was very sorry they couldn't give me a scholarship. The thing is, Mum earns so little she doesn't have to pay anything anyway. The Girls' Public Day School Trust pays. Scholarships go to people who would have had to pay something. Mum went to Oxford University; she wants me to go there too.

What I really want to do is lie here and dream about my imaginary family, the dream world first invented at boarding school when I was four. In bed I can dream all day, be with my family all day.

They do know whether I'm at school or not, but they don't care. I'm just a tiny, depersonalized, slanting inky mark in a little box in the register on a line against "WALLACE, E." Only today, as I'm not there, it will be a circle.

That's all I am, who I am. After the eleven-plus all my friends went to other schools. Who cares if I'm there or not.
In junior school I got prizes for art. Before I came to this school Mum said encouragingly,
"You'll do art there, have *proper* art teaching."
I looked forward to that. The first art lesson we were told to paint a picture of a lady pushing a pram in a park. No choice, we all had to do the same, really boring. Still, I did my best. Then the art teacher came round to look. She spent some time telling another girl how good her picture was. Then saw mine and tore it to pieces – well, not literally, but with words. She said it was no good. So that was a 'proper' art lesson.
We did needlework too. Not embroidery like at junior school. Knickers. (All the same, of course.) And what colour were they? Give you three guesses but you'll only need one. You've got it: *purple*. Well, purple and white gingham. So that was needlework: learning to cut and stitch purple crotches.
This school seems dead, soulless. It's killing the real me, the little *me* deep inside, trying to stay alive. What was left after the woman at that Catholic boarding school I went to when I was four, before junior school, finished knocking me into shape, the shape *she* wanted. Knocking the corners off, which is supposed to be good for you. Here, there's more crushing, more moulding. I just can't lose anymore of myself, have more corners knocked off. There won't be anything left.
What I really want is a family. I thought one day I'd have a normal family, my dream world would somehow come true. Now childhood seems to be vanishing into the past and family hasn't happened. Now I'll never be a child in a family like other children. Mum's not happy either, she thinks were're not normal. Maybe she's waiting for Grannie to die so she can inherit and buy her own home.
Even my dream world isn't coming so easily. Like the older children in the Narnia stories who became unable to go back. I'm lost without it. Sometimes I feel so upset and angry I go for long walks round the streets at night and don't come in 'til after Mum's asleep. My dream world's dying. I'm dying with it. I need to get far away. Begin life again. Be a child before I grow up.

Mother now said she'd never intended Putney High to be permanent. Had she been waiting to inherit from Grannie and buy her own home somewhere far away? Was I to have had yet another change? She'd always

assumed I'd cope with being chopped and changed around. Carrying my own world around inside my head, I usually did. Until it broke down.
When it was clear Putney High wasn't working and I would be leaving, Mother went to see the headmistress, Miss Lockley, who apparently told her they were:
". . . very sorry we couldn't give her a scholarship!"
"I will see her before she goes," she apparently said. But she never did. Because I was never there.
The spring term of '57 followed by Easter holidays were a time of critical decisions which would change my life. Mother came into my room where I lay in bed with an attack of depression,
"You're going to see your father and go to St. Christopher's."
One of these did happen in the near future.

I'm still in bed. Mum's just come in holding a green school prospectus the postman brought, what thumped through the letter box. About a boarding school, St. Christopher's, which is "unconventional", she says, and, "progressive" – no endless depersonalising rules – and co-educational. Boys as well. Not just masses of girls. They don't eat meat there, have lessons outside in summer, and self-government by the children who make rules. Best of all, although they don't *have* to wear it, their uniform's the colour of green-gold oak leaves in summer when I'm playing on the Common.
I'm getting up now, putting clothes on.
I just know that's where I want to go.

Mother showed me an old prospectus from St Christopher School, Letchworth, she'd kept since searching for a boarding school when I was four. The Lyn Harris's, then head teachers, had replied to her enquiry that they didn't take boarders as young as four. I loved the sound of the school, what it was setting out to do, the philosophy, self-government. She wrote for a new prospectus. It arrived, still with a green cover like the earlier one, its symbol a flaming torch as though lighting the way.
Mother also thought of St George's, Harpenden, another co-ed boarding school but more conventional and formal than St. Christopher's; she contacted a Quaker boarding school, Friends' School Saffron Walden; they hadn't a place in the middle of the school year. She phoned an advisory

service for independent schools and discussed other Quaker schools known for taking children with problems.

Educated and having been a teacher, good at getting people to help her, she knew where to go for advice, knew the ropes for applying to independent schools. Years later I discovered less educated parents simply didn't know about the process of applying: writing for prospectuses, sending off a completed application form, going for an interview, waiting for a formal offer to arrive in the post.

I was adamant I preferred St. Christopher's, now had more input with this choice than with Putney High. With hindsight although considerable problems still arose I've always felt this to have been the right decision.

An independent boarding school was far too expensive for Mother to afford on her hospital medical secretary's salary the fees being a daunting hundred pounds plus, each term. She went to County Hall in Central London to ask for a local authority grant, applying for herself on the grounds that she couldn't cope as a the single-parent. A grant was refused.

She wrote to my estranged father to ask if he would help with the fees. He replied,

"I don't think it's the sort of school *I* would have liked." He'd always found it difficult to save money, spending what he had.

Bedridden Grannie in Oxford agreed to Mother having some of her share of Grannie's estate in advance of inheriting before she died. So Grannie paid for the first term, after which I did get a local authority grant, an application made on my behalf rather than Mother's, supported by the headmaster. When my problems were explained to Grannie she'd apparently said,

"Oh Ruth! What did I do wrong?"

Which upset Mother.

*

We travelled to St Christopher's for an interview. Taking a mixed ability range the school had no entrance exam; most years a few brighter pupils got into Oxbridge. Mr King Harris, the headmaster, usually asked if a child had passed the eleven-plus exam.

Getting off the train from Kings Cross at Letchworth we walked the mile from the rail station to the main school entrance at Arundale (house names all beginning with "Arun") and were ushered by a secretary squashed inside a tiny cubbyhole with telephone switchboard, into a room off the main hall known as "the Sitting Room". Informally furnished with comfy easy chairs, and a large potted cactus gracing the windowsill with view beyond of sunny, invitingly green, neatly mowed lawns.

Mr King Harris, entering, asked me,

"Did you count the bridges?"

I hadn't.

"There are *nine!*"

Wanting to make a good start I tried to appear suitably impressed.

"Gosh!"

Comparing notes later with other boarders I discovered he asked this of every prospective pupil newly arrived by train from Kings Cross. Young, energetic, enthusiastic, in sports jacket, white shirt and tie, he would then have been running the school for three years, although aged only thirty-four.

First Mother and I were interviewed together, then walked along the path across the school field to view a boarding house, Arunside (not the one I'd join). After which we were taken back to Arundale where I was interviewed separately in "the Study" next to the Sitting Room. His wife Cate (Cathleen) also there, didn't say much, leaving the interviewing to him. He asked about detentions and order marks, seeming to realise Putney High was rigid, formal, impersonal, and I hadn't settled there.

Apparently he then told Mother, whom he also saw separately while I was told to wait in the hall, that I was obviously a very nice girl but very shy; he asked if I'd been to boarding school before and whether I knew the facts of life. It was agreed it would be best to start after Easter at the beginning of the summer term rather than wait until the new academic year in September.

*

A separate problem arising was my inheritance of the family problem of overcrowded teeth. A visit to an orthodontist was arranged. He prescribed braces top and bottom – quite a mouthful – and wanted to extract all four wisdom teeth which, so he said, would cause trouble coming through later. Presumably, as they hadn't yet appeared, this would have meant a hospital operation. At home, Mother asked if I wanted to have it done.

"No!"

So that absolved her, and I was more than happy to take this decision for myself. She wisely didn't press it. With so many other problems she probably felt it wasn't a good time. My teeth stayed tightly packed but the wisdom teeth did eventually come through without any of the prophesied trouble. Aged twelve, increasingly able to resist authority, this would be my last visit to any dentist for more than ten years, never suffering toothache and needing only three fillings being in my early twenties.

For the remainder of the Easter holiday it was arranged I should go away for a while to a children's holiday hotel in Bournemouth near the Chine, a short walk from the beach. I don't remember how long for, at least a fortnight maybe four weeks. I was put on a train at a London mainline station to be met by a stranger, one of two ladies running the hotel, who took me by bus to a lovely large house in spacious grounds. She said she'd known which passenger on the platform must be me as all the rest were old ladies. Being sent off like this had always been part of my life and I wasn't fazed. In a society in which middle class children were often sent off to boarding school at an early age no one, including myself, saw this as any problem.

There were ten or twelve other children aged about seven to eighteen, a small enough group for us all to sit around a large dining table for meals. I remember two young brothers whose parents were out in India (the remnants of colonialism). They spent term time at a boys' prep boarding school and holidays at this children's hotel in Bournemouth. There were a couple of eighteen year-olds, a public school boy and another said to be an Arab prince. The girl I shared a room with, about my age whose name has slipped from memory, said she told me things she couldn't tell anyone else. I hadn't realised.

As the first year of Christopher's Senior School had already started Latin, which Putney High hadn't, Mother asked them to arrange Latin coaching. This turned out to be with a very elderly ex-teacher at his house who taught me the Latin for,

"The master punishes the boy," corporal punishment being endemic with his generation.

I had quite a nice holiday despite Latin lessons and a septic little finger lanced by a local G.P. We were allowed the freedom to walk down the deep tree-filled Chine to the beach on our own. This was the last place I really integrated. Being used to being sent off to where I knew no one and integrating, as at the Farm, with a different group of children each time I stayed, once more I took it for granted I wouldn't ever see any of these new friends again.

Sent a clothing list for St Christopher's, a few new clothes were bought (including tent and ground sheet), the clothing list checked through, items ticked off. The only compulsory uniform was for games. Enthusiastically I helped sew on nametapes, pack Mother's large blue trunk to be collected by station wagon and sent by train PLA (Passenger's Luggage in Advance). Although there would be problems (there always are) St Christopher's gave me so much help, understanding and support, boarding there did turn out to be the right decision, never regretted. It's been said there's no love for children at boarding schools, probably often true, but St Christopher's turned out to unquestionably buck this trend.

At the end of the Easter school holidays Mother came with me, by bus and tube, carrying a small overnight suitcase, to Kings Cross main line station to link up with the St Christopher School party travelling to Letchworth, supervised by two staff for the hour's journey.

A warm day in the Easter holidays 1957. Back garden with Auntie Gladys's sitting room window immediately behind the green canvas tent for two, bought to take to St Chris.

Above:
with Mother and Scamp.

Below:
Vanessa with Scamp.

Epilogue: A Better World Emerging

This rather lengthy epistle seems to have turned into something of an egotistical trip down ego lane, a remedy for a lifetime's inability to talk about myself. For those of us born during the Second World War, dubbed "The Silent Generation", it's said we didn't protest. Perhaps we sensed that in those post-war years adults were suffering from burn out after six years of bombing, not knowing if they'd survive the next raid, separations caused by conscription, evacuation and homelessness. They'd had enough. So we endured . . . *silently*.

So many family disasters are no longer regarded as skeletons to be locked away in the deepest and darkest of cupboards: sex outside marriage, illegitimacy, marital breakdown, being an only child – whom, it was believed, must inevitably be 'spoilt' whatever the family circumstances, serious illness, disability and mental health issues, how you spoke and where you were in the class system, what you wore – trousers for women being unacceptable, distressed feelings which shouldn't be expressed – might drag others down, the list goes on and on . . .

While chopping and changing a young child around can be damaging this left benefits in the way of broadening experience and learning not to trust too easily. There are advantages in being wary about accepting what strangers might tell you, being not too easily taken in by charm, confidence and a middle class accent combined with impressive surroundings in sunshine, as Mother had been on our first visit to Tubney. It's useful to develop the ability to put out psychological antennae before trusting. And another benefit: coping with difficult people, negotiating tricky relationships, may have made coping with life easier.

Epilogue: a Better World Emerging

Included here are the somewhat dull minutiae of everyday life. Researching family history I wished I'd known more about the more mundane details of ancestors' lives, especially women's, often more involved with minutiae – keeping families going by carrying out everyday chores – able only to guess and extrapolate, possibly inaccurately, what might have been, from published social histories. Huge changes in living standards and thus everyday lives have taken place during my lifetime.

To jump ahead to the 1960s: after early disasters my luck changed enormously, firstly with a boarding place at St Christopher School, progressive and coeducational, unusual for the time – on a generous local authority grant – where an unprecedented amount of support would be immensely healing, a school philosophy of valuing and believing in children giving experience of a mentally infinitely healthier way of life. It's been said there's no love in boarding schools; this wasn't true of St Christopher's. Following came a hugely expensive NHS residential inpatient place at the Cassel Hospital in South West London pioneering group psychotherapy, where seventeen-year-olds had the freedom to come and go 24/7. From a seriously depressed, terrible teenager, together these turned my life around. There must have been many needing that type of help who weren't lucky enough to find it. I'm forever grateful.

In the 1960s with war trauma receding a better world began to emerge, people began to be nicer to each other, more tolerant and understanding towards children. Huge changes in attitudes have taken place in my lifetime. Barring another world disaster things will hopefully continue that way.

List of Illustrations

FRONT COVER, clockwise
Sketch of Claremont, Highdown Road, Roehampton
Aged two c. 1947
Aged eleven 1956
Auntie Gladys (Mrs G. M. Hamilton) on the terrace

R.S.P.C.A. certificate for essay on "Kindness to Animals" iv

BEFORE MEMORY
Ruth and Bill	11
Ruth with Elizabeth, Brambletye	17
Aged 18 months, driveway, "Claremont"	30
Post-war economy pushchair	32
First portrait aged two	34

MOVES AND CHANGES
Sketch of "Claremont", Highdown Road	37
Auntie Gladys on the terrace	38
Sir F. Truby King	47
A is for Apple – children's alphabet book	57
Hunsden House Nursery School group photo 1948/9	58
17 Stephen Road	48
Miss Woods' house and On the Swing	61
Barbara Lamb by Cam – illustrated children's story	71, 72
Little Miss Pink's School children's illustrated storybook	75

TOTAL DISRUPTION
Front view of Tubney House	79
Rear view of Tubney House	90
Ground floor plan of Tubney House and room uses	94
Aged five	104

PRECARIOUS NORMALITY
Favourite grey shorts, Brambletye, Hindhead	145
Frying Pan Holiday	148
Christening gifts: bible and prayer book	156
Godfather and family	158
Dressing up, Ann Robilliard	164
Dressing up, Vanessa	165
1930s technology	168
Doll family and "Lamby"	176
Brand new, sky blue, first bicycle	182
Bexhill holiday camp	188, 189, 190
Swimming pool, Shanklin	192
Andrew	198

SETTLED BUT ONLY TEMPORARILY
School portrait aged 10, 1955   218
Prize giving   221
School report   222
White Boots prize label   223
Cage Birds diploma   224
Mixing things   226
Addison's ironmonger's, Roehampton Village   229
Scamp in back garden   238
Sue in hutch   239
Sue in Scamp's basket   240
Vanessa's birthday party in Richmond Park   253
Ruth and Bill's wedding photo ?   258
First photo   258
Roehampton Village drinking fountain   264
Roehampton Great War memorial and path by Addison's   265
Portrait of Auntie Gladys and china pug   276
Roehampton Church School top junior class 1956   285, 286
School portrait 1956   287
Mr Ayling and Mr Whitaker   288
Group with animals at Hatchgate Farm, Cuckfield   294

DISASTER
Green canvas tent   308

INDICES – see also Illustrations

PEOPLE some with forenames only given to protect identity
Andrew – pupil, Roehampton Church School 152, 159, 197, 201, 204, 207, 224, 285
Anthony, "Little Anthony" – boarder St Nicholas Sch. Tubney 116, 130, 139
Audrey – first cousin of Ruth Isabelle Wallace, née King 40, 131, 147, 151, 163, 295
Ayling, Mr Kenneth – teacher, Roehampton Church School 259, 266, 287
Barber, Miss – teacher, Putney High 300
Baring-Gould, Mrs – teacher, living Tubney Ho. Gatehouse 81, 85, 122, 124, 131, 134
Barnes, Dr – GP Roehampton 143
Beale, Elsie Mary, née Thomson – Ruth's aunt 21
Boving family – Rawlinson Road, Oxford 141, 246, 247, 249
Bradley, Ann – daughter of Daphne 186
Bradley, Mrs Daphne – lived Roehampton & Sanderstead 49, 186
Campling, Canon – vicar Holy Trinity Ch. Roehampton 149, 183, 209, 220, 234, 238
Chaloner, Bill – living Dover Cottage, Highdown Road 182, 283
Chaloner, Joan – living Dover Cottage, Highdown Road 207, 245, 282
Chaloner, John, living Roehampton & Dulwich – pen name "Jon Chalon" 30, 282
Chaloner, Len – pen name, see also "Mrs Chaloner" 42
Chaloner, Mr – living Dover Cottage, Highdown Road 280
Chaloner, Mrs – Dover Cottage, Highdown Rd. 42, 99, 103, 201, 227, 230, 280, 300
Charles – boarder St Nicholas's Sch. Tubney 108, 111
Christine – best friend Roehampton Church School 208, 259, 266, 288
Christopher – boarder St Nicholas's Sch. Tubney 92
Clack, Mrs – teacher Roehampton Church School 150, 208, 212, 221, 223
Coles, Gladys Mary – see Hamilton
Coles, Mrs Eliza – mother of Gladys Mary Coles "Old Auntie" 39
Coles, Reggie – 173
Cooke, Reverend C. K. Hamel and family 157
Florrie – child minder, Roehampton 38
Frazer, Mr – teacher Roehampton Church School 152, 159, 183, 192, 195, 209, 260
Gisborne, Miss L. E. 77, 81, 141, 248
Glyn, Dr – GP Roehampton 300
Hamilton, Gladys Mary, née Coles 21, 35, 174, 239, 273
Hamilton, John H. ("Jack") husband of Gladys Mary 21
Hamilton, "Kitty" – lived Roehampton 174, 239
Hamilton, "Nellie" – lived Roehampton 174, 239
Harris, Nicholas King – headmaster St Christopher Sch. 305, 306
Heard – gardener at Claremont, Highdown Road 70
Herbert, Mrs – dinner lady, Roehampton Church School 199, 209, 213, 214
Higgins, Miss Mabel V. A. – live-in home help Sandfield Road, Oxford 246
Hill, Mrs – nurse, Roehampton Church Sch. 161
Janet – boarder St Nicholas's Sch. Tubney 124, 129, 137

Joyce – land girl, Hatchgate Farm, Cuckfield 291, 293
Kim – pupil Roehampton Church School 217
King, Emma Bertha, née Thomson, "Grannie" 20, 21, 35, 100, 260, 271, 303, 305
King, Isabella "Auntie Bella" – Ruth's aunt, father's sister 15, 242
King, James – Ruth's father 14
King, Janet "Auntie Janey" – Ruth's aunt, father's sister 242
King, Janet Bertha – "Auntie Janet", 53, 55, 67, 76, 147, 198, 204, 231, 251, 254, 262
King, Kathleen Mary, "Auntie Kay" – Ruth's sister 33, 35, 65, 147, 254, 269
King, Ruth Isabelle 1914-1999 – mentioned throughout
Kitty – live-in maid Claremont, Highdown Road 69
Lawson, Miss – teacher Putney High Sch. 298
Lea, Claire Jean, née Wallace – half-sister 91, 105, 122
Leo – boarder St Nicholas's Sch. Tubney 126
Lockley, Miss – headmistress, Putney High Sch. 304
Malcolm – boarder St Nicholas's Sch. Tubney 106, 115, 125, 127, 131, 138
Mitchinson, David Edward "Ted" – distant Australian cousin, Rottnest Is. Perth 231
Murray – boarder St Nicholas's Sch. Tubney 126
Nigel – Andrew's younger brother living Dover House Road 227
Nurse – St Nicholas's Sch. Tubney House 80, 84, 103, 126, 141, 248
Parkinson, twins – living Highdown Road, Roehampton 245, 284, 300
Paul – boarder at St Nicholas's Sch. Tubney 120, 135, 138
Richard, "Little Richard" – boarder St Nicholas's Sch. Tubney 138
Rixom, Norman and Duncan – Rhodesian 2nd cousins 252
Robilliard, Ann – pupil Roehampton Church Sch. 162, 169, 184, 220
Robin – day pupil St Nicholas's School Tubney 127
Seagrove, Mr and Mrs – farmers Hatchgate Farm, Cuckfield 290
Sheila – Ruth's university friend living Wimbledon 33, 185
Susan – Andrew's sister living Dover House Road, Roehampton 178, 184
Susan – boarder St Nicholas's School 129
Thomson family pawnbrokers 67, 205
Thomson, David, Roger and Michael – second cousins 252
Thomson, Elsie Mary – Ruth's aunt, Bertha's sister 21
Thomson, Emma Bertha – see King
Rixom, née Thomson, Daisy "Auntie Daisy" – Bertha's sister, Ruth's aunt 21, 257
Utin, Archie – artist and teacher Hunsden Ho. Nursery 54, 68
Utin, Deborah – daughter of Mary and Archie 54, 55
Utin, Mary – teacher Hunsden House Nursery 54, 63, 68
Vanessa – 2nd cousin 146, 163, 169, 279
Vicky and Toni – twins, boarders, Tubney Ho. 78, 91, 115, 123, 125, 136, 139, 140
Wallace, Elizabeth Ruth b. 1944 – author
Wallace, George Carlton ("Bill") 1903-1980 9, 23, 24, 26, 66, 133, 259
Wallace, Ruth Isabelle, née King 1914-1999   mentioned throughout
Whitaker, Mr – headmaster Roehampton Church Sch. 149, 206, 210, 216, 261, 287, 299

Wixie, Elizabeth – boarder St Nicholas School, Tubney 104, 121, 126
Woods, Miss – founder Hunsden House Nursery School 54, 55

PLACES / INSTITUTIONS /AUTHORS

All place names are in the United Kingdom

Addison's Ironmonger's, Roehampton, London 47, 166, 173, 223
Barnes, Surrey 33
BBC Children's Hour 233, 235
Bentalls, Kingston – department store 179
Bertram Mill's Circus 256
Bexhill 186
Birkbeck College, University of London 6, 16, 45, 301
Bletchley Park 9
Bournemouth – children's holiday home near The Chine 307
Bowlby, John *Child Care And The Growth of Love* 80
Brambletye, Linkside East, Beacon Hill, Hindhead, Surrey 16, 202
Bury Knowle Park, Headington, Oxford, library & clinic 60, 62
Carlisle County High School for Girls 53
Cassel Hospital, SW London 310
Catholic teaching 105
Children's Bookshop, Oxford 250, 257
Christ's Hospital school 212
Claremont, (now no. 8) Highdown Rd, Roehampton, S.W.15. see Highdown Rd.
Clarence Lane, Roehampton 244
Conscientious Objection to military service 5
County Hall, London 305
Crestway, Roehampton 40, 163, 181
Dentist, Putney, Upper Richmond Road 269
Devil's Punch Bowl 243
Dover House Road, Roehampton & Putney 35, 36
Eleven Plus Exam 200, 261, 305
Friends' School Saffron Walden 304
Froebel Training College, Roehampton 155, 220, 266
Frying Pan holiday Wiltshire 146
Fundamental English, Fundamental Arithmetic 85, 131, 132, 135
Gamages – London department store 228
George VI – funeral on radio 139
Girls' Public Day School Trust 297
Gloucester Green bus station, Oxford 97
Gollds, hunting lodge, Tubney House 79
Goodge Street, London 11, 13

315

Gower Street, London 1, 12, 258
Harrods department store, London 238, 240
Headington School for Girls, Oxford 54
Heathersbank Nursing Home, Surrey 16, 17
Highdown Road, Roehampton, London S.W.15. 35 – 37, 171
Hindhead, Surrey 144
Holy Trinity Church Roehampton 148, 154, 155, 184
Hospital, children's, near Hindhead 45
Hunsden House Nursery School, Headington, Oxford 54
Huts Hotel, Hindhead 181
King George VI – funeral on radio 139
King, Sir F. Truby – author *Feeding and Care of Baby* 40
Kingsmere Pond – Wimbledon Common 243
Latymer Upper School 10
Letchworth, Hertfordshire 76, 162
London Airport, Heathrow 241
Long Dene School, Kent 76
Magdalen Bridge, Oxford 62
Magdalen College Park, Oxford 63
Magdalen College, Oxford 82
Medfield Street, Roehampton Village 48
Mee, Arthur *The Children's Encyclopaedia* 230, 233
Ministry of Information, Senate House, London 8
National Health Service 45
North Parade, Oxford 115
Nursery School, Upper Richmond Road, Putney 42
Pathfinder Holidays – Church of England 186, 190
Pelmanism, mind control method 74
Ponsonby Road, Roehampton – 150
Port Meadow, Oxford 249
Potters Bar, Middlesex/ Hertfordshire 27
Putney Heath – "the Common" 73, 155, 199, 200, 217, 243
Putney High School for Girls, Putney, London 261
Putney Park Lane – the "Cuckoo Lane" 175
Putney, London – clinic 269
Putney, London – hospital 269
Putney, London – shops 180, 279
Quaker Lane, Potters Bar 27
Queen Elizabeth II 195
Queen Mary's Hospital, Roehampton 237, 299
Queensmere Pond – Wimbledon Common 73, 243
Radionics 141
Richmond Ice Skating Rink 241

Richmond Park, London, Adams Pond 243
Richmond Park, Pen Ponds 244
Richmond, River at 241
Roehampton Church School 86, 148, 154
Roehampton Swimming Pool 241
Roehampton Village 33, 264, 280
Roehampton Village shops, 1940s and 1950s 47,169
Russell. Bertrand *In Praise of Idleness* 11
Scio Pond – Putney Heath, the "Little Dirty Pond" 73, 177
Senate House, London 8
St Andrew's Church, Headington, Oxford 63
St Christopher School, Letchworth, Hertfordshire 68, 76, 162, 304, 307, 310
St Leonard's School, St Andrew's, Scotland 54
St Marylebone Church 158
St Nicholas, patron saint of children – Christmas story - 128
St Nicholas's School, Tubney House, Berkshire 77
St Paul's Girls' School, South West London, UK 4, 178, 227
St Peter's, Seaford – boys' prep school 207
St Thomas's Hospital, London, UK   13
Stephen Road, Headington, Oxford 54, 61, 100
Tubney House, Berkshire/ Oxfordshire 78, 82, 94, 120, 137
Upper Chine School, Shanklin, Isle of Wight 187, 190
Upper Richmond Road, Putney – day nursery, doll's hospital 43, 72
Wanstead Quaker Meeting, London, UK 5
Where the Rainbow Ends – children's play, London 257
William Willett – architectural style 36
Wycombe Court Garden School, High Wycombe 77, 101, 132, 143